7/12

INSIDE SEAL TEAM SIX

INSIDE
SEAL Team
Six

My Life and Missions
with America's Elite Warriors

DON MANN
with RALPH PEZZULLO

Little, Brown and Company

New York Boston London

*To all the courageous Navy SEALs who put their lives on
the line day after day in defense of our great country and
especially to those who have died, and to their families.*

*"Courage consists not in hazarding without
fear, but being resolutely minded
in a just cause."*

—*Plutarch*

———————————

Little, Brown and Company
Hachette Book Group
237 Park Avenue, New York, NY 10017
www.hachettebookgroup.com

First Edition: November 2011

Little, Brown and Company is a division of Hachette Book Group, Inc. The Little,
Brown name and logo are trademarks of Hachette Book Group, Inc.

The publisher is not responsible for websites (or their content) that are not owned by
the publisher.

The Hachette Speakers Bureau provides a wide range of authors for speaking events.
To find out more, go to www.hachettespeakersbureau.com or call (866) 376-6591.

ISBN 978-0-316-20431-6
Library of Congress Control Number: 2011936625

10 9 8 7 6 5 4 3 2 1

RRD-C

Printed in the United States of America

A NOTE FROM THE PUBLISHER

Inside Seal Team Six contains redactions of classified material as required by three U.S. government agencies. We have left the redactions in place rather than deleting the challenged material, so readers will understand that Don Mann's experience and knowledge go even further than he is permitted to report due to requirements of the U.S. government.

Contents

INSIDE SEAL TEAM SIX

Virginia, May 1, 2011

> Tonight, I can report to the American
> people and to the world that the United
> States has conducted an operation that
> killed Osama bin Laden.
>
> —*President Barack Obama*

It was a quiet Sunday night, and I'd just returned from a long weekend of SEAL training at Naval Amphibious Base, Little Creek, in Virginia Beach, Virginia. I poured myself a glass of wine and was watching an egret rise from the marshland behind my house when my cell phone rang.

Reading my wife Dawn's number on the LED screen, I answered. "Hey, honey, what's up?"

"Don, where are you?" she asked. She sounded excited. Almost out of breath.

"I just got home. Why?"

"You need to turn the TV on. Tune it to CNN."

"How come?"

"Just do it. You are not going to believe what just happened!"

As soon as the TV screen lit up I saw a photo of Osama bin Laden—similar to the one I'd been using for dry shooting practice in my basement. Underneath ran a banner: BIN LADEN KILLED IN PA-KISTAN.

I leaned forward. Adrenaline started pumping through my veins. I'd been in a program to try to nail the bastard. And I had never really gotten over the horror and embarrassment of the attacks on 9/11.

Could it be true that we had finally taken out public enemy number one—the hated and greatly feared leader of the al-Qaeda terrorist group?

Dozens of questions started running through my head, including: How was he killed? Did he put up a fight? Who ran the op? Then I heard Wolf Blitzer mention SEAL Team Six. I couldn't believe my ears.

Then Wolf Blitzer mentioned the name again.

Even though I was stationed at SEAL Team Six from 1985 to 1989 and 1995 to 1998, I'd rarely heard its name uttered in public. Maybe once or twice when the ███████████████████████ appeared on TV. But besides that, almost never, not even by guys on the teams.

Officially, there was no SEAL Team Six (ST-6). ████████████ ██ ████████████████████████████

Unofficially, ST-6 was the most highly trained warfare unit on the planet.

Now Wolf Blitzer was announcing to the world that ST-6 ██████ ████████████████████████

Many of the active-duty SEALs on Team Six were guys I had taught how to shoot and ███████████████████████████ and trained in ████████████████████████████ as well as in ██

████████. I knew how they thought, how they trained, and how they were selected.

A couple months earlier, I'd attended an ST-6 reunion in the building where I had worked for many years, and many of the active-duty guys were serving us beer and liquor. The current SEALs kept pictures of the SEALs I'd served with on the walls.

I spoke with an an active-duty guy who was a member of Blue Team, one of ST-6's assault teams. "During the eighties and nineties we trained and trained and trained but had only the occasional op. Now you guys are conducting missions back to back. With two wars going on, how the heck do you have time to serve us drinks?"

He answered humbly and respectfully. "Yes, but you're the guys who paved the way. We're extremely grateful to all of you."

Later this young, professional, soft-spoken SEAL with a fresh scar across his face took me to his cage and showed me his gear. My attention was drawn to the three-████████████████████ ████████████████ silencer that he kept in the lower left pocket of his ████████████████████.

"Is that for your MP5?" I asked. The MP5 I was referring to was actually an MP5████████████████████ ████████████████████████████████████ ████████████████████████████

"Sure is."

I said, ████████████████████████

He nodded. "Yeah, I like it. A couple of months ago during a raid, we made a silent entry and I entered this room and used it to kill four known terrorists. It worked so well that a couple other terrorists from the same cell remained sleeping in a room down the hall. I killed them too. They never knew what hit 'em." He said this matter-of-factly. He was a professional: killing terrorists was part of his job.

One of the members of ST-6 who went on the raid ████████████

██████ told me later that he'd been on more than seventy raids over the last couple of years. The pace of combat was intense, and important commendations such as Silver Stars and Bronze Stars were handed out so often that the team no longer had time for medal ceremonies. Instead, the Silver and Bronze Stars were sent in the mail.

I listened as Wolf Blitzer on CNN described how the SEAL team had been flown in by Black Hawks from Afghanistan and attacked the compound in Abbottabad, Pakistan, right under the noses of the Pak army. He said that one specially modified Black Hawk helicopter had gone down hard and hit a wall, which had made it impossible for the SEALs to fast-rope into the compound as planned.

But SEALs were trained to prepare for all kinds of contingencies. Something always went wrong. You did your best to "plan your dive and dive your plan."

I knew that there had been hundreds of raids against bin Laden and other al-Qaeda leaders that had come up empty. Dry holes, we called them. Missions that the American public never heard about.

Given that, the SEALs sitting in the two Black Hawks must have had doubts that Osama bin Laden—known as UBL in military parlance—was even in Abbottabad. But some of those misgivings would have evaporated within minutes, after they breached the wall and took fire from the guesthouse. The threats shooting at them were protecting someone. Who?

Adrenaline slammed through their veins as they entered the main house. They were dressed in ████████████████████ ██ ██ ████████████████████████████████ They held their M4s and MP5s at the ready as they scanned the rooms looking for immediate threats. They encountered wives and children, people SEALs generally refer to as nonthreats or, sometimes, unknowns—

because you can never be sure. The SEALs focused on hands first, because hands hold weapons.

They were also looking for suicide vests and booby traps of any kind. ███████████████████████████████████████

██

███████████████████████████████████████

███████████████████████████████████████

███████████████████████████████████████

███████████████████████████████████████

███████████████████████████████████████

███████████████████████████████████████

They were equipped with ████████████████████

███████████████████████████████████████

██████████████████████████

Masters of CQB, the SEALs moved quickly from room to room. Every man had a specialized job and knew what he was supposed to do. They were ███████████████████████████████████

███████████████████████████████████████

███████████████████████████████████████

████████████████████████████████████ They'd previously memorized photos and studied descriptions of everyone in the house.

███████████████████████████████████████

██████████████████████████████

The SEAL motioned to the two operators behind him, and the three men crossed immediately to the bedroom where they found the six-foot-four al-Qaeda leader standing with two of his wives.

UBL's fifth wife, Amal al-Fatah, charged the lead SEAL, shouting in Arabic and waving her arms. Fearing that she might be wearing a suicide vest packed with explosives, the first SEAL to enter the bedroom shot her once in the leg.

Then he pushed bin Laden's other wife aside.

One of the SEALs behind him already had bin Laden in his sights. The al-Qaeda leader stood by the bed wearing a white prayer cap and robe.

███

███

███

██████████████████████

At that moment that ST-6 member must have felt like the luckiest man in the world.

Once the shooting was over, the building secured, and UBL confirmed dead, the commo rep on the SEAL team radioed back to command and control: ██████████████████████████████

███

██████████████

Other SEALs had already started going through the house collecting intel. A treasure trove of computers, cell phones, thumb drives, computer disks, and documents. Amazing!

One of the ST-6 commandos who participated in the op told me, "The mission was so easy, it was like shooting at paper targets."

As I listened to the news on CNN, I felt powerful emotions—tremendous relief and overwhelming pride at ST-6's success and the fact that they got this mission in the first place.

Not too many years earlier I was on a beach in northern California with ST-6 ████████████████████████████████████ We inserted off a mother craft, in a storm.

The waves were enormous. One second we were twelve feet below a rapidly building crest, and the next we were lifted up so high we could see miles beyond the beach.

As in most water ops, we were paired up as swimmer teams. My buddy and I struggled but made it safely to shore. As the team medic, I had to treat three fellow SEALs who almost weren't as lucky. They nearly drowned.

The ███████████████████████████████ who was observing the mission came over to me and asked, "Are you going to be able to swim these hostages out of there on the real mission?"

I said, "Sir, we'll be fine. But the hostages, especially the injured hostages, might not do so well. Some will make it, but some may not. It depends on the intensity of the surf."

He thanked me for my frank answer.

Later, we learned that particular mission had instead been assigned to the ██████████████████████████████████████ ██████████████████████████████████████ ███████████████████

We were pissed. Once again, the big green machine (the Army) had nabbed a mission that should have been ours!

In those days, ████ and ST-6 ████████████████████ missions. But now ████ had to be kicking themselves with envy. They knew the hit on bin Laden would never be topped. Not in our lifetimes.

Soon after SEAL Team Six captured and killed bin Laden, my phone started ringing off the hook. One call after another came from reporters working for ABC, CBS, NBC, Fox, the *Washington Post*, *Newsweek*, and even al-Jazeera TV. They were also e-mailing and texting me.

They all wanted to know the same thing: You were a commando on ST-6, you were the ST-6 advanced-training officer; how did ST-6 train for this op?

Yes, I was the ST-6 advanced-training officer; I knew how the team trained for its raids. But I wasn't about to give away any specific mission- or training-related information that might aid our enemies.

Instead, I gave them all the same answer: "They trained harder than anybody else in the world. They trained for the insertion, actions on the objective, lots of shooting in the shooting house, breaching, emergency medicine, commo, contingencies, hostage handling, intel searches, and for the extraction."

And as I spoke, I felt a strong sense of affirmation. Now fifty-three years old and a veteran of many ops, scrapes with death, broken bones, and ruined marriages, I knew that every minute of my time with the SEALs had been worth it.

Maybe the young SEAL Team Six member I'd met in the team room months before was right: in my own small way, I'd helped to pave the way to this great success.

I wanted to think so. I still do.

CHAPTER ONE

Somalia, 1985

The only easy day was yesterday.
                    —*SEAL motto*

You having fun, Doc?" Lieutenant Haig asked. He called me Doc because I was trained as a Navy corpsman (the Army referred to us as medics), and he and the other two SEALs on our team trusted me to patch them up should the need arise. Lieutenant Haig (we called him LT) was a Lebanese American, about five ten, 185 pounds. Sported a sinister smile and was a student of military history. He was also as gung ho as they come.

"Hoo-ya," I answered, which is SEAL-talk for, roughly translated, "Hell, yes."

I was in my midtwenties and this was my first real-world SEAL mission—a top secret, highly dangerous reconnaissance-and-demolition op; ten years before, I hadn't even heard of the SEALs. Four of us were sitting in a six-by-six-foot foxhole covered with desert-camouflage netting on a beach in an undisclosed part of Somalia, up to our necks in water fouled with excrement and puke. Ours. But despite the less than ideal conditions, I was loving it. I said to myself, *This is incredible. It's what SEAL team is all about!*

Two nights earlier we'd executed a jump out of a C-130 off the coast. First out, our rubber boat—a Zodiac CRRC (combat rubber raiding craft), which we called a rubber ducky. It was followed by our gear—scuba equipment, motor, gas can, paddles, water, shovels, MREs (meals ready to eat), commo supplies, rucksacks, demolitions. Then the four of us with our weapons, belts, and packs.

It was pitch-black when we hit the water. Then the C-130 tore off into the night sky, leaving us to our mission with no support whatsoever, which was almost unheard-of. Under normal circumstances, we would have been given backup and a medevac plan.

But this was a special mission. One of the most dangerous and important ops SEAL teams had gone on since Vietnam. So critical, in fact, that the SEAL commandant had personally selected us from all the SEALs stationed on the West Coast.

When our Zodiac CRRC motored to within a thousand meters of the shore, me and my SEAL buddy Bobby O.—a little Irish guy whose specialties were comms and picking up chicks—donned our black skin suits, which covered us from head to foot, slipped on our fins, slid in the water, and swam to the beach. It was a little finger of land with a harbor area and airport to the west and a big landmass beyond a tributary to the east.

SEALs aren't choirboys. A couple of months earlier, I was trying to get Bobby out of a hotel room in the Philippines. He spoke to me through the closed door, saying, "Don, I've reached the lowest point of my life." When he finally let me in, I saw a naked Filipino woman sitting on the foot of the bed smiling; she was cross-eyed and wore thick glasses and was hugely overweight and covered with freckles.

But despite Bobby O.'s tastes in women, I trusted him with my life.

As I sidestroked through the ocean, I kept checking the water behind and to the sides of him, and he watched the water around me. We'd been warned during the pre-mission intel briefing that these waters were infested with sharks. Seems like the Somali operated a camel-meat processing plant nearby that dumped the camel innards in the ocean, thus attracting hundreds of sharks.

Thankfully, Bobby and I made it to the shore in one piece and the four of us quickly dug two holes, one to bury our equipment in and one to live in, both of which we covered with camo netting.

And that's where we were two days later, me, Bobby O., the LT, and Drake—a tall, lanky guy and weapons expert— ███████ ██ ████████████████████████████████████ It would've been easy work if it weren't for the extreme heat and violent windstorms that filled our mouths and ears with sand. Especially when we were trying to sleep, which we had to do sitting up.

"You still having fun, Doc?" the lieutenant asked.

"Hoo-ya."

Added to the sandstorms were two other challenges. One, our hole had filled up with salt water during high tide. And two, all of us were suffering from serious cases of food poisoning.

███ ██ ██ ███████████████████████ They reciprocated by showing us how to eat poisonous snakes: by snapping their heads against our boots, peeling the skin back with our teeth, pulling out the venom sacs, and eating the meat. Now we were all horribly sick. Running fevers, puking our guts out, and suffering from real ugly diarrhea.

In between frequent bouts of relieving ourselves in our foxhole, we cursed the Egyptians. Soon after we left Cairo, they were sent on a mission to take down a hijacked Boeing 737 Egypt Air jet. ████ ██ ██ on the plane and set it on fire. Fifty-eight passengers died, along with two of the six crew members and two of the three Abu Nidal terrorists. The third, Omar Rezaq, was captured and sent to prison. Until September 11, 2001, it was the deadliest airplane hijacking in history.

The Egyptians considered the mission a success. We, however, were deeply embarrassed and knew we'd get ribbed endlessly about it when we returned to the States. Something like *Nice job, guys. Next time we need to* ████ *foreigners to fry airline passengers, we know who to send.*

Back in the hole on the beach, my teammates were losing patience. Even our lieutenant started to bitch, saying, "I should have trained to become a helicopter pilot. This sucks."

Drake, a total action junkie, said, "I should have stayed living in the desert, racing cars and motorcycles."

Aside from the occasional gripes, we didn't talk much. Instead, we listened to our surroundings and were occupied with our own inner musings about life and the possible dangers that waited around the corner, musings that were intermittently interrupted by the sound of one of us snoring or throwing up. Thick green bile mostly, since we didn't have anything in our stomachs.

LT turned to me and flashed his isn't-life-a-pile-of-shit smile. "You still having fun, Doc?"

"I'm fine, LT. What about you?"

Sitting in a foxhole with sand whipping our faces and shitty water up to our necks didn't seem to be such a hardship, considering the excitement of the op. I mean, no one other than a handful of people back in Coronado, California, even knew we were there. We were completely on our own in enemy territory with limited ammo, on a

████████████████████████████████████

████████████████████

It didn't get more thrilling than this.

Day three, I was on watch with my ████████████████

████████████████████████████████████

████████████████████████████—when, through my goggles, I spotted a local man approaching. Through the rising heat and swirling sand, he looked like a figure out of the movie *Lawrence of Arabia*.

It was about three in the afternoon. The man was skinny, midtwenties, with a short beard. He obviously had no idea that he was approaching a hole with four armed U.S. Navy SEALs inside.

I roused my buddies as I kept my weapon trained on the Somali man's chest. We'd been taught to aim at the center of mass. Despite what you see people do in the movies, heads are too easy to miss.

The four of us SEALs were well versed in the U.S. military rules of engagement, which stated, in part: "Deadly force may be used to defend your life, the life of another US soldier, or the life of persons in areas of US control…when (a) You are fired upon; (b) Armed elements, mobs, and/or rioters threaten human life; and (c) There is a clear demonstration of hostile intent in your presence."

Common sense told us to simply take the guy out with a silenced weapon and feed him to the fish. But warfare is rarely simple, and we'd been trained to operate within the parameters of the U.S. military code.

There was nothing we could do except watch the guy approach and hope he changed course. Which he didn't. Because, according to Murphy's Law, "If something can go wrong, it generally will sooner or later."

When he got within thirty yards of us, he saw us, and the guy stopped in his tracks. I watched his shocked expression as he took in the camo netting and the four of us wearing desert-camouflage uniforms, floppy hats, and goggles, all of us pointing weapons at his chest. For all we knew, he thought we were aliens from another planet.

Then he raised his arms. No, he wasn't giving us the Vulcan salute. He was freaking out, shouting in a language none of us understood—probably Somali. After doing a quick about-face in the sand, he ran away as fast as his skinny legs could carry him. Since we weren't in a position to take him prisoner, we just watched.

"Shit!" muttered my teammate Bobby O.

Now, in addition to being sicker than ever, we'd just been compromised. Which wasn't good at all. We were having trouble keeping down water and MREs (which we called "not really meals or ready to eat"). And our demolition mission and extraction wasn't until the following night.

We waited until nightfall, then slammed into action. The plan was to dig up all our gear, cover the holes so it looked like we were never there, inflate the rubber Zodiac, put it in the water, place our dive gear inside, rig the gas tank and engine, motor toward the harbor, then dive and attach a limpet mine to one of their ships.

We definitely weren't in the best of shape. But the three of us were digging hard, unearthing our equipment, as the LT kept watch. I was psyched to finally be moving; I was heaving shovelfuls of sand over my shoulder when I heard the LT say, "Okay, guys, put your hands up."

"What?"

"Guys, put your hands up!"

I wasn't sure I was hearing him right. But when I looked past the LT I saw about two dozen armed Somali approaching with AK-47s pointed at us. They were climbing over a slight knoll about a hundred meters away, and they looked frightened, as though they were wondering: *What are these strange-looking giants doing on our land?*

Maybe because I was in the company of highly trained teammates I trusted, I wasn't scared. We could have run and jumped in the water. Or we could have reached for our weapons. Either way, we probably would have been shot to pieces by the Somali.

Our lieutenant wisely told us to stand right where we were and raise our arms over our heads, which we did, even though it felt wrong to surrender without a fight.

The Somali circled us with their fingers on the triggers of their AKs. Safeties off. I remember thinking: *They can't shoot us now, because if they do, they'll fire right into one another.*

But these weren't trained soldiers. Besides, what did I know.

Their leader started screaming incoherently. We had no idea what he was saying. His men looked like they wanted to blow us away and return home.

Bobby O. tried addressing the head man in English. "Hold on, chief," he said. "Let me show you something."

As Bobby reached for his rucksack, four Somali put rifles up to his head. I thought they were going to blow his brains out.

Bobby shouted, "Whoa, guys! Back off!" And looked like he was about to shit his pants. All of us tensed up.

Their leader motioned with his arm. Using the few words of English he knew, he said, "Down! Down! We shoot you!"

Screw that.

His volume increased. "Down! Get down!" It looked like his eyes were going to pop out of their sockets.

We weren't moving. No fucking way.

As their leader continued pointing at the ground and screaming, a couple of the other armed Somali discovered the gear we'd started digging up. Thankfully, they didn't look through the bags, because if they had, they would have seen the mines and demolition equipment and quickly figured out that we were up to no good.

Our LT said, "We speak English. Do you know someone who speaks English?"

"Eng-leesh?"

"Yeah, English. We're Americans."

This seemed to register with their leader, who decided to hold us prisoner while one of his men returned to the nearest village to find someone who spoke our language.

Several hours later, his man came back with a dirty-looking fellow who described himself as a local merchant. He wore a robe with a dark vest over it and spoke some English.

It was approaching midnight. The merchant explained that the Somali were going to kill us for trespassing on their land. He said, "Okay, sir. Now you must lie on your stomach, so they can shoot you in the back. Because that's what they do here to trespassers."

No, we told him. That's not going to happen.

What started as a standoff turned into a discussion conducted without anger or raised voices but with loaded AK-47s still pointed at our heads.

After several hours of back-and-forth, the Somali leader gave us permission to show the interpreter one of the ███████████ we had in our rucksacks. "It says that we're only on a training mission," the LT explained. "We're Americans. We're sorry we trespassed on your land. We won't do it again."

The Somali leader considered this, then pointed emphatically to our rubber boat and said, "Go!"

The local merchant elaborated. "He wants you to get in your boat and go back to America."

"Sure thing." That was a long way to travel with a 55-horsepower motor, but it sounded good.

"Go...now!" the leader repeated.

"Yeah. Right away."

We thanked the merchant and the leader, who turned and left with his armed men and the merchant, to our great relief.

Our LT had been right not to resist them. If we'd done anything differently, all four of us would most likely have been shot and left to die on the beach in Somalia.

We were physically and mentally exhausted. "LT," Bobby O. said. "We just cheated death. What do you say we go home?" None of us felt like diving into shark-infested waters.

LT wasn't having any of it. Like I said before, he was a gung ho type. He growled, "Guys, get your gear on. Our mission won't be a success unless we complete it. Let's go!"

"Has he lost his friggin' mind?" Bobby O. asked under his breath.

Still wearing our skin suits, we donned masks, fins, white belts, and rebreathers. Then dove into the warm, pitch-black bay, which stank and was covered with a layer of oily gunk. Our route took us right past the camel-meat processing plant. All I could think of was the sharks. When something brushed past me, my heart almost stopped.

We were going on pure adrenaline and couldn't see a thing other than the luminescent dials of our depth gauges, compasses, and Tudor dive watches. The German diving Drägers strapped to our chests were feeding us 100 percent oxygen so that no bubbles could be seen on the surface.

We had four hours max before that high a concentration of oxygen became toxic. We traveled in two-man teams. I was paired with Bobby. He was the navigator and focused on his dive compass, while I timed each leg of the dive with my watch. After we swam an allotted amount of time on a particular bearing, I'd squeeze his arm, which was the signal for him to stop and set the next direction on the compass.

We doglegged through the harbor for three hours underwater until we located the right ship. Then we extracted the ███████████ from a pack and attached it to the ship's hull exactly where our intel had determined it should be placed. ████████████████████████████
██

We set the timer and checked our watches: we were running out of time.

Now we had to swim back to where we had anchored our Zodiac CRRC. But when we got close we realized we had a problem. We'd left the boat when the tide was high. Hours later, in the low tide, our Zodiac rubber boat was beached and a couple of hundred meters from the water. High and dry.

First light was less than an hour away. Even though we were completely spent from the ordeal with the Somali and then the four-hour dive, we had to sprint over to the boat, carry it to the water, sprint back to pick up the gas tanks, motor, and all our gear, and then carry it back to the boat. This took multiple trips, all of which we had to do while carrying our personal gear and weapons.

By the time we had all our gear in the Zodiac and the 55-horsepower motor cranked up to max, the sun was starting to rise over the horizon.

That meant that we'd missed our primary pickup time; now we had to wait another twenty-four hours and try again.

Instead, our LT decided that we should trek ten kilometers through the desert and then radio headquarters to initiate plan B, which involved meeting a local guide who would take us to a nearby airstrip. This meant that we had to be on alert all day in case the armed Somali tribesmen returned.

Shortly after nightfall we met our guide, a smelly little Ethiopian man who had never worked with Americans before. For some reason, he was constantly touching us and giggling. I was designated the guide handler, meaning it was my job to take the guide out if he should do anything to put us in jeopardy.

The eager Ethiopian led us through some low desert terrain to the far end of an airstrip. As the sun started to rise, we paid our guide, cut through the barbed-wire fence, crawled through on our bellies, then radioed the extraction aircraft.

Then the four of us hid in the low shrubs and waited. No one had slept more than an hour or two in the past four days.

LT, lying beside me, asked, "How are you doing, Doc?"

"Okay, LT. How about you?" We were shivering and sweating simultaneously. Sick, dirty, hungry, thirsty, and exhausted. The sun burned into our backs.

"You still having fun, Doc?"

"Hoo-ya," I answered, with a little less enthusiasm than before. The truth is I couldn't wait to get the hell out of there.

All of us kept glancing up at the cloud cover over the landing strip, hoping for some sign of a friendly aircraft.

As the minutes dragged by, our desperation grew.

Finally, after about an hour, we heard this low rumble that quickly turned into a roar. Sounded as though the sky were exploding. Bobby O. covered his ears.

Looking up, I saw a C-130 cut through the clouds nose-first, like an arrow headed straight for the ground. As the four of us held our breath, the C-130 straightened out at the last second, touched down on the runway, and immediately slammed on its brakes.

Smoke billowed from the landing gear as though the plane were on fire. The smell of burning rubber was intense.

Through the drifting smoke, we watched the rear ramp open. Then the LT said, "Let's go!"

We ran like hell with all our gear. As soon as we boarded, the crew closed the ramp and then the plane took off. Talk about an amazing short-field landing. I'd seen several, but none as dramatic as that.

The C-130 ferried us back safely to the base in Cairo. The mission had been a success, but we were all sick as dogs; at the base, we lay in a stifling fly-filled tent—pasty white, throwing up constantly, running high fevers. I was in the worst shape of the four of us. I couldn't keep fluids down and it was impossible to get an IV in my arm because my veins had collapsed. My fever was up to 104 and rising.

My alarmed teammates summoned an Egyptian doctor. Half awake, I saw him approach me with a nasty-looking syringe that had no cover on it. His hands looked dirty and he was covered with flies.

"Egyptian medicine," he announced with a big smile. "I'll take care of you, sir. I'll fix you."

I said, "No way you're putting the needle and whatever is in it in me."

He backed off. After half a dozen more tries, Bobby O. finally got an IV in my arm. We forced in about 3,000 ccs of Ringer's lactate, and I started to revive.

That night the four of us were invited to go to dinner with some Egyptian military VIPs. We were still weak and exhausted, but we were expected to attend. At around six, a little guy named Mohammed showed up to escort us to the restaurant.

On the way, he took us through a section of town that was crowded with tourist shops peddling jewelry, cosmetics, scarves, and rugs. He stopped in practically every shop we passed to point out the array of perfumes.

He'd say, "Look, Mr. Don. Your wife, your girlfriend will like this."

"No, thanks, Mohammed."

None of us showed the least bit of interest. We just wanted to get the dinner over with, return to the base, and crash.

But Mohammed wouldn't leave us alone. He was constantly at my elbow, saying, "Look, Mr. Don. Fine perfume. Very nice. I get you the very best price."

"No, thanks."

I tried arguing with him, I tried ignoring him, but he wouldn't let up.

After half an hour we arrived at an upscale restaurant where four or five Egyptian military officers were waiting. They escorted us to a round table. My three SEAL buddies sat across from me. The Egyptian officers found places next to them. Mohammed settled to my right.

The waiters placed before us plates of fried falafel, kushari, baba ghanoush, lamb kebobs, and more. All the local delicacies. None of us four SEALs had any appetite. We just wanted to get through the dinner politely and then go back to our tent in west Cairo. It had been a difficult week.

But Mohammed to my right kept bugging me. He kept saying, "Please, Mr. Don. You can't leave without buying some fine perfume. I'll take you later."

"No, thanks."

He wouldn't let up. "Please, Mr. Don. I insist. I'll show you. I'll personally guarantee the very best price."

"I said no."

"Oh, yes, Mr. Don. You'll see. These are the finest perfumes in all the world."

I'd held myself together through the heat and diarrhea, the night of captivity and exhaustion, the collapsed veins, even the sharks. But with this little Egyptian handler refusing to leave me alone, I snapped. I lifted a sharp knife from the table and held it to his throat.

Mohammed's eyes bugged out and his face turned white.

In an even tone—without raising my voice—I said, "Shut the fuck up, Mohammed."

He nodded and I put down the knife.

Nobody at the table said anything about the incident. We finished our dinner as though nothing had happened.

As we neared the base, LT walked beside me and flashed his sinister smile. "You still having fun, Doc?" he asked.

"Sure." But inside, I was saying, *I just want to get out of here alive and in one piece.*

"Teams and shit, huh, Doc?" LT asked. It was a SEAL saying that in a few words described all the training and hardship we had to go through to accomplish what we did. I'd just completed my first real-world SEAL mission.

"Teams and shit. Yeah," I responded, now appreciating what the words meant.

Through all the action, the physical and mental challenges, and the brushes with death, my enthusiasm for SEAL life hasn't dimmed. Call me a maniac, which many people have. Call me crazy. But I've never wanted it any other way.

CHAPTER TWO

New England, 1970s

Looking for adventure
In whatever comes our way...
—*Steppenwolf, "Born to Be Wild"*

During my career I've been called Dr. Death, Don Maniac, Warrant Officer Manslaughter, and Sweet Satan. Over the past three decades I've served as a Navy SEAL lead petty officer, assault team member, boat-crew leader, department head, training officer, advanced-training officer, weapons of mass destruction (WMD) officer, and, more recently, program director preparing civilians for BUD/S (Basic Underwater Demolition/ SEAL) training. I was asked by the U.S. Navy in 1997 to assist with the Navy recruiting command and created the SEAL Adventure Challenge and the SEAL Training Academy, where we taught skydiving, combat scuba diving, small-unit tactics, marksmanship, and land navigation. Up until August of 1998, I was on active duty with SEAL Team Six.

Owing to my long years in service and my career in extreme adventure sports—which has included seventy-five thousand miles of running and three hundred thousand miles of biking—I'm also known on the teams as the high-mileage SEAL.

Over the years I developed a reputation for being one of the ST-6 commandos who liked to push the envelope. Rip it apart if I could.

Like the time I decided to beat the biannual SEAL physical-readiness test record in Panama on a black-flag day. *Black flag* means "dangerously high heat." According to base policy, military and civilian personnel weren't allowed to exercise or work outside on a black-flag day. I said, The hell with that, and set out to beat the course record.

In the hundred-degree, high-humidity heat, I performed 120 push-ups and 120 sit-ups, swam a half a mile, and followed that with a three-mile run. During the run, less than three hundred meters from the finish line, my vision started to blur to the point that I couldn't tell the people from the trees. I kept pushing harder. Woke up on my back looking up at the timekeeper—a senior chief petty officer in a khaki uniform.

"Did I break seventeen thirty?" I asked him, referring to the course record of seventeen minutes and thirty seconds.

"Seventeen twenty-eight, you maniac," he answered.

"Then I'm okay."

Most people have no idea of what their full potential is. One of my mottos is Blood from Any Orifice. Because I figure that if you don't push beyond what you think your limits are, you'll never know your true abilities.

I've always tested limits. People who know me say that despite my intensity, I appear to be soft-spoken and relaxed. Truth is, over the years I've learned to manage the almost uncontrollable fire burning inside me.

But I put my parents through living hell growing up.

I was a bad kid, and I'm not proud of the fact that I was a lousy role model to my younger brother, sisters, and friends. My parents were good, kind, loving people who deserved better than what I gave them.

My dad loved his country so much that the day after the attack on Pearl Harbor he quit high school to join the Navy. He became a distinguished stunt pilot. On the last day of World War II, an officer ordered him and fifteen of his fellow sailors to stand on the platform of an aircraft carrier so that they could be ceremoniously lowered down to the dock.

But the platform mechanism broke and they fell sixty feet. My dad broke his back. One sailor died. Since then he had a soft spot for disabled vets—volunteering long hours at the local VFW (Veterans of Foreign Wars) and serving as the state commander of the VFW in South Carolina. He ended up working as an executive in large insurance companies, and he still liked nothing more than to make other people laugh and have a good time.

My mom was a Limestone, Maine, homecoming queen, the valedictorian of her class, and the salt of the earth—totally dedicated to her family in every way. She was born premature, weighing three pounds, in an early February blizzard. Her parents didn't think she would survive, but they put her in the kitchen oven to keep her warm until the storm eased up enough for them to get her to a hospital.

She had a quick, sarcastic wit that made all of us laugh. She and my dad were like a comedy team at parties—the local Stiller and Meara.

And I was their first son—a bat-out-of-hell, shit-kicker motorcycle punk. I popped out of my mother's womb with a wild, crazy energy that has never let up.

We lived in various spots throughout New England—Limestone, Maine; Orange, Connecticut; Nashua, New Hampshire—but I consider Methuen, Massachusetts, to be my childhood home (it's also where my dad was born). It's situated in the northeast part of the state, right across the border from Rockingham County, New Hampshire. Back in the 1970s, Methuen and nearby Orange were considered Mafia towns. Methuen was rough but bucolic, with ponds, streams, the Merrimack and Spicket Rivers, a bird sanctuary, and lots of forested land.

I was into giving myself impossible challenges from the start. Beginning in second grade, one of my favorite activities was to go into the woods and walk for hours in a random direction, then try to find my way home.

By fourth grade, I was sneaking smokes on the school playground and building go-carts out of shopping-cart wheels and scraps of wood. My buddies and I would slip out at night and meet at the cemetery, which had this wicked long hill. We'd fly down it in the dark, screaming and often crashing into headstones. Part of me knew what we were doing was wrong, but I was young and filled with wild, anarchic energy, and it was so much damn fun.

By fifth grade, I'd graduated to minibikes, which led to dirt bikes and motorcycles. Then I was really gone.

I loved the smell, the roar, the power, the promise of the track, open trail, and road. For me, nothing matched the excitement of riding fast and hitting the jumps hard so I sailed high in the air. The suspense that occurred during flight was incredible.

My dad, bless his heart, tried his best to keep me under some kind of control. Because I was too young to get a license, he told me to stick to riding on the track or on the trails in the woods behind our house. But I couldn't resist the lure of the streets—where the big kids rode their choppers.

I craved danger, action, and adventure, and it won't surprise you that my hero growing up was Evel Knievel—a man who wasn't afraid to look death in the face.

Imitating my idol, I'd roar down the streets on my Kawasaki 175 doing wheelies, scaring old ladies, and getting into fights.

I studied Evel's life and knew he failed as many times as he succeeded. When he attempted to jump the fountains outside of Caesars Palace in Las Vegas, his bike malfunctioned on takeoff, causing him to hit the safety ramp and skid across the parking lot, which resulted in a crushed pelvis and femur, fractures to his wrist and both ankles, and a concussion that kept him in a coma for twenty-nine days.

In '68 he crashed while attempting to jump fifteen Ford Mustangs and broke his right leg and foot. Three years later, in California, while trying to jump thirteen Pepsi delivery trucks, he came down front-wheel-first on the base of the ramp and was thrown off his bike. He broke his collarbone and suffered compound fractures of his right arm and both legs.

He ended up in the Guinness book of world records for suffering the most broken bones in a lifetime—433. But through it all, he never backed down from a promise. I considered that important. Evel said, "When you give your word to somebody that you're going to do something, you've gotta do it," and when he promised an audience he would make a jump, he did it, even when he realized that it was impossible.

Years later, and with both of his arms in casts, Evel Knievel flew out to California and confronted a promoter named Shelly Saltman who alleged that Evel had abused his wife and kids and used drugs. Evel attacked Saltman outside Twentieth Century Fox studios with a baseball bat and shattered his wrist and arm.

He also told kids to stay in school and not do drugs.

I listened to him, even though drugs and failure were becoming more and more common all around me.

Another big influence was the Hells Angels, which was a paradox, since Evel regularly criticized them for dealing drugs.

Motorcycle gangs were big in our neck of New England. Besides the Angels, we had the Huns, Evil Spirits, Hole in the Wall—and given the environment I grew up in, it was probably inevitable that the guys I hung out with started stealing motorcycles and cars. They targeted kids who they thought didn't deserve them. For example, if they heard that some rich kid's father had bought his son a fancy new Honda motorcycle or a Camaro, one of them would say, "That douche bag doesn't even know how to ride; let's go rob the sucker."

No wonder the area I grew up in eventually became one of the stolen-car capitals of the United States. In the early to middle 1970s, many of the stolen vehicles were driven to a place called the Pit, located in a heavily wooded part of Methuen, Massachusetts, where the cars and motorcycles were stripped for parts.

Even though I drew the line at stealing, I got a kick out of driving a stripped car up a steep hill, putting it in neutral, riding down, and jumping out before it crashed into the other cars and trees below. I also liked to fight, ride, and get crazy.

By the time I was in sixth grade, the kids around me were drinking and doing drugs. Our drink of choice was something we called a Tango—orange juice and lots of vodka. We also drank our share of Boone's Farm wine, which to our unsophisticated palates tasted fantastic.

I became a ringleader. I was the only non-Italian in our group, the Flat Rats—so named because we lived in a suburban part of the town called the Flats. Many of my friends had dads and uncles who were members of the Mafia. We had long hair and wore black leather jackets, jeans, tight-fitting T-shirts, and black boots.

Total hell-raisers.

One summer afternoon I was out on the road riding motorcycles with my buddy Greg. I said, "Hey, Greg, if you see the cops, take off. Because if I get caught, my dad will kill me." I was maybe fifteen years old. Too young to have a driver's license. Trying to outrun the cops was always a good time.

We were cruising up a local two-way back-country road north of Methuen when we came to a stop at a four-way stop sign, and I spotted a cop car to my left. I yelled, "Greg. Cops. Take off!"

He pulled back on the throttle but flooded out and stalled.

I hung a right on my Kawasaki 175 and took off. WFO (wide fucking open), we called it. To my mind, WFO was the only way to go.

My bike could only get up to about seventy-two miles an hour max, so on the straight stretches of road, the cop car got right up on my tail. I braked, downshifted, and turned right onto somebody's lawn. Because the grass was wet, I did a quick one-eighty, spitting up a rooster tail of mud and grass.

The cop surprised me and turned onto the lawn too.

This guy wasn't going to be easy to shake.

I peeled off back in the direction I'd come from, thinking that maybe I'd catch up with Greg. My Kawasaki screamed, the cop's siren blared, and adrenaline raced through my veins. Approaching the four-way stop sign, I saw another cop cruiser light up its flashers and join the chase.

Now I had two cop cars on my tail.

I tore through one town after another, running through my repertoire of tricks. My favorite was to stick my right arm out like I was pulling over, then, when the cruisers passed me, gun the bike and scream by, shooting the cops my see-ya smile.

But nothing seemed to work. After forty-five minutes of being chased, I began to worry. None of my previous escapades with the police had lasted this long. I was actually more worried about my father than the cops.

My long hair flying out of the back of my helmet, I tore down country roads with the cops on my tail. Approaching cars had to swerve off to the side to give us room to pass. I was a small kid—maybe five seven at fifteen years old—and the bike was too big for me, so I was bouncing up and down on the seat and gas tank, which hurt.

One police car inched up to my back wheel, and, determined not to get caught, I zoomed faster, past a large farm where some of my buddies and I had worked. Some of the Puerto Rican workers out in the fields picking corn recognized me and started cheering. They yelled words of encouragement.

Salem, New Hampshire, was just ahead. I saw the light at the five-way intersection turn red. To my right was a Dairy Queen parking lot crowded with pickups and station wagons filled with families and kids going out to get a summer afternoon sundae swirl or shake.

I made a split-second decision and turned into the crowded lot.

People panicked. Mothers screamed, "Watch out!" and grabbed their children. They wrapped them in protective hugs while their husbands cursed me: "Lunatic!" "Asshole!" "Hoodlum!" "Stupid punk!"

I wove my way through the maze of vehicles and people, braked when I absolutely had to, and skidded my way through.

The cops had to steer around it, which meant that I gained a little time, but they quickly caught up with me on a long, straight country road. My bike was screaming hot and I was running low on fuel.

One of the cop cars—the one that was aggressively staying near my back wheel—passed and cut in front of me. I braked hard, downshifted fast, and faced two options: One, slam into his car broadside. Two, cut left into unknown terrain.

I chose the second and was immediately confronted with a five-foot-high stone wall. Sudden death. At the last second I spotted a tiny opening and miraculously squeezed through.

Whew!

A second or so later I hit something that stopped me and almost caused me to fly off the bike and do an endo (end over end). A large root had lodged itself between the frame of my bike and the engine.

I tried pulling the root out. No luck.

Looking back, I saw the cops running toward me with their sticks and pistols ready.

I cut the engine and asked myself: *What do I do now?*

Before I could think of an answer, one of the cops grabbed me by the hair sticking out of the back of my helmet and yanked me off seat and over the back fender. I hit the ground and immediately felt a nightstick crash into my ribs.

I felt a sharp pain. Then another. Then dozens in succession from multiple cops.

They beat the living hell out of me until I passed out. I woke hours later on a bench in a local jail, badly bruised and hurting.

I called my mom, who was extremely upset but managed to remain calm. She came and got me released on bail.

I said, "Mom, I'm really sorry."

She looked at me sadly and shook her head. "When your dad comes home tonight, make sure you tell him everything that happened."

Most weeks he was away from home four out of five nights, traveling for work. But because this was a Friday, my dad returned for the weekend at around eight.

When he walked in the front door, I was still wearing the same tank top that I'd had on all day. It was ripped and spotted with dried blood. My bottom lip was badly swollen and I had big black-and-blue bruises covering my ribs, arms, and shoulders.

He asked, "What happened? You have an accident on your bike?"

"No, Dad. I got caught riding on the road."

"You were riding on the road?"

"Yes," I answered. "But look what the cops did to me. I was unconscious by the time the cops hauled me to jail."

I couldn't tell if Dad was angrier at me or the cops. He wanted to know the name of the arresting officer.

"Officer Phil Smith," I told him. "Of the Salem, New Hampshire, police department."

Seconds later he was on the phone saying, "This is Arthur Mann. You arrested my son this afternoon for riding on the road, but you had no right to beat him up the way you did."

I watched the expression on his face change from outrage at them to anger at me as he listened to Officer Smith describe chasing me through four towns and two states, the cars that had been run off the road, and the scene in the Dairy Queen parking lot. I heard the officer explain, "We would have shot your son, but he looked too young."

My father's face was red when he turned to me and said, "You're never riding that motorcycle again as long as you live in this house! You understand me?"

I nodded and said, "Yes, Dad." But I was thinking, *Where am I going to live?*

I mean, I had to keep riding and racing motorcycles.

I stashed my Kawasaki in the basement and worked on it at night. For a couple of weeks, I obeyed my dad, but I knew it was just a matter of time.

One Saturday afternoon a couple weeks later, my dad asked me if I would go pick up my brother at his friend's house.

"On my bike?" I asked, knowing that where we lived, kids were allowed to ride on the back-country dirt roads without a license.

He said, "Okay. I'll make an exception this time."

Excited, I passed through the kitchen where my mom and my sister Wendy were washing dishes.

Minutes later I was screaming down a dirt road, enjoying the wind in my face and the smell and the feel of my Kawasaki. I knew that I'd be passing the house of my girlfriend, Jody, and I wanted to impress her. To let her know that I was back.

She lived on a dirt road by a lake. The lake was on my right; her house was on my left. I did a second-to-third-gear wheelie as I swerved around the corner.

It just so happened that a friend of mine was on his bike speeding in my direction. He was in the process of passing a car around that same corner, and we smashed into each other head-on.

My girlfriend, Jody, was looking out her bedroom window, and she heard a terrible crash and saw both bikes fly in the air. She said they rose as high as the telephone lines.

I hit the ground and broke all the ribs on my right side so severely that bone fragments stuck into my liver. I also broke my arm and several bones in my face and suffered a concussion. I was in a coma for almost a week.

The doctors told my parents that I wasn't going to survive.

I woke up hovering near the ceiling of a hospital hallway. Below, I saw my dad in his suit and tie holding my mother, who was crying. They were watching a gurney being wheeled past by several orderlies. A bloody sheet covered a body.

Months later, I realized that I had had a near-death experience.

I was looking at myself.

It took me months to recover from my injuries, and between visits from my hoodlum friends, I made a decision to dedicate my life to something, and I chose the only thing that really excited me at the time: motocross racing.

It might seem like a strange decision given the fact that I had almost killed myself on a motorcycle, but it gave my life some purpose and direction. Besides, in motocross, all riders travel in the same direction, so the chances of a head-on are very slim. At least, that's the reasoning I gave my parents.

When they asked me what I wanted for Christmas, I said a weight set. They got one for me, and I started working out. Every night at around eleven, I'd come home after working or hanging out with my buddies, put on my headphones, crank up Black Sabbath on my stereo, and lift weights—curls, bench presses, overhead presses—then do rowing, push-ups, and sit-ups. I'd try to do a continuous set of a particular exercise to each individual song. "Iron Man" and "Paranoid" were my favorites.

Often I'd keep going until two or three in the morning, then I'd catch a couple hours sleep before heading off to school.

After school and weekends, I worked various different jobs—pumping gas, washing cars. One of my most memorable jobs was at a place called Raymond's Turkey Farm on Hampstead Street. They hired me even though I was underage because I was willing to do the nastiest job they had, which was working in the cellar and preparing the turkeys for the slaughter.

I was fourteen or fifteen years old and experiencing something that was like a scene out of the horror movie *Texas Chainsaw Massacre*. Or worse.

In the weeks leading up to Thanksgiving and Christmas, I'd work day and night, sometimes fifteen hours at a time, up to my knees in blood. My job was to reach down, grab the turkeys by their feet, and hang them on these racks. Then an old guy with an electric knife cut their heads off.

Next, these ladies put some kind of vacuum cleaner down their throats to suck their lungs out. These were dumped into big barrels that I had to clean out at the end of every shift. It was disgusting, and the smell was awful.

But I was young and making $1.65 an hour, which helped support my motorcycle habit. My parents wouldn't let me go out on the weekends unless I came home with my paycheck and posted it on the refrigerator. That was for bail money, in case I was arrested.

Which happened often.

The guy who got me the job, Bobby, was two years older than me. He used to pick me up on the way to school and drive me home after school. And every time he left my house, he burned rubber, leaving behind tire tracks in our driveway and a cloud of smoke. He drove like a maniac, always over a hundred miles an hour—blasting "Hot Rocks" by the Stones from his eight-track and Jensen triaxial speakers. I don't know how we survived, but somehow we did. Barely.

Between working, school, and training for motocross, I still managed to routinely get into trouble.

One of my best friends, Gary DeAngelis, was the mechanic for my bikes at the motocross races. He was a big, heavy guy with a thick black beard and long matted hair, and he was on probation to be a member of the Hells Angels. As part of his initiation, the whole chapter had urinated on him, and he wasn't allowed to change his clothes or take a shower for a year.

One night, he and I and three or four other bikers went to a bar together; a fight broke out, and someone kicked a glass door in. I ran out because I was underage and didn't want to get caught.

Instead of calling it a night, we rode to another bar, where we were all arrested. I was handcuffed to Gary for an entire weekend. Man, did he stink!

When I turned sixteen, in October of 1973, I finally got my license. Christmas Eve I borrowed my dad's station wagon because I was going out to buy my girlfriend, Kim, a Christmas present. On the way to the mall, I stopped at her house and ran into her dad, who was a World War II veteran, and his best friend, Nicky, who was a member of the Hells Angels, the Lawrence, Massachusetts, chapter.

Nicky said, "Don, I heard you just turned sixteen. Come have a drink with us."

"I'd better not."

"Come on, man. Let's celebrate. Don't be a pussy."

Nicky was one of the craziest, funniest people I'd ever met. I looked up to him as a role model of a sort.

I said, "Okay," had some drinks with them, then got into my dad's station wagon. While I was inside, a blizzard had blown in. The roads were slick, and visibility was terrible. But I still had to get a present for Kim.

Seeing a snowplow ahead of me, I decided it might be a good idea try to catch him.

I hit the gas hard, did a three-sixty, smashed into some trees, and ended up in a frozen swamp.

I'd just gotten my license and now I had wrecked my dad's car.

Sitting in the frozen swamp waiting for the tow truck, I felt like the guy in the Albert King song—the one later recorded by Jimi Hendrix and by Cream: "If it wasn't for bad luck, I wouldn't have no luck at all."

I didn't realize for a long time how lucky I was to have parents who loved me, despite everything, and to still be alive.

CHAPTER THREE

Graduation, 1976

Don't go 'round tonight.
Well, it's bound to take your life.
There's a bad moon on the rise.
—*Creedence Clearwater Revival, "Bad Moon Rising"*

It was the mid-1970s, and my friends and I were teenagers filled with wild, rebellious energy.

The mood in the country had turned dark and angry. Nobody trusted anyone. It was the tail end of the Vietnam War. President Nixon was in the White House trying to find his way out from under the debris of Watergate. Kids marched in the streets and burned the flag. Talk of revolution and repression filled the air.

My friends and I didn't understand what was going on around us. Nor did we know what to believe in. All we knew was that the world our parents had helped create was coming apart.

Were we aware that by emulating our neighborhood's motorcycle gangs, we risked getting drawn into a vortex of drugs and violence that seemed to grow faster and more powerful every day? Maybe on some level.

But what did we really understand?

Somehow, thank God, I managed to stay right on the edge of the whirlpool and never got completely sucked in—partly due to motocross training and racing. I practiced relentlessly at a track in Salem, New Hampshire. Every day, like a teenager possessed.

Friday after school my buddies and I would tear our bikes apart, clean them, and get them ready for the race on Sunday. Saturday afternoon we'd drive to some track in the New England–New York area in a '63 Chevy van, which we'd sleep in overnight.

I was raw and fearless, and drawn to the energy, excitement, and danger. (Some things never change.)

My goal was to become a professional. By tenth grade I was racing 125 cc and 250 cc, and in the open class and I already had a sponsor: Dave McCullen, the owner of New Haven Suzuki.

That changed one Sunday at a race in Pepperhill, New Hampshire. I was in fourth place, trying to catch Dave himself, who was in third. Even though he was my sponsor I was determined to beat him. Because that's the way I rode—WFO.

Motors screaming, mud spitting from our tires, Dave and I started climbing up a rocky slope. He was eight feet ahead of me, bouncing all over his bike. I bore down.

As I started to pass, his leg flew out of the peg. I whipped by, fighting to control my bike, with no chance to stop. My front tire smashed right into his leg. The leather motocross pants and boots Dave wore didn't save his leg from snapping.

Sorry, Dave. Good-bye, sponsor.

Despite the danger and my many accidents, I raced as often as I could, and I hung out with my rowdy friends at night.

School meant nothing to me. Some years I never once opened a book. When textbooks were handed out on the first day of class, I'd stash them in my locker and not look at them again until the last day of school, when we had to turn them in.

Once, at the end of the year, when a teacher asked for her textbooks back, I remember answering, "I'm sure they're in good condition, but they're in my locker, and I don't remember where my locker is."

I attended Amity High School in Woodbridge, Connecticut, where my Flat Rats friends and I were known as torks.

The jocks were from rich families. They played football, drove Chevy Camaros, and dated pretty girls. We torks wore dirty jeans, black boots, and black leather jackets, rode motorcycles, had muscular arms, and got into fights. Our girls were tough, drank and did drugs, and rode on the backs of our bikes.

There was a third group called the ziegs—the hippies who listened to the Grateful Dead and smoked pot.

Whenever torks and jocks were in the same room, you could feel the tension crawl up your neck. Insults were exchanged, and usually threats.

I shared a class after lunch with tall, blond Bobby Savage, the captain of the football team and leader of the jocks. At the time I'd reached about five eleven and weighed 165. Bobby was about six inches taller and fifty pounds heavier than me. He made snide remarks and tried to intimidate me all year long.

One day during class, I dropped a pencil that rolled under Bobby Savage's chair. When I went over to get it, he kicked the pencil to the back of the room.

All the kids in class stopped what they were doing and waited to see how I was going to react.

I walked to the back of the room and calmly picked up the pencil. But inside I was seething, thinking, *I can't let him disrespect me like that. I've got to do something. What am I gonna do?*

I blew off the next class and met up with a group of torks sitting at a table in the cafeteria. They were all Italian Americans and had fathers who were associated with the Mafia. Tough guys.

I leaned on the Formica tabletop with my foot resting on a chair behind me; the other torks huddled around me. As I started telling them what had just happened, one of my friends said, "Here he comes."

"Who?"

"Bobby Savage."

"Where?"

I turned to look over my shoulder and saw the big football player stride into the cafeteria with a tall, blond friend of his from the basketball team by his side. They even had the gall to walk by our table.

"Son of a…"

Without thinking, I kicked the chair my right leg was resting on, hard. Bobby's friend coolly stopped the chair and pushed it away.

I turned to face Savage, cocked my right arm back, and smashed him in the face.

Shock registered in his eyes. Blood shot from his shattered nose.

As his friend and my friends looked on, Savage crumpled to the floor. Immediately, I jumped on him and pounded him in the face about seven more times.

Then I got up and walked away.

The school was in an uproar. A tork had beaten up the big, tough captain of the football team—the leader of the jocks.

What was going to happen next?

I knew I was in trouble. About an hour later, I was walking down a hallway alone on my way to the bathroom when I saw Bobby Savage and his basketball friend come out of the nurse's office. Bobby's nose was covered with bandages and he had two black eyes.

He saw me and charged. Before I could react, the two big jocks grabbed me and pinned me against the wall.

"You asked for this, asshole."

"Take your best shot."

As Savage brought his arm back to slug me, I lifted my knee up as hard as I could into his crotch. His torso bent in half, and he lowered his head.

I brought up my knee again, this time into his face. Crunch!

A couple months later, I was sitting in a bar with three of my tough Flat Rats friends, flirting with four girls we'd just met. I was particularly interested in this cute brunette who had a mischievous smile and dimples in her cheeks.

The eight of us were sitting at a table laughing and drinking when we heard a loud commotion at the front door. Looking up, we saw this big, greasy guy in a black motorcycle jacket push his way through the crowd. He looked like an ex–football player who'd put on some weight.

He appeared to be out of his mind on drugs.

The girl sitting to my right looked alarmed. She picked up her purse from the chair and slung it over on her shoulder, as if she were getting ready to run.

I asked, "Who is he?"

One of my buddies answered, "That guy's a real scumbag. He used to deal drugs in front of the elementary school and just got released from jail."

Another friend added, "I heard he beat this one girl up so bad that her parents had to bring pictures of her to the hospital so the doctors could reconstruct her face."

The guy was clearly looking for someone, scanning the crowd. His bloodshot eyes came to rest on the girl beside me.

"You know that guy?" I asked her.

Before she had a chance to answer, the big, greasy scumbag stomped up to her and grabbed her arm.

He shouted, "You're coming with me, bitch!"

The brunette beside me started to tremble. The other girls at the table froze.

I felt like I had to protect her, so I said to the drug-crazed guy, "Back off. She's with me."

He brought his finger to within an inch of my face and snarled, "You, shut the fuck up!"

All the people in the bar stopped what they were doing to watch.

Then the big drug dealer yanked the purse off the girl's shoulder, which caused her chair to fall backward; her head slammed against the floor.

"Hey, man. What the hell!"

A bolt of fear passed through the packed crowd.

Then, while the girl was still moaning on the floor, the big scumbag grabbed her purse and stomped out of the bar. No one tried to stop him.

I got up and followed him outside, hoping my buddies would come with me. They decided to help the injured girl instead.

Now I was in the parking lot running after the big thug, wondering, *Why did he take her purse? Where the hell is he going?*

I saw his wide body ahead, pushing through the pools of light, and yelled at his back, "Hey, man, give back her purse."

He spun around and looked at me with cold fury. The guy was twice my size and clearly out of his mind on drugs. I knew that if he hit me, I'd be in serious trouble.

So I tried my best to defuse the situation. I said, "Look, man, I don't want to fight you. I just want the girl's purse. You walk one way, I'll go another. We'll forget this whole thing."

He growled back, "I'm going to rip your head off and shit down your throat."

Nice image.

I was standing about five feet away when he reached into the girl's purse, removed a set of keys, and threw the purse to the ground. Spewing a stream of curses at the girl and me, he stomped over to a light blue Corvette parked nearby and removed the hard T-top roof.

I expected him to jump into the Corvette and drive off.

Instead he raised the hard T top over his head and started coming at me. He looked like he wanted to kill me with it. He probably did.

I shouted, "Hey, put the roof down. I'm not here to fight you!"

He kept getting closer, the T top raised as a weapon. I backed away.

"The cops are coming. They'll be here any minute!"

When he got within five or six feet, I picked up a rock the size of a large toaster to defend myself with. Then I started to back away from him, down a path that led into the woods. He followed me with the T top held over his head and murder in his eyes.

We were descending into the dark woods, away from the well-lit parking lot.

I was growing increasingly nervous because I didn't know where I was going. I said again, maybe a little more desperately, "The cops are coming! I don't want anything from you. Just drop the roof and go!"

He kept bearing down on me with the T top held over his head. I backed downhill until we were out of sight of the bar. Probably out of earshot too. Then I stumbled on something, and he swung the hard roof at my head. I recovered just in time to jump out of the way.

"Hey!"

"You're a dead man. I'm gonna kill you!"

My heart was pounding wildly. I was alone with this crazed lunatic and scared.

At the bottom of the hill, we reached a little clearing with a junked car in it. The drug dealer swung the roof again. I ducked.

This time his momentum caused him to spin around, so he landed

45

with his back against the grille of the car. He froze for a minute, and I saw the panic of a trapped animal flash in his bloodshot eyes.

I still held the rock over my head but backed away to give him space.

I was in the awkward position of confronting him and trying to defuse the situation at the same time. I didn't want to fight, but he was growing increasingly aggressive and intense.

To my great relief I heard footsteps running down the trail. Three of my buddies entered the clearing, out of breath.

One of them shouted, "What's going on here? Don, you okay?"

"Not really," I answered, not taking my eyes off the thug. "This big guy's trying to kill me."

The big drug dealer, looking confused, wheeled and swung the roof at the biggest of my friends—a bodybuilder named Jay.

I shouted, "Jay, watch out!" and simultaneously threw the rock I'd been holding at the drug dealer's head, thinking, *If I have to, I'll kill him, but I don't want me or my friends to get hurt.*

The crazed man ducked his head at the last second, so the rock missed him, smashed the windshield of the junked car, and slid down the hood to the ground.

"You're a dead man now!" the drug dealer roared.

If he was crazed before, now he was completely unhinged. He threw down the roof, picked up the rock, and lunged at me.

I charged into him as hard as I could. My right shoulder sank into his stomach, knocking the wind out of him. The big man grunted, reeled backward, and crashed into the car.

I kept pushing my shoulder into his stomach.

From near the ground, I reached with my left hand, grabbed his nuts, and pulled down with all my might. The big man screamed and bent over. At precisely that moment, I punched up with my right hand and hit his face straight on.

Blood poured down my arm.

My friends descended on the guy, kicking and punching him. With my ears against his stomach, I could hear each impact, and I pulled away and shouted, "Guys, let up!"

We watched the drug dealer slump against the grille of the car. His face was a mess.

We left him bleeding into the ground and scrambled up through the woods to the parking lot. I told my friends to go home. I'd call them later.

One of them asked, "What about you?"

"I'm going to go back to the bar to see if the girl is okay."

"Are you crazy, Don? You can't do that!"

I said, "No. No, I'm fine."

Figuring that maybe it was better to wait for things to calm down, I walked to another bar nearby and headed to the bathroom.

When I walked in, people looked at me like I was a mass murderer. It wasn't until I looked in the mirror that I realized I had blood all over me—down my arm, splattered across my tank top, and smeared along the side of my face.

I washed up and went outside, where I heard police cars and saw a police helicopter hovering overhead. I ducked into a nearby miniature golf course, feeling like a fugitive. Actually crawled inside one of those doghouses people putt through, thinking, *Boy, am I in trouble!*

After forty minutes or so, I got out and started making my way carefully across the big parking lot. I planned to run into the woods if I saw the police.

Halfway across the lot this car came speeding around a corner and stopped beside me. To my relief, there was a couple inside. The guy who was driving rolled down his window, but the girl seated next to him leaned over and did all the talking.

She asked, "Are you okay?"

"Yeah, I'm fine."

Focusing on my ripped tank top that was stained with blood, she said, "You don't look fine. You got into a big fight, didn't you?"

"Yeah. Why?"

"Because the police were here and they took the guy's body. We're happy you did what you did. We'll help you get out of here."

I said, "That's okay. I'm going back to the bar to look for the girl."

"Don't do that," she warned. "The police are looking for you and your friends."

"I'll be okay."

"No," the girl said. "Let us give you a ride."

I climbed in the backseat. As the car approached the entrance, police officers emerged from the bar. I ducked down, waited for them to drive off, then I got out of the car.

The two bouncers standing in front recognized me immediately and put their hands on my shoulders.

One of them said, "Get out of here, right away. But thanks so much for what you did."

The second bouncer put in, "That big asshole is like public enemy number one around here. He's been terrorizing this town for years. They put him in an ambulance."

"Really?"

That's when it hit me: I might have killed him. But I remember thinking that if I did, I didn't feel bad.

He was a scumbag, a menace to society who got what was coming to him.

That incident was just one more example of how the scene around me was turning darker and more violent. The drugs that kids were taking got stronger. Guys I knew were starting to get hooked on heroin and cocaine. Girls I dated were turning to prostitution to pay for their drugs.

A quiet Flat Rat kid I knew and liked and who had been trying to stay out of trouble went out into his backyard one day, cut both his wrists, and shot himself in the head with a shotgun.

Not long after, Nicky, the Hells Angel I looked up to, got out of prison for stealing a police car and running over a cop. He returned to the one-bedroom apartment he shared with his father and brother and asked them both to sit with him at the kitchen table.

He said, "Dad, you've always hated me. We've never gotten along."

As his father and brother watched anxiously, Nicky started putting bullets in his mouth. Then he pulled a .38 out of his pocket and said, "I should blow you both away."

Finally, Nicky said, "To hell with you both," put the pistol in his mouth, and pulled the trigger.

I was shocked and deeply saddened by both deaths.

By the time I was finishing high school, kids I knew were stealing air conditioners out of their parents' homes to buy drugs. My own younger brother, Ricky, joined a car-theft ring and became addicted to cocaine.

And it kept getting closer to home. Just after I graduated from high school, my parents held a big party at my house. Hundreds of our friends showed up. The streets outside were jammed with parked cars and motorcycles.

People young and old were dancing, drinking, and having a good time. My parents told jokes and made people laugh.

As the party was winding down, two girls I knew asked me if I could drive them home. Before I left, a friend of mine said she was cold, and I let her borrow my black leather motorcycle jacket.

While I was gone, three punks from a rival gang in nearby Milford, Connecticut, showed up at the party, roughed the girl up, stole my jacket, and left.

When I returned home, around three in the morning, I was told what happened and I immediately tore off on my motorcycle to go after them. Two fellow Flat Rats known as the Monaco brothers followed me.

The Monaco brothers and I drove all over but couldn't find them. When we returned to my house hours later, the three punks from Milford pulled into my driveway.

"Unbelievable!" I got off my bike and walked up to the driver's side of the car. Two of the Milford punks got out of the passenger side holding baseball bats. The guy wearing my jacket was sitting in the passenger seat with the window down. Before he had the chance to get out, I punched him in the mouth.

Then I grabbed the bat he was holding and charged after the other two, who ran off.

It wasn't a big deal. But I'd recovered my jacket and made a point—don't mess with me, or the Flat Rats.

I hoped it was over. But a couple days later, Mrs. Monaco was standing in a phone booth in a strip-mall parking lot when some guys from the Milford gang saw her and stabbed her to death.

It was an ugly, horrible, senseless act of retaliation.

I said to myself, *The hell with this place. I've got to get out of here.*

When I invited my parents to come to my high school graduation, they'd asked if I was going to get a diploma. I barely squeezed through, graduating near the bottom of my class. But I was graduating, and moving on. Class of '76.

Wanting to improve my chances of finding a decent career, I decided to go to Mattatuck Community College, in Waterbury, Connecticut. I remember going with my dad to register for classes and buying a T-shirt that read TUCK U.

I thought it was cool. My dad wished I had selected a different one.

But for first time in my life, he seemed proud of me, his first son. My parents were even more pleased when I made the dean's list the first semester.

But the transition from hell-raiser to college kid wasn't easy. I had a burning desire to do anything but sit in a classroom listening to a professor and taking notes.

I thought maybe I'd be suited to being a policeman, because cops saw action and carried guns. I could be like my hero Evel Knievel, who had switched from black leather to white. So I signed up for a course in criminal justice.

The first day of class, the instructor asked, "How many of you here think you want to become cops?"

Practically everyone in the room raised his or her hand, including me.

He said, "You want to be cops because of what you've seen on TV. The chases, the shootouts. Isn't that right?"

A bunch of us answered, "Yes."

"Well, those things will never happen," he said. "You pull your weapon from your holster, and you're in court the next day defending yourself. The hours are terrible. So is the pay. The divorce rate is the highest of all civilian jobs. You spend most of your time writing parking tickets."

Now I had to find something else. The question was, What?

I was still racing motocross, and even though it was expensive and dangerous, it remained a good outlet for my relentless energy. My friend Dave Kelliher, who was a professional rider, told me that if I wanted to get serious, I needed to start training.

"What do you mean? I'm at the motocross track all the time."

"I'm talking about physical training," he answered. "I run ten miles three times a week."

At that point, I'd never run in my life.

The next morning, I met him at this house in North Haven. Dave had measured this one-mile loop in his neighborhood that he ran ten times. I completed the first mile with him at a leisurely pace but didn't feel good. The second mile I was breathing hard and felt like I was going to be sick.

After the third, I sat on the grass and watched. I'd had enough.

By the time Dave was on his sixth mile, I was thinking, *I'm watching a professional motocross racer get fitter and stronger. And I'm sitting here on the grass like a quitter.*

As I watched him complete the tenth mile, I felt completely pathetic.

The next day, I started running, and I haven't stopped since.

When I ran with Dave a month later, I beat him.

About four months after that, I ran the Boston Marathon. It was brutal, but I promised myself that I wouldn't stop running until I crossed the finish line. Bill Rodgers won that year, with a time of two hours, nine minutes, and fifty-five seconds. My time was three hours and forty-four minutes.

I was determined to get better. I trained hard every day. A month after that, when I ran a second marathon, my time was three hours and thirty-three minutes.

My third marathon, I got it down to three hours and fifteen minutes and finished in the top 20 percent.

A month after that, I clocked in at three hours and six minutes.

Now I had to beat three hours. A couple weeks later, I did, crossing the finish line at two hours, fifty minutes. I'd made the top ten.

I started to realize something important: if you push yourself, you can accomplish great things.

I wanted to channel all the energy I had into something worthwhile, to find a way to make up for some of the bad things I'd done and the misery I'd put my parents through.

I just needed to find the right outlet.

I joined the Navy like my dad.

CHAPTER FOUR

The Navy

If you only do what you think you can
do, you never do very much.

—*Tom Krause*

The funniest story I've ever heard about joining the Navy involves a buddy of mine, a fellow SEAL. His name was Don, but we called him Boats because he was a boatswain's mate.

Boats, a big, gruff guy covered with tattoos, described himself as a skinny, geeky kid in high school—the kind of boy that girls had zero interest in.

On the afternoon of Boats's seventeenth birthday, one of the most beautiful girls in school approached him in the hallway. Her name was Patty.

She stopped in front of him and said, "I heard that today's your birthday. Is that correct?"

Looking down at his shoes, he answered, "Uh, yes, Patty."

Just being near her and speaking to her was exciting. When she actually touched his arm, he felt a tingle shoot through his body.

She purred, "That's great. Congratulations."

"Uh, thanks, but it happens to everyone."

Patty trained her beautiful blue eyes on his and said, "You know, my parents are going out tonight. Why don't you come over to my house at seven and I'll make you dinner?"

Boats couldn't believe what he was hearing. He stammered, "Wh-wh-what did you just say?"

"It's your birthday and my parents are going to be out tonight. So why don't you come over and I'll cook you dinner? Would you like that?"

"Of course. Yeah. I mean … Are you sure?"

"Come on. Don't you want to celebrate your birthday?"

"Yeah. What time?"

"Seven. You know where I live?"

Of course he did. How many times had he made a deliberate detour to go past her house on the chance that he might catch a glimpse of her through a window?

Now she was standing there before him like a dream come true, waiting for his answer.

He said, "Seven o'clock. I'll be there."

Boats went home, showered, put on his nicest clothes, spritzed himself with his dad's cologne, then drove to a neighborhood florist to buy a bouquet of flowers. He splurged and bought red roses, arrived at Patty's doorstep at seven, and rang the bell.

He stood rehearsing what he was going to say when Patty answered the door. She opened it and said, "Hi. Come in."

Her smile was radiant. Almost blinding.

He mumbled, "Thanks," and followed her inside.

She looked resplendent in a yellow and white sundress and smelled incredible. Patty showed him a place on a sofa and sat beside him.

She started to talk about how he was one of those people that she had always wanted to get to know better and how she was really excited that she'd finally gotten this opportunity.

Boats was having trouble thinking clearly. Just sitting next to a sexy, beautiful girl with perfect skin was driving him crazy.

When she touched his arm, he felt wild sparks travel through his body. Then she put her hand on his leg.

He nearly fainted.

Maybe Patty had only intended it as a friendly gesture, but the sensation sent a bolt of electricity into Boats's groin. The sexual charge he felt was almost overwhelming. The second time she did it, Boats was in agony. He crossed his legs, squeezed them together, and bit down on his lip.

Then he heard Patty say, "If you'll excuse me a minute, I think I'll go upstairs for a minute and freshen up."

Not knowing exactly what she meant, he said, "Sure. No problem."

He watched her leave, then looked down at the lump in his pants. He realized he had to do something fast. It was a choice of fleeing the house or relieving himself immediately so he didn't humiliate himself in front of Patty.

He chose the latter.

When he heard her reach the top of the stairs, Boats removed a handkerchief from his back pocket, unzipped his pants, kneeled in front of the sofa, and got to work.

Just as Boats was about to peak, he thought he heard something stir in the next room. A few seconds later a chorus of people shouted, "Surprise! Happy birthday!"

Looking up, he saw twenty-four members of his family—his mother, father, grandparents, brother, sisters, aunts, and uncles—rush into the room. Then he watched as their expressions changed from excited expectation to shock and horror.

Boats quickly yanked up his pants, ran out of the house, and drove himself directly to a Navy recruiter. By the time he got up the nerve to return home, five years later, he'd completely transformed and become a Navy SEAL.

My recruitment story wasn't nearly as dramatic or embarrassing. But like Boats, I realized I had to get out of my hometown. In my case, I wanted to escape the cycle of drugs and crime that was consuming so many of my friends.

I took a train to get to Navy basic training in Great Lakes, Illinois, determined to make something of myself. It was my first real trip away from home and I spent most of the train ride flirting and making out with a young schoolteacher and then playing poker with a pimp who complained about how he had to keep all his girls supplied with cocaine. Just the thing I was trying to leave behind.

I took to military life immediately. Civilian life seemed chaotic and confusing, and the structured, ordered, and disciplined environment in the military enabled me to thrive.

A former basic-training bunkmate named Bob Klose, who is now a college professor in Maine, remembers me as something of a lunatic.

When I spoke to him recently, he said, "Don, do you remember how you used to push the bunk bed into the middle of the room so you could run around it three hundred times?"

"Sort of."

"You measured the length of all the tiles and calculated the distance. I think your longest run was seventeen miles."

"Sounds right."

"What about all those times you used to get under the bunk and bench-press it?"

"Yeah, I remember that."

Bob said, "I asked you, 'Hey, Don, how many times are you going to bench-press the bunk?'

"And you answered, 'Until my nose bleeds.'"

One day after swimming they asked all us new recruits if we wanted to watch a movie about the Navy SEALs.

What the hell are SEALs?

I saw a group of four very fit guys covered from head to toe in camouflage and riding a rubber Zodiac boat over high surf. The narrator said, "These elite commandos are defined by their extreme fitness and training and what instructors call the 'fire in the gut.'"

I learned that the acronym SEAL comes from *sea, air, and land,* and that SEALs worked in small units and trained to perform the most difficult military tasks under any type of circumstance, in any type of environment—from deserts to frozen mountain peaks, jungles, and urban areas.

I was fascinated. I'd loved pushing myself since I was a kid, and I said to myself, *That's the job for me!*

Over the next few days I soaked up as much info about the SEALs as I could. From a book at the base library I found out that the SEALs had been created in the early 1960s when President Kennedy was looking for small units to resist the Vietcong in the jungles, coasts, and rivers of Vietnam.

Developed as a more versatile, state-of-the-art-of-war version of the Navy's underwater demolition teams (UDTs), which had blown up bridges and tunnels during the amphibious phases of the Korean War, the SEALs quickly distinguished themselves by going behind enemy lines, raiding enemy camps, sabotaging supplies, cutting off enemy communications, and destroying stored ammunitions.

And I learned that their training was brutal—the toughest of any military force in the world.

All Navy SEALs have to graduate from a BUD/S selection and training course. I went to my commanding officer a few days later and said, "Sir, I respectfully request permission for orders to BUD/S."

He read me the requirements. The candidate:

1. Has to be an active-duty member of the U.S. Navy
2. Has to be a man twenty-eight years or younger with good vision
3. Has to be a U.S. citizen
4. Has to pass the Armed Services Vocational Aptitude Battery

Check, check, check, check.

"Is that all?" I asked.

"You also have to pass a stringent physical screening test."

"I'm ready, sir."

A couple days later, I swam five hundred yards in fewer than 12.5 minutes; completed forty-two push-ups in under two minutes and fifty sit-ups in under two minutes; and did six pulls-ups. Then I had to run one and a half miles in boots and long pants. (Of course, these were Navy standards, and the SEALs wanted a lot more than that. Also, the standards in the 1970s were a bit different than they are to-day.)

Piece of cake. Now I had the score qualifying me for BUD/S noted in my new service record. Boy, was I proud!

I said, "All right, sir, I'm ready to join."

"Not so fast, recruit."

"Why not, sir?"

He said, "You think the SEALs want brand-new recruits with only eight weeks of training? You've got to go to corpsman school first."

The Navy recruiter in New Haven—a real charming character who called himself Diamond Jim Brady—had told me that my aptitude test showed that I had the ability to be a corpsman.

"What's a corpsman?" I had asked.

"It's basically the Navy's version of a medic. You'll get to work with some pretty nurses, and you'll get a chance to take care of people."

So after basic training, I went to corpsman school, where I learned how to run sick call, stop bleeding, administer CPR, and give medications.

After completing two months of hospital corpsman training, I asked about joining the SEALs again. This time I was told that I needed at least a year of experience on a ship or at command or clinic first.

The Navy assigned me to the Naval Regional Medical Center in Newport, Rhode Island. It was an old brick hospital built at the turn of the century; seeing it today, you'd think it was the setting for the movie *Shutter Island*. And it reeked of mildew and disinfectant.

But Newport was gorgeous, had great places to run, and was near where my parents lived. So, all in all, it wasn't a bad assignment.

I did rotations in the ER and OR—where I administered to all the young Marines who got into fights and accidents on the weekends—and in the ARS (alcohol rehab service), where I developed a friendship with a young drug addict named Ron. When Ron was told he was being released, he protested loudly, because he didn't think he was ready.

I tried to calm him down by telling him that he'd be okay, he'd make new friends, and I'd come visit him. When that didn't work, I went to the counselors to see if I could get them to change their minds.

But when I went back to look for Ron, I couldn't find him. I searched his room, the rec rooms, the cafeteria, the halls.

Then I noticed that a door to a room that was normally left open had been closed. I turned the knob, but it was locked. After I knocked and got no answer, I kicked the door in, only to discover that the bathroom door was locked too.

"Hey, Ron, you in there? It's me, Don."

No answer. Just a faint gurgling sound.

I kicked that door in too and found Ron slumped on the floor in a pool of blood. He'd cut his inner forearms lengthwise from his elbows to his wrists—the serious way. Blood oozed out of his mouth.

Where was it coming from?

I'd learned the ABCs of emergency medicine during corpsman training. Airway, breathing, circulation: clear the airway so the patient can breathe, establish a pulse, stop the leaks.

I used my smock to wrap one arm, pulled off my T-shirt and used it to wrap the other. As I reached into his mouth to sweep his airway, something cut my finger.

I carefully extracted what turned out to be a razor blade. Ron had apparently tried to swallow it.

I shouted to my fellow corpsman, "Dennis! Dennis, I need some help here! Bring a stretcher!"

We lifted Ron onto the stretcher, then quickly ran him over to the ER, where the surgeons sewed him up. Ron survived.

Most of my shifts weren't as eventful. They usually ran from 9:00 p.m. to 7:00 a.m. As soon as all the patients were in bed and I'd helped out wherever I could, I'd go to a little room downstairs that contained a couple of old Lifecycles and start pedaling. Most nights, I'd keep going past the time the TV stations went off the air, finish at 6:00 a.m., do my chores around the ward, then go home.

The hospital staff considered me something of a wild man but enjoyed that my name was being mentioned in the local newspapers and even on the evening news. That's because I was competing in and winning races throughout New England—bike races, 10 Ks, marathons.

Then a friend named Wally who worked in the ICU told me about a new race that involved swimming, biking, and running in succession, something called a triathlon.

I thought, *That's wild. A new challenge that combines three events. Bring it on!* At that point I wasn't much of a swimmer, so Wally helped me learn the crawl stroke at the base pool.

At the Sri Chinmoy triathlon six weeks later, competitors swam one and a half kilometers, biked forty kilometers, then ran ten kilometers. I finished in the top ten.

My parents had come to cheer me on, and they were standing near the finish line after the race when my dad heard a few of the top competitors talking about something called an Ironman.

"What's an Ironman?" he asked.

Someone told him that there was an article about it in the May 1979 *Sports Illustrated*. I rode my bike to the library the next morning to look it up.

It turned out that a Navy commander named John Collins had organized the first Ironman competition in Hawaii in 1978 by combining three local events—a 2.4-mile swim, a 112-mile bike race, and a 26.2-mile run.

"Whoever finishes first," Collins declared, "we'll call him the iron man."

The first race held had attracted eighteen people; fifteen of them started, and twelve finished. The winner was a twenty-seven-year-old Honolulu taxi driver and former military pentathlete named Gordon Haller.

I cut out his picture and pasted it on my wall for inspiration, then trained like a maniac. Several months later, in early February of 1980, I took a military plane from snowy, icy Rhode Island to sunny Hawaii.

I felt like a stranger in paradise as I lugged my $109 Motobecane bike through the terminal in a cardboard box, my Navy seabag slung over my back. Through the windows I saw palm trees, tropical foliage in bold colors, and tanned girls in sarongs.

I was winter white and marathon thin. The race owner—a woman named Valerie Silk Grundman—felt sorry for me and let me sleep on her sofa.

One hundred and eight people raced, and I finished in fifty-seventh place. But my result didn't matter to me that first time out; now I had a better idea of how to train for and compete in an ultradistance race.

Having completed my first Ironman, I couldn't wait to get to BUD/S, the initial phase of SEAL training. But when I returned to Rhode Island, I was told that a new Navy policy had been handed down: all recently trained Navy corpsmen had to choose between the Marines or ships. I didn't want either.

I said, "I've passed the test to qualify for BUD/S twice. Now I want to go to SEALs."

"Regardless, you have to pick Marines or ships."

I picked Marines and was ordered to report to the Marine Corps training school in Camp Pendleton, California. I thought, *That's perfect, because it's not too far from Naval Amphibious Base Coronado.* That was the home of BUD/S and SEAL Team One, the West Coast SEAL team (SEAL Team Two was East Coast).

The Navy allowed me ten days to travel there. That night, as I was sitting in my room listening to the Doors on my stereo, I looked at my trusted Motobecane and wondered if I'd get the opportunity to ride it when I was stationed with the Marines.

That's when an arguably insane idea hit me: *I'll ride it across the country!*

I figured three hundred miles a day for ten days wasn't out of the question.

The next day I pedaled over to a local bicycle store, Ten Speed Spokes, and asked Ted, the owner, if he wanted to sponsor me. It helped that I was still getting publicity for being the first New Englander to complete the Ironman, and he said, "Absolutely."

Ted contacted Guinness World Records in London. They told him that I could set a record by completing a transcontinental bike ride in ten days. They also pointed out that it would be easier if I rode west to east, since the other way was against the trade winds.

But I had only one destination—BUD/S.

Guinness had a few additional requirements. First, I needed to find a car to follow me the whole time. Second, I had to start at a town hall or other official place and finish at an official end point with someone there to time me. Finally, volunteers had to be recruited so that every twenty miles or so along the route there was someone there to record my progress.

My mother offered to loan her station wagon to serve as my support vehicle, and my girlfriend, Kim, and my sister Wendy agreed to drive it.

When I spoke on a local radio station to publicize my upcoming cross-country attempt, I received a call from a University of Rhode Island football player named Jay who said that he wanted to ride with me.

I told him we had to share expenses and ride at least eighteen to twenty-two hours a day.

He said, "No problem."

Jay and I started training together and planning our route—from New York City to the Mississippi, across the Rocky Mountains to Los Angeles. A week or so later, when my military orders allowed me to travel, the four of us—Kim, Wendy, Jay, and I—arrived in New York City in the middle of a major transit strike.

We drove to City Hall and asked if there was someone who would officially start our race across the country.

The person I spoke to told us to get lost.

I explained our situation and said, "All you have to do is sign my official Guinness logbook."

"No dice."

So I called Ted back in Rhode Island, who telephoned Guinness World Records in London. They suggested that we start in Florida and end in San Diego because it was a shorter route.

Ted located a small coastal town in Florida that was willing to officially start the race and provide a police escort and even offered to film it.

Excited to finally get under way, we drove down there immediately.

Jay and I climbed on our bikes on a sunny Saturday morning as a crowd of well-wishers cheered us on. I was optimistic and filled with energy.

But it became apparent right away that Jay was struggling. The first night, after we'd clocked about 260 miles, Jay turned to me and said, "Hey, Don. I'm completely gassed. Let's stop for the night and rest."

"Jay, that means we're going to have to do three hundred and forty miles tomorrow."

"Fine. But I'm done for tonight."

The next day he wanted to stop after 240 miles. Two days into our trek, and we were already falling behind. I was upset.

In the middle of Texas, Jay said, "I only want to do a hundred miles a day."

"A hundred miles a day means it will take us eighteen more days! We'll never set a record. And I only have ten days to get to Camp Pendleton."

"Then I'm quitting."

"Come on, Jay, we can do this. I know we can." My mind-set was so strong that I knew I could make it despite the bleeding hemorrhoids that stuck to my shorts.

But Jay was mentally fatigued and sore and had lost his enthusiasm.

So we packed our bikes in the station wagon and drove the rest of the way.

As disappointed as I was about the bike ride (and it's a failure that still haunts me), I was still psyched about arriving at BUD/S.

I understood the new procedures and my Marine orders, but had other ideas. Soon after we arrived at Camp Pendleton, I drove south to Coronado and walked into the Quarter Deck of SEAL Team One, where I was directed to the command master chief's office.

I said, "Master Chief, I'm the Navy corpsman who called earlier and set up an appointment. I've passed the screening test twice and I request orders to go to BUD/S. I don't want to go to Marine Corps training. I'm ready to go to BUD/S."

He looked me over and said, "We really need corpsmen, and it's hard to find corpsmen who are in shape."

"I'm here and I'm ready, Master Chief."

"Great. Wait outside."

After he made some calls, he called me back in his office and said, "Looks like you're going to have to complete your five-week course with the Marines first."

"Then I can come back and start BUD/S?"

"Yes. Don't give up hope."

I returned to Camp Pendleton and completed the five-week Field Medical Service School with flying colors. In fact, I scored the highest of all the students and was named the top graduate.

But when I went to the Navy admin officer and requested orders to go to BUD/S, he told me, "Not after we've just invested all this time and training in you. You've got to complete an assignment with the Marines first."

The Navy sent me to Okinawa, Japan, where I treated Marines who were hurt in training, and had a blast. The Marines actually flew me all over Asia to compete in races—including the Western Pacific Cross Country Championship and the Marine Corps marathon in DC—all on their dime. I was running marathon after marathon now, averaging close to one a month and using each one as training for the next.

Among the races I competed in was the third Hawaiian Ironman in February of 1981. I arrived in Oahu from Okinawa carrying my $109 Motobecane in a box.

Around the baggage-claim area stood these incredibly fit and muscular athletes. One cut and tanned guy with blond hair spotted me carrying my bike and looked at me as though he were thinking, *Who the hell are you, and what are you doing here?*

Even though I was a veteran Ironman, I felt intimidated and out of place.

The next morning, I and the other 537 athletes who had entered in the race lined up to be inspected and weighed. Race officials were worried about people getting too dehydrated, so they told us that we would be weighed twice during the race, and anyone who lost more than 10 percent of his body weight would not be allowed to continue.

I was more concerned about the waves I saw crashing over the seawall and washing across the street. I started to feel small and wanted to return home.

Then the cocky blond guy I'd seen at the airport came over and stood in front of me with a beautiful lime-green five-thousand-dollar Bianchi bike by his side.

He asked loudly, "Are you in this race?"

"Yup."

He pointed at my bike. "What's that?"

"It's a Motobecane."

"A Motobecane. No shit. What do you have on it?" he asked with a big smirk on his face.

"It is what you see. I've got nothing special on it."

He said, "My pedals are worth more than your bike. They're made of titanium."

"Whatever."

"So that's a Motobecane, huh?"

When the starter gun sounded, we all ran into the water. I watched the blond guy swim past me.

But no way I was giving up.

I fought through the waves, swallowed water a couple of times, but completed the swimming section without too much difficulty. Then I climbed on my bike. As soon as I started pedaling, something lit up inside me.

Feeling a burst of energy and confidence, I started passing people and quickly moved from 175th place to 150th.

I said to myself, *I've done a great deal of training and have run thirty marathons in thirty-six months. There's no reason in the world I can't place near the front.* I passed more riders—149th, 148th, 147th, 146th—then spotted the ripped blond guy on the green Bianchi ahead. I picked up speed and blew past him, then looked back and said, "So that's a Bianchi, huh?"

I knew that Gordon Haller, the winner of the first Ironman, had completed the course in eleven hours and forty-four minutes. It was my goal to break his record.

I was in 110th place and I was thinking, *Only a hundred and nine more to go.*

About twenty miles away from the end of the biking section, I saw this helicopter hovering ahead. Crowds of people were cheering. News cameras were filming one of the riders.

When he came into view, I read the name on the back of his shorts.

"Gordon Haller. Holy shit!"

I passed him, thinking, *This is amazing! I'm about to pass the champ!*

I finished the bike portion, pulled off my bike shoes, laced up my running shoes, and took off like I was on fire. A couple of guys I passed running up the first hill, shouted at me, "Hey, dude, you'd better slow down. You've got a whole marathon ahead of you."

They had no idea what was burning inside me.

Hours later, now in thirty-seventh place and nearing the finish line, I noticed the helicopter approaching me from behind. Someone in the crowd shouted, "Watch out, man, the champ's after you and he's a runner!"

I turned and saw Gordon Haller behind me on my right.

He was starting to pass me, but I picked up speed. Then he picked up speed.

We made a right-hand turn together and I saw the finish line ahead. Now we were both running as fast as we could, completing the last two miles doing better than six and a half minutes per mile.

The crowd grew louder and louder.

We both broke through the finish line and ran chest-deep into the ocean. When we emerged, Gordon Haller took my hand. He said, "Great race. And thanks so much for pushing me."

I said, "It's an honor for me just to be talking to you. Thank you. You're my idol."

We lay on mats on the ground. Hawaiian girls came over to put leis around our necks and rub our shoulders. I'd just finished thirty-eighth out of 538 of the world's top athletes. I had achieved something that had seemed almost unimaginable months earlier.

The race changed my life. It proved to me once and for all that anything is possible if you work hard and prepare yourself.

I said to myself, *Now that I completed this goal, I need to focus on getting to BUD/S and getting in SEAL shape!*

I determined that everything I did and everything I ate would contribute to making me stronger for BUD/S. That meant three healthy meals a day and no candy bars, sodas, or junk food. I had micro goals—to win individual races—but the macro goal was to become a SEAL.

I started doing visualizations. For example, I knew that BUD/S involved a lot of swimming under difficult circumstances, and I still wasn't a strong swimmer, so when I was doing laps in the pool, I'd imagine myself in freezing water looking up at a black sky, every part of my body numb from the cold, from swimming for hours.

One weekend I completed a 240-mile ride around Okinawa in fourteen hours, setting a course record that stood for a long time afterward. And when I wasn't swimming, running, or racing, I worked at the USMC Futenma base clinic improving my medical skills.

Most days involved routine tasks, but given the constant activity going on all around us, it seemed like things could change in an instant. I was on sick call at the clinic one afternoon when I heard two very loud pops outside. Someone shouted that an OV-10 turboprop light attack aircraft had lost an engine just before landing and had hit the runway. I grabbed my medical bag and ran the quarter mile to the scene of the accident.

The pilot had ejected first and seemed okay. But the copilot had bailed at an angle that shot him across the cement runway. I ran over to where he was lying and saw that the skin along the right side of his body had been scraped away, exposing his bones and organs. The poor guy was dead, but the Timex watch on his wrist was still ticking. Just like the ad.

Once I got a call that a Marine had passed out in the barracks. I ran there and leaned over the Marine to check his pupils. I knew that the Marines didn't like the fact that a Navy corpsman with a beard and long hair continually aced their PRT (physical readiness test), but I wasn't there to do anything but help.

The Marine was drunk. When he opened his eyes and saw me looming over him, he punched me full force.

I recoiled; my face throbbed, and blood trickled out of my nose. I was ready to smash him, but part of me said, *Don, try to remain professional.* Besides, there were eight Marines who were standing around watching.

One of them said, "Let it go, Doc. This guy's usually not like this. He's just really shit-faced."

I was pissed, and the guy who sucker punched me didn't even apologize.

So a couple days later, my eye still black and blue and my lip swollen, I walked into the clinic, found his shot records, tore them into pieces, and flushed them down the toilet. Then I left a note for the staff sergeant telling him that the Marine was behind on all his shots.

A month later, after the Marine had come in to get all his shots but still hadn't apologized, I tore up his shot records again. Screw him!

One night around two a.m., I was on duty at the clinic when the bell rang. My buddy and I got up and answered the door.

This drunk Marine staggered in and asked, "Doc, can you help me out?"

"What's the matter?"

"I got a real bad case of acne and it's bothering me a lot."

"Really?"

"I'm sorry for coming in so late after hours, but the bars just closed and I figured I'd stop by on my way back to the barracks."

I looked at Kevin, my fellow corpsman, and he looked at me. We were both thinking the same thing: *Can you believe this guy made an emergency call at two in the morning because of acne?*

I said, "Look. We've got all kinds of drugs in the pharmacy. Some work, some don't. But the best cure for acne is this old Indian remedy."

"What's that?"

"When you get up in the morning and urinate, cup the urine in your hands and splash it on your face. You do that for a month and your acne will disappear and never come back."

"Really, Doc?"

"It works like a charm every time."

About two weeks later, this Marine master sergeant called the clinic sounding irate. He said, "What's the name of the doc who told my private to put piss on his face? I saw him in the head this morning splashing it on his face like it was some kind of cologne."

We laughed our heads off. Don't mess with the docs.

I finished up my assignment to Japan and finally, in May of '82, when I was back in the States assigned to a Navy Reserve unit in Easton, Pennsylvania, and working temporarily as a prison guard, I received my orders to report to BUD/S.

I was ecstatic. This was it. I called my parents and my girlfriend, Kim, and said, "Finally, finally, my goal is within reach!"

I had no backup plan. It was SEALs or nothing.

CHAPTER FIVE

BUD/S

The more sweat and tears you put into
the training, the less blood you'll shed in
time of war.

—Basic Underwater Demolition/
SEAL motto

Have you ever heard of something called heart-rate variability
(HRV)? It's a real medical phenomenon discovered by a guy named
Dr. Charles Morgan of Yale University that's used to predict which
soldiers are likely to perform most efficiently under the stress of combat.

Most people have a large degree of variability in their heart rates
during the course of a day. In other words, your heart speeds up
and slows down all the time, depending on conditions—like whether
someone is pointing a gun at your head or you're lounging by the pool
drinking a Dos Equis.

But many SEALs and other Special Forces types have what is
called a metronomic heartbeat, meaning the heart thumps like a
metronome, with the beats evenly spaced, not speeding up or slowing
down.

And no, we're not cyborgs.

Our hearts do this, it turns out, because our brains release a higher level of a neurotransmitter called neuropeptide Y (NPY) than most people's brains do. NPY works as a natural tranquilizer that controls anxiety and buffers the effects of stress hormones like norepinephrine.

Dr. Morgan found that those with metronomic heartbeats perform better than others in survival school, underwater-navigation testing, and close-quarters battle because their systems are able to manage a very elevated degree of stress. Today, HRV is one of the factors used in the selection of SEALs.

But there's a downside. Dr. Morgan also found that the metronomic effect is often associated with early heart disease and even sudden death. Apparently, the body chemistry that allows young people to survive under high stress does not translate into optimal heart health past the age of fifty.

I realized my own unusual response to danger the first time I had a gun pointed at me.

I was a newly licensed sixteen-year-old driving like a maniac down the Boston Post Road, my arm around my girlfriend, Lynn, and a beer in my lap. I had my '68 Pontiac Firebird cranked up to ninety-five miles an hour and was trying to hit a hundred.

We were flying, passing other vehicles as if they were standing still, when this dark Chevy sedan pulled up beside me. The driver wore reflector shades, and his hair was buzzed short. You know the type.

Figuring that he was a cop, I slowed down to eighty. He motioned for me to pull over.

Lynn didn't want me to.

I stopped and got out.

The thick-necked guy stomped over and grabbed me by the arm. He said, "You're coming with me, punk. I'm an undercover cop and I'm hauling your ass in."

I asked, "If you're a cop, where's your badge?"

"I'm not showing you shit! Come with me!"

He was big, loud, and aggressive.

I said, "No, I'm not."

Lynn grabbed my other arm and said, "Let's go with him, Don. Come on."

"No!"

For some reason I had a feeling that I could talk my way out of it if I held my ground.

Red-faced now, the big guy pulled out a gun and stuck it in my stomach. He said, "Now you're coming. Let's go, punk."

We were eye to eye, so close that I could smell his breath. I said, "I'm not going with you."

Lynn pleaded, "Please, Don! Stop arguing. Let's just do what he wants."

"No."

We stood nose to nose for half a minute, then the big guy put his revolver away, walked to his car, and drove off. Lynn was a mess, but I was perfectly calm.

Sometimes I think I'm at my best in dangerous situations. I thrive under stress and like living on the edge.

Another time, shortly before I went to BUD/S, my father and brother and I went to Easton, Pennsylvania, to see heavyweight champion Larry Holmes fight. We parked our car in a lot and walked to the arena, passing by this car parked across the street with a couple in the front seat.

They were both hysterical and holding a baby upside down by the ankles. I ran over to the car and said, "I'm a medic. Can I help you?"

Apoplectic with fear, they couldn't answer.

The poor baby's face had turned blue. I took it from them and held its head in my hand.

Immediately, my combat medic training kicked in. My brain was shouting at me, *Airway, Don! Airway! Check the airway!*

The baby was close to death, but I remained calm.

I looked down the baby's throat, saw something stuck there, then reached in with my little finger and popped a white piece of plastic out of the way. The baby started making sucking sounds and crying. The blue around its lips started to fade and then changed to a healthy pink.

The parents grabbed the baby, thanked me quickly, and drove away.

In March of 1982, bursting with excitement, my girlfriend, Kim, and I packed our stuff and hopped in my black TR6, which didn't have working brakes. We drove across country in three and a half days with only a handbrake. I arrived at BUD/S in Coronado (about five miles south of San Diego) on March 31, 1982, fired up and ready for action.

When I looked out on the field where guys from the previous BUD/S class were running around with scuba tanks on their backs, with instructors yelling at them, I thought, *This is for me! I've arrived.* The first two weeks, known in those days as pretraining (it's changed since), were intense. There were over a hundred men in my class. Most looked fit, but some looked like they'd been spending a lot of time drinking beer and eating pretzels.

Then the instructors handed all of us phase one green helmets and immediately started kicking our butts.

Phase one, which started on June 18, consisted of two months of grueling physical conditioning and training. It included:

Timed runs in the sand
Swimming
Calisthenics

Timed obstacle course
Small-boat seamanship
Hydrographic surveys and creating charts
Rock portage in a rubber raiding craft

We were constantly in motion and ran everywhere, including to breakfast, lunch, and dinner. I'm talking roughly six miles a day in boots just to eat, in addition to long daily runs on Coronado Beach.

First thing in the morning after the 0430 muster, the instructors would order us on the asphalt grinder and we'd do all kinds of calisthenics—flutter kicks, good-mornings, dive-bombers, push-ups, sit-ups, triceps push-ups, pull-ups, and rope climbs. If it was chilly, they'd spray us with cold water just to place another challenge in our way.

From their perspective it was all about seeing how much pain and discomfort we could take and how willing we were to push ourselves.

Being a wiry triathlete type with little extra meat on my bones, I developed an oozing sore on my tailbone from working out on the asphalt and had a constant bloodstain on my shorts.

From the grinder we'd run to the obstacle course, where we'd climb up ropes and walls, run through mud, crawl under barbed wire, hang by our arms, and so on. The instructors would launch a trainee every thirty seconds and challenge him to pass the guy ahead of him.

"Come on, push! For your sake, I hope you can move faster than that!"

And each time you ran the course, you were expected to beat your previous time. The instructors evaluated each candidate at the end of each phase of training and took great pleasure in eliminating the weak candidates, whom they referred to as "shit birds."

Our first-phase proctor looked like he'd been ripped from the cover of *Soldier of Fortune* magazine. His name was Bob Donnegan and he happened to be the world arm-wrestling champ at the time—hard, and tough, with huge arms.

One morning he'd climbed up three towers to show us some aspect of the course when he lost his footing, fell about thirty feet, and landed on his back with a thud. The ground around us literally shook, and we thought he was dead.

My training kicked in again and I ran over, knelt by his side, and shouted, "Instructor Donnegan, can you hear me? Are you okay?"

He turned his head to look up at me and growled, "Get the hell out of here."

Then he stood up in his blue and white dive shirt and UDT dive shorts, brushed himself off, and said, "Listen up, you hooligans. I never, ever want to see any of you do anything like that. You understand?"

"Yes, Instructor Donnegan."

We stood in silent awe, figuring the guy must have bones made out of steel.

I found out right away that my reputation as an Ironman and long-distance athlete had preceded me, which was both good and bad. The instructors sort of grudgingly respected me but expected more from me too.

The reason for that was Ray Fritz, who happened to be a SEAL from my Navy Reserve unit and the friend of a BUD/S instructor.

Funny guy, Ray. Because when I met him, he actually tried to talk me out of becoming a SEAL.

Knowing that I was corpsman, he said, "Don, why do you want to go to BUD/S? Hell, you've already proved yourself physically. You and I should go into sports medicine. There's a fortune to be made there."

I said, "No, I want to be a SEAL. That's my one and only goal."

So before I got to BUD/S, Ray—who went on to become a very successful orthopedic surgeon—called his friend at BUD/S in Coronado, a guy named Steve Simmit, to let him know that I was coming.

The first week of BUD/S I ran into Steve as we were assembling before our weekly four-mile timed run on the beach. Steve was another amazing physical specimen—a pentathlete with a body so fit that it looked like it had been turned inside out, leaving all of his muscles on the outside.

I said, "Instructor Simmit, a friend of mine says hello."

"Who is your friend?"

"Ray Fritz."

He grunted. "Drop down and give me fifty."

No problem. It was a beautiful California summer day with a fresh breeze blowing in from the ocean. I enjoyed doing push-ups and I loved that I was finally at BUD/S.

As I was lifting myself up for the fiftieth time, he said, "Now get in the water and make a sugar cookie." Sugar cookies meant getting wet and rolling in the sand.

So I'm in my shorts covered with sand when he barks, "All right, Mann, give me another fifty."

"Yes, sir." I did another set.

"Fifty more!"

The inside of my thighs were starting to bleed because of the chafing from the sand.

Then he beckoned me closer and said in confidence, "What you gotta do now is win the run. I know what you can do, and I expect you to win every time."

My swim buddy Jeff Hobblit and I always ran at the front of the pack. Steve Simmit said, "Don, you gotta beat him today."

"Yes, sir."

I did, and I beat him the next time too.

Instructor Simmit started acting real friendly and I was honored. When somebody told me that the instructors were taking bets on whether Jeff or I was going to come in first, I understood why.

So a couple days later, I ran down the beach as hard as possible to catch up with Jeff. When I finally pulled alongside him, I said, "Jeff, instead of us killing each other each time we run, why don't we tie?"

"Good idea."

For the next four months we ran at 99 percent instead of 100 and crossed the finish line side by side. I'm sure it threw the oddsmakers for a loop.

Jeff was on my boat team too, along with four other trainees, during small-boat-tactics training. We were the power guys up front—I was on the port side, Jeff was starboard. We paddled every day, some days for as long as eight hours.

One night the IBS (inflatable boat, small) we were in was lurching all over the place and we were losing speed so that the team behind us was closing.

I yelled at Jeff, "Come on, Jeff. Paddle harder!"

He turned to me and shouted, "I am paddling hard. You paddle harder!"

I looked behind me and saw that the officer, the coxswain, who only had to steer the boat, had fallen asleep. No wonder we were zigzagging all over the place. It took all my self-control not to smack him with a paddle.

Training was always highly competitive, and often highly dangerous. Rock portage was hairy as hell. The goal was to get your IBS through the surf and onto a forty-foot-high rock formation near Coronado Cays. Guys broke arms and legs all the time. The less fortunate broke backs and cracked their skulls.

When the waves reached their violent peak, a BUD/S instructor standing on top of the jetty would signal with his flashlight. If the moon wasn't out, you couldn't see squat.

Most times you'd get smeared and flip over. Sometimes you'd end up sailing over the bow. The boat would go flying. You're getting tossed around, flailing through huge waves, doing your very best not to drown or hit the rocks. Then you had to regain control of your boat, paddle out, and try again.

I never hit the rocks hard enough to get hurt. But I saw plenty of guys from previous classes walking around the BUD/S compound with broken arms or hobbling around with broken legs or ankles from rock portage.

Hydrographic surveys and drawing beach charts were a snap in comparison. The instructor would give you a lead line and a slate board, and drop you into the water. The idea was to measure depths and check for obstacles.

The part I was the least proficient at was swimming. The BUD/S instructors had a fast way of testing our fight-or-flight response. They'd tie our hands behind our backs, bind our feet, then toss us in the pool.

Some trainees quickly figured out that the only way to avoid drowning was to relax, sink to the bottom of the pool, kick off powerfully toward the surface, get your mug above the waterline, gasp for a bit of air, then drop to the bottom again.

Many panicked, swallowed water, then coughed, choked, and eventually passed out. Divers retrieved them from the bottom of the pool, and the unconscious trainees were rolled on their sides and revived. Then instructors screamed in their faces, "Are you gonna quit? Did you get uncomfortable? What are you wasting our time for, quitter? You want to quit now?"

They were given thirty seconds to answer before they were tossed out of the program. Some guys left voluntarily—it was a challenge that got to the core of what it meant to be a SEAL, to face something profoundly uncomfortable and come out the other side.

Those who said they wanted to keep going were thrown back in the pool.

Who passed? The guys who refused to give up, who could suppress the need to breathe, who trusted that they'd be rescued if something went wrong and were prepared to lose consciousness—or even die.

The instructors called it drown-proofing.

I remember one particular trainee, a cocky EOD (explosive ordnance disposal) guy who went around bragging that he was going to finish at the top of the class. He tried to outsmart the instructors by resting the back of his head on a buoy in the pool. But an instructor saw him, grabbed the pool pole, and smacked him in the head. The EOD guy passed out and sank to the bottom.

The BUD/S instructor in charge motioned to the Navy safety divers to pull him out and resuscitate him. Like a number of the other big cocky men, the EOD guy ran home immediately with his tail between his legs.

I almost failed too.

It happened during an exercise in which we were instructed to stand on the side of the pool, do a forward flip above the water into the pool, then complete a fifty-meter swim underwater—twenty-five meters to one end, then a flip-turn and twenty-five meters back—without coming up for air.

I swam twenty-five meters, did my flip-turn, and, feeling that I needed air, came up for a breath. Almost immediately an instructor shouted, "Hey, you quitter! Get out of the pool and stand over there!"

Feeling about two inches tall, I joined the majority of my class along the side of the pool.

The instructor shouted to the eight or so guys who had passed, "These losers quit. You want to go to war with these quitters? They were feeling a little uncomfortable and had to come up to breathe. The hell with them. We can't allow lower than whale shit quitters into the teams." I was scolding myself, saying, *What the hell's wrong with you? You came this far and just because you were a little uncomfortable you had to come up for air? That's pathetic!*

Meanwhile, a couple of the instructors were huddled together talking. One of the them announced, "All right, let's give these quitters one more chance."

I thought, *Whatever happens, I'm not coming up for air. I don't care if it gets so bad that my head explodes. I'm not quitting this time.* I swam underwater, did my flip-turn, and started back. My lungs started screaming. I desperately wanted to take a breath.

Please! Please! my brain was saying.

I forced myself on and blacked out just before I reached the wall. I don't remember seeing it or feeling it. All I know is that the divers pulled me out, and I heard one of the instructors say, "Okay, you passed."

Huge relief.

I learned later that the first time you think you need air, it's really the CO_2 receptors in your brain telling you that it's time to exhale. If you exhale a little you can last a minute or so longer.

I met some real characters during BUD/S. One guy who stands out was Chris Klauser, who paddled up to BUD/S in a rubber boat on the first day. He beached his boat and removed his dry suit; he was wearing his white dress uniform underneath.

He marched up to the quarterdeck, stood at attention, and said, "Petty Officer Klauser reporting for duty."

Klauser was a short, bald guy who weighed about a hundred and fifty pounds and had one long eyebrow. He looked kind of odd, but he could bench-press four hundred and fifty pounds—three times his weight! There were guys who could lift even more, but for muscle-to-body-weight ratio, Chris was at the top.

He gave the BUD/S instructors a hard time right from the start, which all of us thought was insane.

One of our instructors caught him clowning around one morning and shouted, "Hey, you, Klauser. Who do you think you are?"

Chris leaned against a palm tree and mimed smoking a cigar. "Burt Reynolds?"

The instructor, who didn't find it funny, barked, "Drop down and give me fifty."

Chris's comeback was "Which arm?"

He passed BUD/S with ease and went on to become a distinguished SEAL pilot and cigarette-boat captain.

Cockiness and apparent fitness weren't necessarily indicators of future success in the SEALs. It was impossible to tell which guys were going to pass. Big tough-looking football-player types were falling out. Bodybuilders broke legs and ankles. Cocky guys broke down and cried.

My third roommate (the first two washed out) was a soft-looking Mexican American who seemed to be failing everything. He was a weak swimmer, a slow runner, and did mediocre on all our tests. I kept wondering when he was going to quit or be sent packing. But he toughed it out, slowly improved and ended up having a very distinguished career in the SEALs.

A trainee who wanted out at any point during those two months had to ring a bell outside near the grinder and place his helmet beside it. Guys usually did this at night to avoid embarrassment. You'd be half asleep and hear the bell ring. And in the morning you'd look out and see more green helmets.

There was actually one BUD/S class a couple of years before mine where no one passed. From my perspective, BUD/S was 90 percent mental and 10 percent physical.

Halfway through phase one, the forty or so of us who remained began hell week—five days and five nights of continuous training on a maximum of four hours of sleep. Torture, some people might call it, from sundown Sunday to sundown Friday. We didn't know when it was coming.

Hell week started with the instructors tossing smoke grenades in our tents while we were sleeping and firing blank rounds, yelling and screaming. That initial high-anxiety moment was followed by nonstop boat exercises, carrying inflatable Zodiacs over our heads, timed runs, crawling through mud, calisthenics. Seems like we never got a chance to catch our breath.

The instructors almost never gave us time to sleep either, and when they did, they made sleeping difficult. Once four of us were told we had an hour to nap, but we had to do it under a sprinkler. And one of us had to be on patrol the whole time, running around the other three.

During meals you'd see guys pass out and their faces fall into their plates. Guys actually closed their eyes and dozed off while they ran. A couple of times I managed to paddle in the ocean and sleep at the same time.

It was nonstop cold, wet, sore, and exhausting. I thought the Ironman race was tough. Hell week was like ten Ironman competitions in succession.

Day five I was hiking through the Tijuana mudflats at night, thinking I was following a guy with long black hair, a black leather jacket, and black pants. I followed him for about an hour and was trying to remember who he was when I realized there was no one in front of me. I'd been hallucinating the whole time.

Guys imagined they were seeing witches, pigs, and babies in trees. Beautiful mermaids smiled at them and waved. Rocks turned into talking turtles.

About half of the class managed to make it through phase one. Those of us who did got to exchange our green helmets for blue ones.

Phase two consisted of eight weeks of rigorous dive training. We were still required to do all the runs and PT (calisthenics, obstacle course, and so on).

Included were something called jock-up drills. We'd be down on the cement holding ourselves in push-up position for hours while wearing weight belts and twin scuba tanks on our backs as the instructors screamed at us, "Straighten up your back! Get all the way up! Hold it! Hold it longer!"

Your hands would be burning into the asphalt; your back would be sagging under the weight. The instructors didn't stop until all of us gave up. Added to that were at least two dives a day. We learned both open-circuit diving (using tanks with compressed air) and closed-circuit diving with the Dräger LAR V (breathing 100 percent oxygen).

With the Dräger, exhaled breath passes through a chemical filter that removes the carbon dioxide and replenishes the oxygen. The advantage of the Dräger is that it produces no bubbles that can be detected by an enemy. The disadvantage is that breathing 100 percent oxygen for more than four hours or deeper than thirty feet leads to oxygen toxicity.

We also learned how to dive using another closed-circuit re-breather system—the MK 15, which is a closed-circuit mixed-gas underwater apparatus especially suited to deep-water dives.

We worked in two-man swim teams, starting with two-mile ocean swims and going all the way up to five-and-a-half-mile swims. Instructors taught us how to approach land undetected and how to attack ships.

At the end of phase two, all remaining trainees exchanged their blue helmets for red ones and began phase three—nine weeks of land-warfare training. The second half took place on San Clemente

Island—an uninhabited island owned by the Navy since 1934, about fifty-five nautical miles south of Long Beach, California. A beautiful place.

Again the intensity of PT went up. We ran and swam longer distances (five and a half miles in the ocean) and still had to continually lower our time on the obstacle course run, and swim. But the twenty-six of us who had made it this far were now in terrific shape.

The training became more operational in a sense. Instructors taught us how to fire, take apart, and assemble different weapons—9 mm SIG Sauer P226 and MK23 Mod 0 .45-caliber handguns, MK43 and M2HB machine guns, HK MP5 9 mm automatic submachine guns, an M16. We fired mortars, shoulder-held rockets, and grenade launchers. And we learned how to blow up underwater obstacles with C4, dynamite, and TNT.

We spent many days and nights practicing land navigation, small-unit tactics, and patrolling techniques. Then we were taught how to both rappel and fast-rope from a helicopter.

Since rappelling is safer (and slower), we learned that first. From a helicopter hovering anywhere from twenty to seventy feet off the ground, the trainee was taught how to snap into a rappel line using a locking carabiner that was strapped to his shoulders. A beener or D ring was attached to each trainee via a rappel seat that went around his waist and upper thighs.

From a sitting position with the legs out the door of the helicopter, the trainee pivoted 180 degrees on the skid so he faced the inside of the helicopter—feet shoulder-width apart, knees locked, balls of the feet on the skid, body bent at the waist, the brake hand on the small of his back.

On the go signal, he had to flex his knees and push away from the skid gear, allowing the rope to pass through the brake and guide hands.

Optimal descent was roughly eight feet per second with no jerky stops. The trainee had to start braking about halfway down by releasing tension on the rope and moving his brake hand (the bottom one) out at a forty-five-degree angle.

One guy fell in front of me and broke his back in two places, both his feet, and his right femur.

Fast-roping is a whole lot quicker. Wearing a pair of leather gloves, the trainee grabbed the rope with both hands held at about chest level and then put the rope between his boots and stepped out. The idea was to slide down using hands and feet as brakes.

We practiced slowing our descent and stopping. And when we started carrying fifty-plus pounds of gear on our backs for a seventy-foot descent, we had to pull our gloves off fast when we hit the ground because the leather felt like it was on fire.

By the last days of November we felt like warriors. But even at the very end of BUD/S, guys were selected out if they didn't keep improving steadily.

Over a hundred trainees had started BUD/S with me, and only twenty-three of us stood on the podium in our white dress uniforms on December 3, 1982, to receive our BUD/S graduation certificates.

It would be another six months at least, during which we were on probation and completing our advanced SEAL training, before we could earn our coveted Navy SEAL tridents and become SEALs.

CHAPTER SIX

Goat Lab

Success depends upon previous preparation, and without such preparation there
is sure to be failure.

—*Confucius*

Back in the early 1980s there were only two ███████████
SEAL teams in existence—ST-1, on the West Coast, which covered
operations in all of Asia; and ST-2, stationed in Virginia Beach, Virginia, which was responsible for operations in Europe, Africa, and
Central and South America. My goal at the time was to serve on
both.

Each coast was also home to two UDTs (underwater demolition
teams)—elite, special-purpose forces established by the U.S. Navy
during World War II. Their primary function was to reconnoiter and
destroy enemy defensive obstacles on beaches prior to amphibious
landings. The Navy's top combat swimmers, UDTs breached the ca-
bles and nets protecting enemy harbors, planted limpet mines on
enemy ships (as we did in Somalia), and located and marked mines
for clearing by minesweepers.

A precursor to the Navy SEALs, UDTs pioneered closed-circuit diving, underwater demolitions, midget submarine (dry and wet submersible) operations, and combat swimming—a more efficient variant of the side-stroke that reduced the swimmer's profile in the water.

Even though I knew about SEAL Team One and Two and the UDTs, I was still in the dark about SEAL Team Six, ███████ ███

Before I checked into SEAL Team One, I had to complete Special Dive Technician School (SDTS), with the only other corpsman in my BUD/S class, a guy named Bob. SDTS was basically a crash course in how to diagnose and treat dive injuries and dive illnesses, including decompression sickness, emphysema, and dive embolisms, and how to administer hyperbaric-chamber treatment.

Since I was responsible for the safety of the divers on my team, I was eager to learn.

I found out that decompression sickness (aka the bends) occurs when a diver who has spent a long period of time underwater or has been breathing gas at a higher pressure than the pressure on the surface ascends and then develops bubbles of inert gas within the tissues of the body.

Symptoms include severe joint pain in the shoulders, elbows, knees, and ankles. Some divers develop itching and mottled skin; others, headaches and blurred vision.

It's initially treated with 100 percent oxygen until the diver can be placed in a hyperbaric chamber for recompression. I handled some cases of dive embolisms and decompression sickness levels one and two later in my career, but they were rare, since SEALs are expert divers.

Following the two-week course, Bob and I took Christmas leave. He flew home to Texas to go on a hunting trip with his dad, and I flew to Pennsylvania, where my parents were living.

Then I returned to ST-1 in Coronado, and before starting advanced training, I volunteered for Survival, Evasion, Resistance, and Escape (SERE) School.

Bob questioned my choice, and he wasn't the only new SEAL who did. "Why are you going to SERE School?" he asked. "You don't have to, and I've heard it's a pain in the neck."

"Because a Vietnam vet SEAL told me that if we're captured in combat there's a good chance we'll be beheaded or skinned alive," I explained.

███

███

██████████████████████████████████

Most of the twenty people in my SERE class were Navy pilots and aircrew personnel considered to be at high risk of capture. Since I was the only SEAL, I was known to both instructors and students as Baby Killer—a derogatory term left over from Vietnam that described a commando who raided small villages and killed indiscriminately.

The night after my arrival, I received a call from Bob, who told me that soon after he had gotten home, his dad had gone out to the store, and three guys had stopped him and tried to rob him. Bob's dad had resisted and was shot dead.

"Jesus, Bob. That's horrible. I'm so sorry."

Bob said, "Don, I need your help. They caught the asshole who pulled the trigger. He's in prison. I need you to show me how to get inside and kill him."

Bob knew that I had worked briefly as a prison guard when I was waiting for orders to BUD/S.

I said, "Bob, forget it. Your dad's gone. You don't want to murder anyone."

"You don't understand. The asshole's in prison waiting for arraignment. I'm going to go in there and take him out."

"Bob, you're one of my best friends. I don't want you to do this."

"I have to do this, Don."

"When you go into the prison, they're going to use a metal wand to check you for weapons. Then you go through a door and you wait there. There's a table. They check the table. Then the guards bring the prisoner in. You've got to call first to make an appointment. Say that you're an attorney and you want to meet with the guy. Make sure you carry a briefcase and business cards. And tape a razor blade to the back of your watch. Wear a short-sleeved shirt so it looks like you don't have anything to hide. While you're talking to the guy, lean over and whisper something, then do what you need to do."

Bob decided not to do it—thank God. And he ended up serving on the SEAL teams for twenty years.

SERE training was intended to provide the skills to live up to the U.S. military code of conduct when operating in an uncertain or hostile environment.

The COC was drilled into our heads.

You've probably heard pieces of it grunted through the gritted teeth of actors stripped to their waists in cheesy action movies. But for the record, here it is:

Article I. I am an American, fighting in the forces which guard my country and our way of life. I am prepared to give my life in their defense.

Article II. I will never surrender of my own free will. If in command, I will never surrender the members of my command while they still have the means to resist.

Article III. If I am captured, I will continue to resist by all means available. I will make every effort to escape and to aid others to escape. I will accept neither parole nor special favors from the enemy.

Article IV. If I become a prisoner of war, I will keep faith with my fellow prisoners. I will give no information nor take part in any action which might be harmful to my comrades. If I am senior, I will take command. If not, I will obey the lawful orders of those appointed over me and will back them up in every way.

Article V. When questioned, should I become a prisoner of war, I am required to give name, rank, service number, and date of birth. I will evade answering further questions to the utmost of my ability. I will make no oral or written statements disloyal to my country and its allies or harmful to their cause.

Article VI. I will never forget that I am an American, fighting for freedom, responsible for my actions, and dedicated to the principles which made my country free. I will trust in my God and in the United States of America.

Once the twenty of us knew the COC backward and forward, we were given some basic lessons in land navigation; identification of poisonous plants, animals, and insects; water procurement; fire making; building shelters; and evasion, escape, and resistance techniques.

Then we were dropped off in the desert without food or water and ordered to find our way to a safe area while trying to avoid contact with the "enemy."

Thirsty and hungry, we drank from prickly pear cacti and searched for edible plants to eat. Spotting a small rabbit running under a bush, I threw my Ka-Bar knife, and to my surprise it pinned the rabbit's neck to the ground. By cooking the rabbit meat with edible plants, I made a half-decent rabbit stew.

But one little rabbit was hardly enough to feed twenty hungry men.

Hungry, thirsty, and exhausted, all of us were captured over the next several days.

██
██
██
██████████████████████████████
████████████████████

I figured that if they were going to act tough, I'd play it for real too.

When one of my captors stepped out of the jeep, I got my bound hands in front of me, grabbed his PRC-77 radio, and tossed it under the wheels.

I also managed to steal a knife and lighter, which I hid in my boots.

██
██
██
██████
██
██
██
██
██
██████████████████████████████████████
████████████████████

Every opportunity I could find, I escaped from my tiny ████████
████████████ and, after numerous attempts, managed to smash all of the bulbs that lit the inner camp. ████████████
██

Once while I was out stealing bags and hiding them alongside the fence, a guard started calling us for roll call by banging on the roofs of the cells; this happened with no warning day and night.

We were tired, hungry, and thirsty. Our bodies were breaking down from the lack of sustenance and sleep.

One of the more hostile guards started to harangue us over the loudspeaker, denouncing the United States, telling us that our leaders were rotten and that we were fortunate to have the opportunity to give up the information they were asking for.

A number of the people in my class capitulated right there and were rewarded with warm drinks, warm food, and clean clothing.

The guards asked one more time, "Who knocked out the lights? Who's been stealing the bags from the empty cells? And who was liberating the prisoners from their cells?"

They grabbed the smallest captive and pulled him over to the board. As they started to strap him down, he broke.

"It's the SEAL," he shouted, pointing at me. "He cut a hole in the fence and is sneaking people out whenever he gets a chance. He's the covert escape leader!"

The guards grabbed me and tied me down.

Eventually the guards gave up and hauled me back to my cell. A couple of hours later, they returned and marched me to the commandant's office.

There, I was pushed against a wall and directed to stand at attention. The camp commander walked in—a fit man in a crisp khaki uniform with his hands clasped behind him. He stopped in front of me, looked me directly in the eye, and asked, "Are you the one who is helping the other captives to escape?"

"No, sir," I answered.

"Where's my PRC-seventy-seven radio?"

"I don't know, sir."

"Where are all the burlap bags?"

"I don't know, sir."

"Did you smash our lights?"

"No, sir."

His face started to turn red, and he barked, "I need to know the truth!"

I repeated my name, rank, and service number the way I'd been taught.

Shaking his head in exasperation, he said, "You don't understand, Petty Officer Mann. I'm being serious."

So was I.

We kept going back and forth like this until the commandant finally broke role and shook my hand.

"Congratulations," he said. "You've been selected as the class honor graduate."

"Thank you, sir."

"I'd go to war with you anytime. But now I need to know the answers to my questions."

I told him what he wanted to know, and he gave me the honor of raising the Stars and Stripes to signify that the course was over.

That's when I learned that the commandant's real name was Captain Ralph E. Gaither and he was a U.S. Navy hero who had spent 2,675 days in captivity in Vietnam.

SERE School had lasted ten days.

When I returned to the ST-1 base in Coronado I was told that my platoons hadn't been formed yet.

Determined to become a better corpsman, I requested permission to attend the Special Forces medical lab in Fort Bragg, North Carolina—known in the military as Goat Lab.

The executive officer at ST-1 said, "It's not required. Are you sure you want to go? The course is long and difficult."

"Yes, sir."

Goat Lab proved to be the most demanding and useful eight weeks of training I've ever had, because the Special Forces medics in attendance had spent the past ten months learning lab work and diagnostics at Fort Sam Houston, in Texas. Goat Lab for them was the combat-trauma phase of a larger course of study.

Although I had ER experience, I'd never learned how to do blood work and diagnose diseases. As the only SEAL in a class of twenty, I was very much behind the other guys and trying to catch up.

Day one, each one of us was given a patient in the form of a diseased goat. (Back in the Vietnam era, they'd used sick dogs.) Mine was a big fellow with a long red beard, so we named him Barbarosa, after the character Willie Nelson played in the movie of the same name.

I've always loved animals and don't hunt. But now, after two other SF guys strapped Barbarosa down, I had to shoot him in the leg with a thirty-aught-six. *Bam!*

For the rest of Goat Lab it was my job to keep Barbarosa alive.

The bullet left a small entry wound and a large exit hole in his upper thigh. First thing I did was stop the bleeding. Then I cut away the damaged tissue, which is called a primary wound debridement.

The other SF medics and I took turns in surgery. I acted as the primary surgeon on Barbarosa and served as assistant surgeon and anesthesiologist for other guys in the class on their animals. And they did the same for me.

It was hard work. Every four hours, day and night, you had to check your patient's vital signs—temperature, pulse, and respiration. And during the day, you did blood work. A classmate would hold the goat's head back while you found a vein, inserted a catheter, and took blood. Then you'd put a sample of blood under the microscope and examine and measure red blood cells and white blood cells, and check for diseases.

I spent days and nights with Barbarosa and grew fond of him.

One cold morning in January, we were doing the morning report with the course veterinarian and he asked how all the patients were doing. I was seated in the back of the room. Once again, as the only SEAL, I was known as Baby Killer.

I'd been up late into the night studying medical manuals in my effort to catch up with the rest of the class.

The vet asked, "How did everything go last night?"

One of the SF medics answered, "Things went fine. But we had one patient that died."

"What do you mean, he died?"

"He died," the SF medic answered. "We went in the pen this morning to look and he was dead."

"How do you know he was dead?" the vet asked.

"He was lying there and he wasn't breathing."

The vet raised his voice and said, "A patient is never dead until a doctor pronounces him dead. Now get out there and resuscitate him."

Since I was the closest one to the door, I got to him first. The goat had rigor mortis with frozen saliva on the side of its mouth. It was obviously dead.

I got down on the ground and performed mouth-to-mouth for a good twenty minutes, up until the vet said, "Okay, the patient is now confirmed dead."

The dead goat's mouth was disgusting, which probably explains why none of the SF medics offered to relieve me.

That episode taught me a lesson that helped me save some lives over the years: never assume someone is dead on the basis of how he looks.

Our final test, called trauma day, was intense. I waited with my medical bag as Barbarosa was led around a corner by two SF guys. Minutes later I heard a loud boom followed by the SF guys screaming, "Medic! Medic!"

I tore around the corner to see Barbarosa on the ground. He was a bloody, smoldering mess. His face had been set on fire. One of his eyes had been pulled out, his right leg had been amputated, and he had two sticks impaled in his chest. In addition, he had suffered several slash wounds that weren't obvious at first.

I slammed into action: ABCDE.

First, I checked for an airway. Barbarosa didn't have one, so I did a sweep with my fingers. You do this with a patient whose mouth has been damaged in order to clear away broken teeth, broken bones, blood, mucus, or vomit.

I discovered that Barbarosa's tongue had been cut and stuffed down his throat; I pinned it to his lip, which is exactly what you would do with a human patient on the battlefield with a prolapsed tongue.

Once he was breathing again, I started to stop the leaks. The slash wounds were treated with direct pressure, but a lot of the bleeding was coming from the sticks that had been impaled in his chest. I chose to leave them in, because I knew that pulling them out would cause more damage.

I made a one-inch slice in his throat and inserted a tube so he had an airway. Then I managed to get two large-bore IVs in him. His vital signs started to stabilize.

I checked Barbarosa's pupils and saw that they were unequal and not reactive to light, which indicated that he'd probably suffered a severe head injury too. So I had to be careful in terms of moving him. I made a backboard from a camo-colored poncho liner and two bamboo sticks and dragged him over to the vet, who was seated near the incinerator a few hundred meters away.

If I had failed to check something or Barbarosa had died, I would have flunked the course. A lot of guys did.

The vet said, "Okay, you passed. Now throw him in the incinerator."

Goat Lab was gruesome, and it certainly was hard for someone who loves animals, but the skills it taught me enabled me to save human lives.

In January, I went to Army jump school in Fort Benning, Georgia. All the military services attended this training, which qualified you as a rope jumper, or a static-line jumper. After doing five static-line jumps, I earned my silver jump wings. But static-line jumping isn't the same as free fall, which is typically what we did in the SEAL teams. The difference is that in static-line jumping, the line that deploys the main canopy is attached to the inside of the aircraft. In free-fall jumping, the parachutist falls to a designated altitude and then deploys the canopy himself.

My first free-fall jump occurred when I returned to ST-1 in Coronado. I remember the thrill of floating down through a beautiful clear blue sky near where Kim and I were living in a double-wide trailer in the community of San Ysidro. As I tried to locate the top of our trailer from the air, I noticed dozens of police cars gathered nearby with flashing lights.

Soon after I reached the ground, I learned that a brutal massacre had taken place at our neighborhood McDonald's. A mentally disturbed unemployed welder named James Oliver Huberty told his wife he was going "hunting humans," walked into the fast-food restaurant after lunch armed with an Uzi submachine gun, a 9 mm Browning pistol, and a 12-gauge shotgun, and killed twenty-one unarmed people ranging in age from seven to seventy-four.

There were so many victims that the town's funeral homes had to use the local civic center to accommodate all the wakes.

That horrible incident underlined something I'd learned in SEAL training and that I believe even more strongly today: You can't anticipate all the challenges that are going to be thrown your way. All you can do is prepare yourself to the best of your abilities.

CHAPTER SEVEN

SEAL Team One

Let your plans be dark and as impenetra-
ble as night, and when you move, fall like
a thunderbolt.

>   —*Sun Tzu,* The Art of War

In June of 1983, fourteen of us from Foxtrot platoon assembled on the grinder and Commander McCurry, commander of SEAL Team One, pinned a coveted SEAL trident on my chest and congratulated me.

I was not only extremely proud but also fired up and ready for war. Not like some crazed psychopath, but as a professional commando prepared to fight for God and country.

But the reality was that in the early 1980s, there wasn't a whole lot going on. The Vietnam War had ended years earlier.

That didn't mean that we sat around doing nothing. Quite the opposite. When we weren't doing ops, we trained nonstop.

At the time, SEAL Team One consisted of six fourteen-man platoons and a headquarters element commanded by a Navy commander. Sometimes platoons were divided into two seven-man squads or three- and four-man elements. All platoon personnel were dive, parachute, and demolitions qualified.

A typical SEAL platoon is made up of two officers, a chief, and eleven enlisted men. Responsibilities are divided into positions on patrol (point man, patrol leader, commo man, M60 gunner, corpsman, and rear security), department leadership (diving department head, air department head, ordnance/demo department head), and by rank.

The officer of each platoon is called the platoon commander. Under him is a junior officer, the senior enlisted man known as the platoon chief, and the next senior enlisted, the leading petty officer, who is in charge of the day-to-day management of the enlisted platoon members.

In addition to ST-1, UDT-11 and UDT-12 were stationed at the Naval Amphibious Base Coronado, and in 1983, soon after I arrived at ST-1, those UDTs were converted into SEAL Teams Three and Five; they continued to be based in Coronado. In 2002 a fourth West Coast SEAL Team was commissioned, ST-7.

SEAL Teams One, Three, Five, and Seven are organized under Navy Special Warfare Group One (NSWG1), which is commanded by a Navy captain. Its geographical responsibilities include the Pacific and Central commands.

On the East Coast, UDT-21 was converted into SEAL Team Four in 1983, and SEAL Teams Eight and Ten were added in 2002. SEAL Teams Two, Four, Eight, and Ten fall under Navy Special Warfare Group Two (NSWG2), based in Little Creek, Virginia.

The team that no one talked about was SEAL Team Six. All you heard was that SEALs in ST-6 were the cream of the crop. They had the best equipment, got the most important ops, and received the most money. You couldn't request orders to go to Six; you had to be selected.

ST-6's very existence was classified. Even though in 1980 it was still very new, it already had a special aura around it.

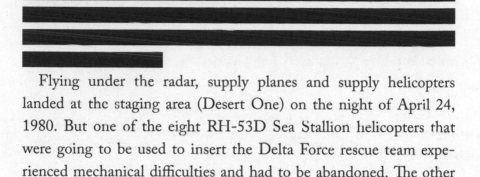

Flying under the radar, supply planes and supply helicopters landed at the staging area (Desert One) on the night of April 24, 1980. But one of the eight RH-53D Sea Stallion helicopters that were going to be used to insert the Delta Force rescue team experienced mechanical difficulties and had to be abandoned. The other seven ran into a sandstorm, known as a haboob, that caused severe navigation problems and forced one to turn around and go back to the aircraft carrier USS *Nimitz*.

The six remaining RH-53Ds arrived at Desert One an hour late. And one of them was badly damaged.

With only five functioning RH-53D helicopters left, the commanders on the scene requested permission to abort the mission. President Jimmy Carter gave his approval.

Now things went from bad to worse.

As one of the RH-53 helicopters prepared to leave, it crashed into a C-130 Hercules transport plane. In the ensuing explosion and fire, five USAF aircrew in the C-130 and three USMC aircrew in the RH-53 died.

In the aftermath of the mission—which also damaged President Carter's chances of being reelected—

The members of SEAL Team Six were considered the most highly trained and lethal warriors in the world.

As soon as I heard that there was a special group of longhaired undercover SEALs stationed on the East Coast, I knew I wanted to be part of the team. But at the beginning of 1983, I was a wet-behind-the-ears SEAL corpsman on a year of probation with the following mind-set: Don't talk, listen. Do what you're told, and work as hard as you can.

Most of our leaders at ST-1 were hardened Vietnam combat vets. Legendary soldiers, like Master Chief Claude Willis Jr., who was the most decorated African American in the military. He was a short guy who was loved by everyone on the team. Whenever anyone got in trouble with the police, which happened a lot when SEALs and Marines drank together, Master Chief Willis would put on his uniform with all the medals on it and go talk to the police.

He served as a jumpmaster when we jumped. We'd be on a plane at about ten thousand feet ready to jump. We'd watch the light go from red, to yellow, to green. Then the jumpmaster would yell: "Go!"

I remember seeing a SEAL standing in the door looking nervous just before a night water jump when Willis tapped him on the shoulder and said, "Holy shit! What's wrong with your chute? Go."

Then he pushed him out.

Under normal circumstances, each SEAL platoon operates according to two-year deployment cycles: twelve to eighteen months of pre-deployment workup, followed by six months of active deployment in a theater of operation. This is so that at any given time, at least two of the six platoons in a particular SEAL team are on active deployment.

It involves a tremendous amount of training, which gives each individual operator a chance to acquire and develop specific skills.

The normal workup or pre-deployment cycle is divided into three phases. Phase one is called the professional development phase (PRODEV), during which individual operators attend formal schools and courses. These can include learning:

Scout/sniper operations (Special Operations Target Interdiction Course, or SOTIC)
Breacher operations (learning barrier penetration and methods of entry)
Surreptitious entry (mechanical and electronic bypass)
Technical surveillance
Advanced driving skills
Climbing/roping skills
Advanced air operations (jumpmaster or parachute rigger)
Diving supervision or diving maintenance and repair
Ranger training
Unmanned aerial vehicle operations
Languages

Phase two is a six-month block of unit-level training during which the whole platoon trains in core mission areas, including:

Small-unit tactics
Land warfare
Close-quarters combat
Urban warfare
Hostile maritime interdiction
Combat swimming
Long-range target interdiction
Rotary and fixed-wing air operations
Special reconnaissance

In phase three, squadron integration training (SIT), as many as six platoons conduct advanced training with the support of special boat squadrons, medical teams, EOD, interpreters, intelligence/ HUMINT teams, cryptologic teams, and so forth.

When I first got to ST-1 we did lots of shooting, jumping, fast-roping, diving, and swimming. We recorded all our jumps and dives in logbooks.

These weren't scenic freshwater dives, but night dives in the bay or ocean for combat-diver training.

Static ship-boarding was one of my favorites. We practiced these a lot in ST-1.

We practiced dives like that all over the world. We also trained for sub ops in Subic Bay, Philippines, in Guam, and in Bremerton, Washington.

I liked the sub ops and the lock-ins/lockouts the least. The first time I did them was on the USS *Grayback*. Earlier, the diesel-electric *Grayback* had served as a launching platform for Regulus II sea-to-surface missiles. In the late 1960s, the ship's cavernous, twin-missile bays had been converted into diving hangars for Special Forces operations.

The idea of being cooped up in the tight quarters of a submarine didn't appeal to me at all. Submarine sailors are pasty white and alternate using the beds in twelve-hour shifts.

Usually it took us a few days to load all our gear on our host sub and was a challenge to find a place to put it.

Most times there were as many as fourteen of us and we'd have to sleep on the deck with all our gear. When the sub was underwater, the stale air would start to make us feel sick after a couple of weeks.

If the sub was the extraction vessel, we'd swim back to the boats and motor back to the sub.

We also trained with SDVs (swimmer-delivery vehicles), which are minisubs that accommodate two to five men. We'd be stuck underwater for four hours in this cramped little thing, shivering and trying to clear our ears.

It wasn't just a sense of unease that kept me from enjoying these maneuvers. Near midnight on January 16, 1982, one of these mini-subs returned to the USS *Grayback*, which had bottomed off the coast of the Philippines. Then divers secured the SDV within the submarine's starboard hangar.

After stowing the SDV, *Grayback*'s support divers and the SDV crew (a BMC, an ensign, two petty officers, a seaman, and a fireman) remained within the flooded starboard hangar making preparations to reenter the submarine. They received permission to shut the outer hangar door, the step just before draining and venting the hangar.

For divers, the vent-and-drain operation was considered routine. But while you're draining water from any manned space, it is critical that breathable fresh air flows in through a vent pipe to replace the water. Aboard *Grayback*, a vent valve, operable from the wet or dry side through a linkage, controlled this airflow.

The dry-side supervisor ordered the vent valve to be opened. The BMC in the hangar acknowledged, and the petty officer complied. But when the venting alarm didn't sound as it should have, neither the BMC nor the petty officer questioned the problem or did anything about it. The dry-side supervisor directed the drain valve to be opened, and draining commenced.

Soon, both the BMC and petty officer felt dizzy and short of breath. The BMC checked valve positions but couldn't open the vent any farther. Someone in the hangar keyed the microphone but didn't speak.

Five of the divers in the hangar, including the petty officer, passed out and fell into the water (some possibly losing their scuba-regulator mouthpieces). The BMC managed to hook his arm on or through a pipe to avoid falling, and then he also passed out.

On the dry side, watch standers heard the microphone keying but dismissed it as an inadvertent action. When they didn't hear the expected reports of water level and when they noted that the usual draining noise had stopped, the watch standers attempted communications with the wet-side occupants. When that failed, they tried standard tap signals, repeating them several times.

Then one dry-side watch stander entered the transfer lock that separated the dry from the wet side and peered through the small deadlight window. He saw only material from a wet suit within.

According to the report of the Navy investigators, after several more minutes of communications attempts, the BMC began to revive and reported that he needed help. Dry-side operators then entered the hangar.

They removed the BMC and the bodies of the ensign, the petty officers, the fireman, and the seaman. For two hours, crewmen tried to revive these men. Five SEALs—William Robinson LT, Chuck Bloomer MM2/DV1, Richard Bond QM3/DV2, Rodney Fitz FN/DV2, and Leslie Shelton SN/DV2—had passed out from lack of oxygen and drowned.

A subsequent investigation revealed several design flaws in the system and concluded that the wet-side operator had opened the vent valve only partway, thereby causing a vacuum to form.

Shortly after the accident, the USS *Grayback* was decommissioned.

When we weren't in the water, we practiced on the land and in the air. And we were taught by the best. Harry O'Connor, who did some of the wild James Bond skydiving stunts, worked with us on our free-fall skills. And Jeff Cooper trained us on pistols and shotguns at his Gunsite facility.

Jeff taught us four rules that every gun owner should commit to memory:

1. *All* guns are *always* loaded.
2. *Never* let the muzzle cover anything that you are not willing to destroy.

3. Keep your finger *off* the trigger until your sights are on the target.
4. *Always* be sure of your target.

Fast-roping and close-quarters-battle skills had just started being utilized in Navy special warfare. Many of these new CT techniques we learned from the ████████████████████████████ ██ ██ ████████████████████████████

Fire movement and fire maneuver quickly evolved. From Jeff Cooper we learned the double-tap (two shots to the chest fired in quick succession to assure maximum incapacitation of a threat). We trained using the modified isosceles stance (which has since been adopted by law enforcement worldwide), and the Mozambique drill used to such effectiveness to this day (two shots to the center of mass followed by one to the head).

As the techniques of urban warfare became more important, we practiced all over the world, breaching building doors, windows, and walls using C4, detonation cord, other specialty demolitions, and rams. We'd rappel or fast-rope down from the roofs and upper decks.

For some ops (training or real), we'd split into squads of six or seven men. Squad one would typically be run by the officer in charge (OIC) and the senior enlisted, the lead petty officer (LPO); squad two by the assistant officer in charge (AOIC) and the chief.

A target would be set up in a building. Squad one would approach on the vertical axis, the other squad on the horizontal. The chief would initiate the order, then it was *boom, boom.* Depending on the op, there might be at least one M60 in each group and the rest us shooting M16s, M14s, or MP5s—point shooters.

When we used this standard operating procedure, the enemy had no place to hide. Every threat on target would be found and captured, or killed.

On command from the OIC, I'd fire a white star cluster from my 40 mm M203, signaling the other squad to shift fire so they hit any-one trying to escape from the back of the building. Meanwhile, squad two would move into the structure and shoot until the ceasefire order was given.

Captured prisoners would be tie-tied at the wrists and ankles and blindfolded. We'd put them on their knees, with their foreheads touching the ground and their wrists behind them. Then we'd search them for weapons, demos, or intel. They weren't allowed to communicate. We'd hold them until the military intelligence guys arrived to debrief them.

We also conducted a lot of land, desert, and mountain warfare training, in and out of helicopters and indigenous vehicles at Camp Kerry, located in the Sonoran Desert outside of El Centro, California.

One night we were rehearsing an op▆▆▆▆▆▆▆▆▆▆▆▆▆▆▆▆▆▆▆▆▆▆▆▆▆▆▆▆▆▆▆▆▆▆ The driver, an ▆▆▆▆▆▆▆ ▆▆▆▆ and our officer sat in front, and eight of us SEALs were in back, four to a bench. We all had our weapons, gear, and rucksacks, and we were camouflaged. With all the op gear, we were probably carrying about three hundred pounds each.

The driver, who was the only one wearing night-vision goggles, was fresh out of BUD/S. The rest of us couldn't see a thing as the ▆▆▆ ▆▆▆▆ flew down a dirt road that dropped off sharply to our right into a canal thirty feet below.

All we heard was the grind of the engine and rushing water as we were tossed around.

I yelled, "Slow down."

The officer in front responded, "Quiet back there."

I told the SEALs who were with me to unbuckle their web gear and hold their weapons away from their heads in case the vehicle had to stop abruptly or went off the road.

Minutes later the ambulance fishtailed around a turn that had no shoulder or guardrail.

We heard the ████████████████████████ guy up front shout, "Cut it! Cut it sharp!"

Then our officer shouted, "Here we go!"

The ████████ shot off the road and flipped over onto its right, so that the guys on the opposite bench fell on us. It felt like we were flying, and then we hit the water hard. We were all severely jolted, and then we felt the ████████ start to sink.

The guys in back with me remained calm. I thought, *At least it's not filling up with water.* Almost as soon as I had that thought, water started pouring in the back. It filled up quickly. The eight of us positioned ourselves so that we could hold our mouths above the waterline and breathe. We tried pushing open the back door but were hindered by the strong current in the canal.

Luckily for us, the driver and SAS guy up front had been thrown from the vehicle. The SAS swam around and tried to pull the back door open while we pushed. After a couple of tense minutes we managed to pry the door open and swim out.

But we couldn't find the driver. Thinking that he was trapped underneath the ambulance, I dove to find him, but he wasn't there.

Turned out he had suffered a head injury and had been carried with the current about a half a mile down the canal. We found him sitting on the bank wondering what had happened.

We trained hard and sometimes partied hard. One night after a long seventy-mile hike in the heat, three of us were sitting outside against some CONEX ammo boxes. One of the SEALs, a big, muscular guy who I'll call Ed, was drunk. He had a deathly fear of snakes.

It didn't help that the area was full of rattlesnakes. The third SEAL, Tommy—who went on to become the command master at ST-6—killed and cut the head off a large rattlesnake, then threw it in Ed's lap. Ed jumped to his feet and started doing this herky-jerky dance as he screamed bloody murder. His movements apparently scared a big, black rat; it came running out from behind the CONEX boxes and started charging right at Ed.

"Holy Mary, Mother of God!" he screamed.

Tommy coolly raised his .45 and shot the rat dead in its tracks.

A couple days later, we were out on patrol again, resting on some rocks, when a large rattlesnake slithered past us. Everyone was so exhausted, including Ed, that no one moved a muscle.

Snakes seemed to be a constant nuisance. Another time during jungle-warfare training in the Philippines, a Marine who was working with us went missing in the jungle for a couple of days. His body was finally found and brought into camp, where a pathologist performed an autopsy to ascertain the cause of death. He found two fang marks four inches apart; they had penetrated four inches through the Marine's skull.

He'd apparently been struck by a king cobra when he stood up to take a piss.

We could be working anywhere on the planet at any given time. One month we'd be slogging through the jungles of Thailand. A month later, we'd be shivering our way through winter-warfare training in Alaska.

It was around this time that me and three other SEALs were selected to go on the ▇▇▇▇▇▇▇▇▇▇▇▇▇▇▇▇ which was so sensitive that it was never even mentioned in our records.

Our platoon also trained for months for a highly sensitive op (that is still classified) that was supposed to take place behind the Iron Curtain. To our great disappointment, we never deployed.

In the winter of '84, seven of us were selected to perform a winter-warfare op in Korea, which involved getting intel from someone who had contact with a North Korean defector. We jumped from an aircraft at night into the freezing water, but we didn't have room on the boat for all our winter gear.

By the time we climbed into our Zodiac and started motoring through the rough sea to shore, our hands and feet were numb, our clothes and gear were frozen, and we were all suffering from hypothermia.

Thankfully we warmed up a little as we climbed into the mountains. The rocky landscape was covered with frozen snow and ice.

We slept outside huddled together on beds of sticks that we'd gathered to keep our bodies off the frozen ground. One night my feet slipped off the sticks, which caused me to suffer frostbite in both feet.

But still we made it through three days of humping over the mountains until we reached our target, and got the intel. Mission success!

Unfortunately, the frostbite stayed with me, and to this day I experience pain and numbness every time my feet get cold.

Despite the occasional discomfort, I loved the pace, constant movement, interesting places we visited, and the characters we met.

There was no one more colorful than Ray Bosco, who taught us hand-to-hand combat in the Philippines. He was a big tough ex-con who had a gym in Subic City; the gym had a bar upstairs and we all gathered there at night.

Once two robbers attacked him at the bar—one armed with a gun, the other with a knife—and Ray, who was unarmed, killed both of them with his bare hands.

He told us that if we ever had any trouble, we should come to him.

I'd gotten away from the kind of trouble I'd had as a kid, but occasionally it still found me. Around this time, I bought my wife, Kim, a new custom-built high-end bike for her birthday. When I was away with my platoon in Guam for a month, our house was broken into and the bike stolen.

I went to the kids who were on the streets riding bikes and I said, "If you ever see my wife's bike, I'll give you a hundred-dollar reward."

They were back in half an hour and said, "The guy who runs the booth down the street where he sells jewelry has your bike. But he painted it bright orange."

I filled my wallet with money, went to his booth, and bought a little piece of jewelry. Behind the vendor was an old bike leaning against a building. I asked him if he was selling it. He gave me a price. I could tell right away that it wasn't my wife's.

"Do you have anything lighter?" I asked him. "I'm in a bike race next weekend and am looking for a lightweight bike."

He said he did but didn't want to sell it. My initial instinct was to grab the vendor by his throat, pull him into the open doorway behind him, and beat the hell out of him. But I decided against it because the bike wasn't even there.

So I paid the kids their reward and I went to Ray Bosco.

Ray, who liked breaking people's legs, said, "I'll kill that motherfucker."

I said, "Ray, I don't want you to kill him. I just want my wife's bike back."

"In that case," he said, "let's call the police."

Ray and a Filipino cop picked me up and drove up me to the jewelry booth, where I identified the crook. They grabbed him, threw him in the back of the cop's jeep, then dropped me off at the police station. Ten minutes later they were back with my wife's bike, which had indeed been painted bright orange.

I thanked Ray and the policeman. But that night as I was getting ready to go to bed, three other Filipino cops knocked on my door and arrested me. They accused me of stealing the vendor's bike and beating him up, which was absurd.

But they refused to drop the charges against me until I dropped the charges I had filed against the jewelry seller. Faced with the prospect of spending the night in a Filipino jail, I relented.

A short time after I told Ray what had happened, my wife's bike reappeared and the jewelry seller was gone. I didn't ask.

When we finished our seven-month deployment in the Philippines and returned to Coronado, ███████████████████████ ███████████████████████████ of SEAL Team Six, would soon be arriving to interview guys who were interested in joining the team.

I figured that everyone would jump at the chance to go to ST-6, but a lot of guys didn't, for one reason or another.

On the designated afternoon, I was escorted into a room where Commander Gormly and four intimidating plank owners (founding members) from ST-6 were sitting. They started going through my records and firing questions.

I felt I was ready, because I'd been giving ST-1 everything I had. Not only was I rated the top corpsman at the command and the top performer in my platoon, I was also very gung ho about joining ST-6.

The guy interviewed before me was a big, tough biker named Rocky. When Gormly asked him if he'd even seen combat, Rocky said he'd answered, "I see it every weekend at the bars in Imperial Beach."

Rocky wasn't chosen, but I was. I had been waiting for this day, and it was here.

My captain protested. "You're not taking Doc Mann, are you?"

Gormly responded, "We can take anyone we want."

CHAPTER EIGHT

Train as you fight, fight as you train.

—*SEAL team motto*

When I arrived at ST-6, based in Dam Neck, Virginia, in November of 1985,

████████████████████████████████████

████████████ And they weren't happy.

The Boeing 727 flight from Athens to Rome had been hijacked by two Hezbollah Shiite terrorists armed with pistols and grenades and redirected to Beirut, Lebanon. In a bid to force airport officials to refuel the plane, the terrorists grabbed twenty-four-year-old U.S. Navy diver Robert Dean Stethem from his seat, pushed him toward the cockpit door, bound him with rope, then proceeded to torture and then beat him beyond recognition. When a battered, bleeding Stethem refused to plead to the tower through a transmitter to send a fuel truck, one of the hijackers shot him in the head and dumped his body on the tarmac.

What's not generally known is that a SEAL Team Six operator had the hijacker in his sights but was never given the order to shoot. Other ST-6 ████████████████████████████████

The standoff ended two weeks later when the remaining passengers were set free in exchange for the release of over seven hundred Shiite prisoners in Israel.

Both of Stethem's brothers became Navy SEALs.

Later, when the pilot of Flight 847 was asked for his impression of Robert Stethem, he answered, "He was the bravest man I've ever seen in my life." Stethem was posthumously awarded a Bronze Star for bravery, and the Navy's thirteenth Aegis destroyer was christened the USS *Stethem* and commissioned in 1995.

Soon after the TWA Flight 847 hijacking, ST-6 prepared to raid the *Achille Lauro*, an Italian cruise ship that had been commandeered by four heavily armed Palestine Liberation Front terrorists off the coast of Egypt on October 7, 1985. While President Reagan was considering whether to disable the ship or launch a full-scale rescue op, the terrorists murdered an elderly Jewish passenger named Leon Klinghoffer and tossed his body overboard.

After two days of negotiation, the hijackers agreed to abandon the liner in exchange for safe conduct to Tunisia. But President Reagan was determined to bring them to justice, and he ordered F-14 Tomcats to intercept the Egyptian airliner the hijackers were traveling on and then direct it to the U.S. Naval Air Station Sigonella, in Sicily. SEAL Team Six waited there to take the hijackers into custody, but Italian authorities insisted on arresting the terrorists themselves.

When I reached ST-6 ███████████████████

███████████████████████████████████

███████████████████████████████████

███████████████████████████████████

███████████████████████████████████

███████████████████████████████████

██████████████████████ ST-6 █████████

███████████████████████████████████

████████████████████████████████

███████████████████████████████████

███████████████████████████████████

██████████████████████████

███████████████████████████████████

███████████████████████████████████

███████████████████████████████████

███████████████████████████████████

██████

███████████████████████████████████

███████████████████████████████████

███████████████████████████████████

███████████████████████████████████

████████████████████████

██████████████████████ ST-6 █████████

███████████████████████████████████

██████████████

Back in March of 1979, the New Jewel Republic, led by Maurice Bishop, had overthrown the newly independent government of the small Caribbean island and established a socialist regime called the People's Revolutionary Government; it was allied with the Soviet Union and Cuba, thereby raising the concern of officials in Washington.

On October 12, 1983, a hard-line faction of the Central Committee led by Bernard Coard seized control of the government. Over the next several days, Bishop and many of his supporters were killed, and the country was placed under martial law.

President Ronald Reagan, alarmed by Coard's hard-line Marxism and concerned about the welfare of nearly a thousand U.S. medical students in Grenada, launched an invasion of the island, code-named Operation Urgent Fury.

Right from the start, commandos from ST-6 ran into problems. Their first mission: to secure the airfield at Port Salinas, emplace beacons, and wait for an airdrop of Army Rangers. But one of the two C-130 cargo planes carrying the SEALs veered off course, then got caught in a storm. Four of the eight SEALs that made the drop were blown out to sea and drowned.

The SEALs' next mission was to secure Governor-General Paul Scoon and his family. But as the ST-6 commandos fast-roped onto the grounds of the governor's mansion, they took fire. My buddy Rich H. was hit in the elbow.

He shouted, "I've been shot! I've been shot!"

Bobby L., who later served as our ST-6 free-fall instructor, responded, "What the hell do you think is supposed to happen in war?"

The SEALs moved Governor-General Scoon and his family to a safe part of the house. Then the mansion came under fire from men armed with AK-47s and RPGs and wearing Cuban uniforms.

Meanwhile, two assault teams from ST-6 sent to secure Grenada's only radio station were met by Soviet-made BTR-60 armored personnel carriers and truckloads of armed Grenadan soldiers. Facing overwhelming firepower, the SEALs decided to destroy the radio transmitter and head to the water following a preplanned escape route. That's when a round from an enemy AK-47 hit one of our officers, Kim E., in the arm and shredded his triceps muscle.

Grenada proved to be a tough baptism by fire for ST-6.

Informal post-ops and hot washes were still being discussed around the command when I arrived. Many of the operators were recognized for the show of great bravery. But as happens in battle, the team had also made mistakes, and they were determined not to repeat them.

ST-6

Even the PTs were harder. We did weekly long swims, long runs, obstacle courses, sessions in the weight room, and, usually on Friday mornings, what was known as a Monster Mash—three to five hours of insane nonstop paddling, running, swimming, O-course drills, as well as carrying simulated wounded men and stopping at various stations to shoot at targets, assemble weapons, put together the radios, and establish comms with HQ.

The days of static-line jumps were over. Bobby L., the tough, Vietnam-era Texan vet who had fast-roped into the governor's compound with Rich H. in Grenada, taught us free fall, HALO (high-altitude, low-opening), and HAHO (high-altitude, high-opening).

He walked up with a beer in his hand and growled in a deep voice, "If there are any of you assholes here who don't know how to free-fall, you're gonna learn to pack and jump by morning."

And he meant it. Those of us who already knew how to free-fall helped the guys who didn't.

We trained in HALO and HAHO, jumping at night in full stacks. Our team would do a mass exit at 17,999 feet, and each jumper would count somewhere between four and eight seconds before pulling.

Much more tactical than the jumping we did at ST-1!

We planned our jumps so we hit the ground at nautical twilight. That way no one on the ground could spot us coming.

Sometimes, we'd be under canopy for forty-five minutes or more. Passing through thick cloud cover was dangerous, because if another jumper happened to drift off his compass bearing and came at you in the whiteout, the two of you could hit each other at a combined force of over two hundred miles an hour.

So we kept track of one another. Each of us always knew how many jumpers were supposed to be in front and how many were behind. We'd spot the low man, ensure no one else was coming in for approach, flare our canopies, and try to land within twenty-five meters of one another.

Once you landed, you buried your parachute in the dirt. Then you'd get your op gear in order, form a 360-degree security perimeter, receive any last-minute communications, get in patrol formation, and start moving toward the target or the objective. This all took place in less than ten minutes.

███████████████████████████████████████

███████████████████████████████████████

███████████████████████████████████████

██████ ██████ most of our over-18,000-foot jumps in either Australia or Germany because the allowable ceiling for skydivers was much higher there.

In Germany we jumped at 22,000, 24,000, and 26,000 feet, and we worked our way up to do a 30,000-foot team jump, which would have set a world record as the highest mass-exit full-military-team HAHO.

At the higher altitudes, the jumper would typically pass through three levels of clouds. He'd exit the aircraft, do his four- to eight-second count while staying on bearing, deploy his main canopy, and watch everyone disappear in a haze that would quickly turn completely white. After that he'd enter a patch of clear sky before sinking into clouds again. Once he fell through the third level of clouds, he'd finally see land.

The jumper and the rest of the stack would do their best to stay in formation and on bearing through the clouds and land within thirty seconds of one another.

The higher the jump, the further away from the target we would exit the aircraft, depending on the direction and velocity of the wind. The advantage of jumping at such high altitude is that the enemy doesn't hear or see the aircraft.

But jumping that high changed the game.

Once airborne in the plane but before we jumped, each of us would do a half hour of breathing from an oxygen tank to flush the nitrogen out of the body. Then we'd disconnect our oxygen lines from the large aircraft O_2 tanks and connect them to the smaller tanks on our gear.

We received a thirty-minute warning, which was followed by a six-minute warning, a three-minute warning, a one-minute warning, a thirty-second warning, and then standby. Then each of us jumped a split second apart, staying flat and stable, each jumper keeping his eyes on the jumper below. If the guy below pulled early, the jumper above didn't want to free-fall into his canopy, because that would kill them both. Because of the two-hundred-mile-an-hour speeds, our oxygen masks would sometimes blow off our faces. So we had to duct-tape the masks to our helmets minutes before exiting the aircraft.

We were falling much faster than on the typical twelve-thousand-foot jumps. And because of the added speed and air pressure, guys were hurting their necks and straining their backs when they deployed their chutes. We joked that there were boot prints on the backs of our helmets, because the shock of opening at those altitudes and exit speeds was so violent that the jumper's back arched to the point where his boots kicked the back of his head.

My buddy Foster frequently lost his oxygen mask and passed out under canopy. He'd wake up after his automatic opening deployed his main chute.

After dozens of jumps, we were ready to try for thirty thousand feet, but I was worried. The rear ramp lowered. A ███ support para-rigger stood behind me on the ramp as I tightened my straps. I cinched down my mask and did a couple practice wave-offs.

My heart pounding, I was ready to go.

But just as the red light turned to yellow, I heard a loud crash. When I looked behind me I saw the ███ ███ on the deck convulsing. His arms, legs, and neck were thrashing uncontrollably. The jumpmaster immediately radioed the cockpit. The ramp was closed and we flew back to the base.

The doctors discovered that the ███ para-rigger had cocaine in his system. He was kicked off the team, and we were pissed that he'd ruined our world-record attempt.

A legendary badass from New Jersey named Al Morrel taught us defensive tactics (DT)—commonly known as hand-to-hand combat. Al was a heavy man who wore thick glasses and had huge bear-paw-like hands. He'd served as General Westmoreland's personal bodyguard during Vietnam and had worked as bodyguard for Elvis Presley.

He stood before ten of us and said, "I can't prove everything I'm going to tell you, but I can tell you this: The ten of you can't take me down. There's no one on this planet who can take me down. But all I can prove right now is that the ten of you can't."

The ten of us looked at him, thinking, *Is this old man crazy?*

Al said, "Give me about a second apiece and come at me one by one. Try gouging my eyes out, putting me in a choke hold, whatever you want to do."

We charged, one after the other. Being one of the smaller guys in the group, I figured I'd jump up at his neck and put him in a choke hold. But when I ran up to him, that mountain of a man threw me, and I landed flat against a wall. He smeared all ten of us good.

Al had an amazing ability to use the assailant's own energy against him. If the guy came at Al with a knife or a baseball bat, Al would use the weapon against the attacker.

Al loved knives. He said to us once, "If I really get to know my knife, I can cut a person without the blade even touching them."

What?

He made incredible statements, and proved many of them to be true.

One day Al walked up to the biggest guy in our class—Mack. Mack stood out not just for his size and his big mustache but also for the big, ugly scars on his face, which he'd gotten from his wife. He explained that he'd been in the shower with his wife and she'd pissed on his leg because she thought it was sexy. Mack didn't agree and slapped her face. She reached up and gouged his face with her long fingernails, which resulted in the scars.

Al said to Mack, "Kick me between my legs as hard as you can."

Mack didn't want to do it.

"Go ahead and kick me!"

Mack kicked Al in the balls. Al didn't even twitch.

The rest of us guys couldn't believe what we had just seen.

Al said, "If I wanted a freakin' girl to kick me, I would have asked one. Go ahead and kick me like a man."

Mack reared his leg back and kicked him so hard it was painful to watch. Al's body rose a couple of inches off the ground, but his face didn't register even an iota of discomfort.

Holy shit!

He straightened his shoulders, walked past us, and said, "Men, I never want you to show how much pain you're in. Under any circumstances."

He never explained how he did it, but we couldn't have been more impressed.

Unfortunately, Al's tolerance for pain knew no bounds. Al had developed a triple hernia years before we met him, which protruded quite a bit. One day before class, he accidentally sliced open his protruding belly, causing his large and small intestines to spill out of the wound. One of the guys in our class found him bleeding on the floor and called an ambulance. Al died from complications in the hospital. We couldn't believe it, and we'd never forget what he taught us.

The diving at ███████████ was much more complex and dangerous than anything we had attempted at ST-1. Now, we dove as a boat crew of six rather than in pairs. And the six of us swam while holding on to a five-foot-long telescopic pole with a caving ladder secured to the end.

Try to imagine swimming with five other guys for four hours underwater at night. All of you are holding on to this pole, all trying to swim at the same depth, in and around pilings and piers. It is fairly difficult maintaining buoyancy as a single diver in the darkness, and trying to maintain the buoyancy of yourself and five others while diving in and around pier pilings is extremely difficult.

We'd dive into a harbor with maybe forty ships in it and have to locate the target vessel from underwater in the dark. The only lights we used were the luminescent green lights on our watches, depth gauges, and compass boards.

We did vertical de-rigs, which they don't do anymore because of the danger. Six of us would swim up under a ship and rig a vertical line from its hull. The line had loops attached to it so each diver could secure his dive gear as he de-rigged underwater. We'd secure our weight belts, fins, and Dräger rebreathers.

On the signal—*toot, toot, toot*—we'd silently surface.

As lead climber, I would climb the ladder and attach it for the rest of the team. This was always an adventure because I never knew how securely the ladder was hooked, or what it was hooked on to. We climbed in order and we each had specific duties once we boarded the vessel.

Weapons training and CQB were also a lot more intense. In fact, we did more CQB training than any other unit in the U.S. military, and probably in the world. And we ████████████████████

██

██

We learned how to take down a house room by room and how to infiltrate an aircraft or a bus. We could secure a vessel compartment by compartment after boarding by sea or air. And we were surgical shooters trained in various breaching and explosive-entry methods.

██

██

██████████████

One of our sniper instructors was the famous Carlos Hathcock, known as the Marine Corps sniper, who had recorded ninety-three confirmed sniper kills in Vietnam. He held the record for distance: a twenty-five-hundred-yard confirmed kill with a .50-caliber rifle during a five-day standoff with the Vietcong.

We also had four incredible lead-climbing instructors, including the amazing Jay Smith and Danny Osmond.

On ops in the jungle, desert, or wooded areas, we'd often extract from a target with ████████████████ helicopters shooting right behind us to ensure that we weren't followed by anyone who might have survived the initial assault. They'd fire so close, hard, and hot that you could literally feel the ground shaking. We trusted those ▆▆▆ pilots with our lives—over and over again. They became famous with the book and movie *Black Hawk Down*.

▆▆▆▆▆▆▆▆▆▆▆▆▆▆▆▆ ST-6, ▆▆▆▆▆▆
▆▆▆▆▆▆▆▆▆▆▆▆▆▆▆▆▆▆▆▆▆▆
▆▆▆▆▆▆▆▆▆▆▆▆▆▆▆▆▆▆▆▆▆▆
▆▆▆▆▆▆▆▆▆▆▆

Rich, one of my teammates and a guy who had distinguished himself in Grenada, was doing live CQB training with his boat crew. The shooting house, or as we called it in the '80s, the kill house, was dark. There were paper funny-face targets placed in different locations. Upon entering with his weapon, Rich spotted a darkened hallway that extended between two rooms. He went down it to make sure it was clear. But the guys who had set up the shooting house and placed the targets didn't plan for anyone to go all the way down the hall. Rich did.

Meanwhile, a second team entered the shooting house through the other entrance, spotted a threat target set up on the other side of the hallway wall, and opened fire. Two rounds hit the paper target at the center of mass, passed through the wall, and hit Rich between the one-inch gap in his body armor. They damaged his lungs, liver, and spleen. Rich died a couple of days after.

He wasn't the only brave warrior we lost in training. We trained like we fought and said that our SOPs were written in blood, so none of our teammates who died in training died in vain.

Training-based scenarios helped us identify our individual strengths, weaknesses, and vulnerabilities. The goal was for each of us to learn how to stay in control and remain confident when faced with life-threatening situations.

Through BUD/S and SEAL training we developed a combat mind-set, and that strengthened even further during ▆▆▆▆▆

We understood that all human beings responded to threat with a fight-or-flight response. Typical reactions included muscle tension; headache; upset stomach; tunnel vision; increased heartbeat; shallow breathing; anxiety; poor concentration; feelings of hopelessness, frustration, anger, sadness, and fear; and auditory occlusion.

Visualization (picturing ourselves in dangerous scenarios), anticipation mind-set, and contingency training were some of the techniques we learned and practiced. *If such-and-such happens, what's the best way for me to respond?* The idea was to develop well-thought-out, sound actions in advance of possible threats. We always said, "Plan your dive and dive your plan."

We all learned the importance of developing situational awareness. According to Colonel Boyd's OODA loop, this involves observation, orientation, decision, and action. In other words, always find the threat before it finds you, orient yourself to your surroundings, trust that your conscious mind will offer the action with the highest probability of success based on your previous training and experience, and act on your plan. Because a poor plan poorly executed is better than no plan at all.

At ███████ we were evaluated constantly—during work and on liberty. We were graded on whether or not we went drinking at night with the guys, how early we got up for PT, how effectively we cleaned our weapons, how neatly we packed our parachutes, and how well we got along with the others.

During the last week of my training, without any warning, an officer and two enlisted men were pulled from ████████ and told, Pack your bags and go, you're not going to an ST-6 assault team.

███████████████████████████████████████

███████████ ST-6 █████████████████████

███████████████████████████████████

██

██

███████████████████████████████ after the team extracted. And the coxswains spent most of their time in the water, traveling in cigarette boats at seventy miles an hour, in all types of weather—rain, snow, hailstorms, lightning—training and chasing down ships.

██

██████████

██

██

██

██

██

██

██

██████████

██

██████████

██

██

███ It's where I belonged.

CHAPTER NINE

SEAL Team Six

Break glass in case of war.

—*SEAL team motto*

When I got to SEAL Team Six, ███████████████ was still under investigation. As a result, all of us were audited. Navy officials sat me down and went through all my hotel receipts, taxi receipts, receipts for the cold-weather gear I had purchased for winter-warfare training. Everything.

I was squeaky clean. But a few guys got in trouble and had to leave the command.

Overall, I found the commitment and professionalism of the team members to be off the charts. They were the very best of the best— serious, smart, tough, dedicated, professional, mission driven—and I was extremely proud to be among them.

██
████████████████████████

During standby, we all met early in the kill house or on the range and fired weapons. We shot a lot—before, during, and after work!

Every morning we'd have something called the head shed meeting, which included officers and boat-crew leaders. During the head shed meeting, we'd discuss the plan of the day—who was going where, and what activities would be taking place. For example, boat crews one and two will conduct over-the-beach training in a.m., boat crews three and four will be at long-gun range in the a.m., the entire assault team will execute a night water jump from a C5 in the p.m. We worked with outstanding air assets, including ███████████████████████████████████ ST-6 █████

Most mornings, the head shed meeting lasted forty-five minutes. Then we'd have individual PT—one to two hours of running, swimming, obstacle course, or circuit work in the weight room.

In the other SEAL teams, the PT was much more structured and mandatory. Running one day, weight training the next, and so on. If you missed PT, you generally had to answer to someone. But at ST-6, PT was the responsibility of each individual operator. All of our operators were always ready physically for battle. We did not train to get big, ripped, or cut—we PTed so we could do our jobs.

During standby, in addition to shooting every day and staging competitions with long guns, MP5s, M4s, shotguns, and handguns, ███████████████████████████████████████ ███████████████████████████████████████ ███████████████████████████████ rehearsals, and discuss tactics—and that we did all the time.

We also rehearsed recalls. Only the command head shed team would know the time of recall beforehand. Once the signal went out, all members of the team would assemble, listen to the warning order, and then run a full mission profile, in full gear—NVGs, gas masks, live rounds. We changed scenarios constantly, juggling the variables, such as the number of hostages and threats.

We had to be ready with all bags packed—one bag loaded with jump and air-ops gear, another with dive gear, a third with counter-terrorist gear, a fourth with winter-warfare gear, a fifth with desert gear, and a sixth with jungle gear. We were constantly tweaking, trying to make the recall lighter, quieter, and easier to assess.

Recalls occurred at least once a cycle and we never knew when they were coming. More than once, we were all at a party at a team member's house when our beepers went off. Each time, all the operators straightened up, hurried to their cars, and drove to work as fast as possible.

Once there, we had four hours to get dressed, pack our gear, have our intel briefing, and go to our cage to get our weapons and ammo. We always kept our wartime ammo separate from the training ammo.

If you were a demolitions guy, you packed all of the demolition. If it was a jump op, the riggers would pack all of the chutes and related gear; if it was a dive op, the men in the dive locker would pack all dive-related gear.

Typically, a recall involved the entire assault team with coxswain and sniper support. We were the only maritime counterterrorism team in the world that could be wheels-up in fewer than four hours!

Once we were recalled the day before a team member named Conrad was going to be married. It was a big wedding, and all of us were invited. But Conrad was the only one who got permission to attend. Later, when we saw the pictures, we noticed that he was just one guy in the company of all our wives and girlfriends. The joke around the base was that it had been a lesbian wedding.

All the operators on ST-6 were trained to be shooters, jumpers, divers, and so on. But each one of us had a specialty. For example, some were breachers, some were coxswains, some were snipers, some were communications reps. I was the medic, a dive supervisor, and a lead climber. So as a lead climber, I was the guy who went up the ladder first, whether we were climbing up the side of a ship, oil rig platform, or building.

During specialized training (SPECTRA, we called it), each of us would work on his specific skills. I climbed at Yosemite; Red Rock, Nevada; and Cabo San Lucas, Mexico, to train with some of the world's top climbers. I also attended advanced para-rescue medical training courses with the USAF Pararescue (PJs) and advanced mini goat-lab courses with the Army Special Forces, and I worked at the Womack Army Medical Center at Fort Bragg as an "intern"—which meant that I was allowed to assist in all types of procedures in the emergency and operating rooms.

Then, during the team's deployment cycle, all of us would pack up and deploy somewhere in CONUS (the contiguous United States) or OCONUS (outside the contiguous United States). We might travel as a team to Puerto Rico for a three-week dive trip, or to Arizona for two to three weeks of HAHO jumping. Sometimes we ███████

██

███████████████████████████████████████

The person or persons who had that specific specialty planned the trip. So I designed the climbing, medical, and dive deployments.

We trained for land, air, water, and mountain, arctic, jungle, desert, and urban terrain. No other maritime unit in the world was better trained, more versatile, or could deploy to as many locations in the world.

Given the level of expertise of the individual operators, we had spectacular advanced-training runs. Instead of static ship boarding, we practiced complex under-ways, which required the split-second timing of numerous components.

During under-ways, we'd parachute into the ocean and drop up to four cigarette boats on pallets approximately five miles away from the moving target ship.

We'd hit the water as close as possible to the cigarette boats, jettison our chutes, swim to the boats, and cut the assault boats free from the pallets. A steer-and-throttle man would board each boat and start the engine.

Then each boat crew would load its respective boat. Once all boats were loaded, we'd take off at a high rate of speed toward the target, generally a cruise liner.

These ops were always conducted at night. Sometimes we'd drop an extra boat, because if one hit the water at the wrong angle, it would sink to the bottom like a lawn dart.

Once the target ship passed, the assault boats moved into position. Two would attack from the starboard side, and two from the portside, in tandem.

With the assault boats bobbing up and down and the target moving at a good speed, a pole man would stand on the bow of the boat, with two men holding him, then extend a telescopic pole with the cave-in ladder attached and try to hook it to something solid on the deck of the target vessel.

At the same time the pole went up on the starboard side, one was also going up on the portside. If one boat dropped its pole or couldn't attach its ladder, the cigarette boat behind it would move into position. If the worst-case scenario happened, we needed only one ladder to go up, because everyone could climb up the same ladder.

Once the pole was hooked, the pole man would pull the pole, which released a small caving ladder attached to it that unrolled down into the assault craft.

The ladder extended as far as forty feet. For ships with higher decks, we'd use two ladders attached to each other and conduct a multi-pitch climb, which was basically a two-stage climb. You'd climb up a good portion of the ship to a landing, then hook again for another climb to the main deck.

Every part of an under-way is quite dangerous. I had a buddy who fell off the caving ladder near the deck of the ship and landed thirty feet down in the assault boat. He was beat up pretty badly and ruptured his spleen. Our team doctor, who was on the ship, saved his life that night. And I witnessed plenty of other lead climbers being flung off the caving ladder once it went taut from the ship going in one direction and the ladder being secured down.

We typically assaulted ships in thin (three-millimeter) wet suits or, in warm climates, black skin suits. We each wore a holster with an S&W 686 revolver and carried gear on a black web belt—Ka-Bar knife, hostage gear, tie-ties, commo, medical supplies, and so on.

As the lead climber, I went up the ladder first and secured it to something on the deck with a piece of one-inch tubular nylon and a carabiner. Attached to the right side of my belt was a carabiner with two to three nylon runners I could sling over something solid and then attach a safety line from the runner to the ladder.

With the ladder secured, I would take up a position of cover and signal the rest of the team to board the ship.

As we reached the deck, helicopters would swoop in, and another element of SEALs would begin fast-roping in. Timing was critical. If the helicopters arrived before the guys on the boats were on deck, the assault boats and their crews would be sitting ducks.

The SEALs from the helicopters would clear from the deck on up, leapfrogging from one position to another. And then they'd proceed to wherever they'd been tasked to go—a ballroom or a stateroom, maybe, in the case of a hostage rescue.

The guys on the boats would clear from the decks on down, and maybe secure the engine room; it depended on the op. Afterward, the assault boats were picked up by the helicopters, or they were driven somewhere and recovered.

Under-ways were by far the hardest thing we did, and we got very, very good at them.

We worked with ███████ the best helo pilots in the world. They liked to mess with us. Like the time we were sitting outside on the skegs during a training op in Puerto Rico and the pilot flew fewer than two feet over the treetops at 120 knots. At times, we thought they were crazy, and the feelings were mutual, I'm sure.

Our HAHO capabilities would have given them good reason to think so. We'd fly in thirty-man stacks, and after we jumped, we'd time it so that all thirty chutes opened at the same time and at the same altitude. We would exit the bird up to twenty-five miles away from the target and land just before sunrise.

Every man in the stack would be in communication with the others. You knew who was supposed to be in front of you and who was supposed to be behind you. You would count off from the rear, "Thirty okay," "Twenty-nine okay," and so on. In the case of a low jumper or a malfunction, a member of the stack would split away and accompany the distressed jumper to the alternate DZ (drop zone).

I loved the sensation of free-falling. But these weren't recreational jumps. We were going down in full combat gear with oxygen and weapons.

Guys suffered serious injuries—I broke my back in two places on a HAHO, and I have seen broken legs, ankles, and backs; some men even died.

One night we did a 17,999-foot HAHO jump outside of Tucson where we exited the aircraft about twenty miles from the target. I was carrying a seventy-five-pound rucksack, my weapon, oxygen tank and mask, my compass board, and my altimeter, and I was wearing my jump helmet with comms.

Before opening the main chute, the procedure is to wave off and then look left and right before pulling; this way, when you open, you don't have another jumper falling or flying into you, which can be fatal.

That night, when I exited, I waved off. But when I pulled, I flipped right through my parachute risers and started falling backward.

This caused my risers to quickly spiral all the way down to my helmet and jerk my neck, helmet, and jaw sharply to my left, knocking off my O_2 mask. I thought I'd broken my neck and jaw. And when I looked up and saw the other jumpers way above me, I knew that I was dropping like a stone. My parachute wasn't even partially opened.

When experiencing a malfunction, the jumper pulled his cutaway pillow with his right hand, which freed the main parachute. Then he'd pull the reserve handle with his left hand, which hopefully would deploy the reserve chute.

I performed my cutaway, enjoyed a short free fall, and seconds later saw a nice full reserve expand above my head.

All of us were wearing push-to-talk radios. The comms wire extended down my right arm from my radio and helmet to my right hand. Generally, when you push the button and talk, everyone on your stick is supposed to hear you.

I wanted to alert my team and tell them that I would meet them on the drop zone. But when I pushed the button and talked into the radio, I could manage only a mumble. The pain in my neck and jaw was so intense that I couldn't open my mouth enough to make anyone understand what I was saying.

I palpated my jaw and realized that it was dislocated and way to the left of where it should be. So I did to myself what I had done to dozens of other people in ER. At around eight thousand feet, I placed my thumb on my bottom teeth, pushed down hard, and jerked my jaw right. It popped into place and hurt like hell!

Then I got back on the radio and said, "Guys, I had a cutaway."

I landed approximately a thousand feet away from the target, grabbed my chute, and jogged over to catch up with the rest of the team.

Another time, on a deployment in Key West, I came very close to drowning during a night static-ship takedown. We were doing a four-hour oxygen dive on Dräger with a six-man boat crew, navigating in a crowded harbor through pilings, with all sorts of ship noises overhead.

Once we arrived at the target ship, we set a vertical de-rigging line from the hull of the ship, with loops in it for each diver. We attached the pole and ladder to the line as we all removed our Drägers, fins, and weight belts and attached them to the de-rigging line, continuing to breathe through the mouthpiece attached to the inhalation hose.

As I was waiting for the verbal signal to surface in the pitch-black water, I suddenly realized that I couldn't breathe. My first thought was that the inhalation hose had gotten twisted with the constant moving up and down around the de-rigging line.

So I felt along the hoses, but I found no kinks or twists. I also rechecked to make sure that the open/close valve on my mouthpiece was open. It was.

Next, I reached for the O_2 bottle, thinking it had somehow been shut, but it was open too. I repeated these procedures three times.

Meanwhile, my head started to hurt. So I reached up to my swim buddy and shook his fin. I motioned to him that I was out of air. But neither of us could see anything.

I put my hand on his mouthpiece, indicating that I wanted to buddy breathe with him, but he didn't understand my signal and backed off.

All I could think to do was repeat my emergency procedures again. So I checked my hoses, mouthpiece, and O_2 bottle. My head felt like it was about to explode. Now my only option was to swim up to the bottom of the ship with my hand over my head in case I hit the hull headfirst. I desperately wanted to take a mouthful of seawater and end the agonizing pain that I was in. It was a horrible thought, and one that still shames me.

Using the hull as a guide, I made my way to the side of the ship and approached the surface. But the ship was close to a large structure and I couldn't squeeze through.

By this time it felt like someone had thrust an ice pick in my brain. Every nerve in my head was screaming.

With no idea how much time had elapsed or how many seconds I had left, I kicked on a steady course, hoping to find an opening to the surface. My body started to sink. I was running out of steam.

During the last moments underwater, I saw a light and followed it. I swam from midship to bow and surfaced! Then quickly uttered a prayer of thanks.

I swam to the portside of the ship, where my teammates were going up the ladder, and joined the stack. The light I saw was actually a moonbeam.

After the op, during the hot wash, where we discussed all phases of the op in detail, I told the team what had happened. It turned out to have been a very unusual malfunction in which the inhalation butterfly valve in my mouthpiece had sealed in the shut position.

I was lucky to be alive.

Despite the constant training activity, guys on the team complained that we weren't getting enough real-world ops. Some felt that ST-6 had become a political show horse, something the military trotted out to impress the big money folks in DC.

Since I was the only corpsman on my assault team, I rarely got time off. Anything we did as a team that involved danger—which was everything—required my presence. Even if a small group of guys was sent off to do breaching or ordnance disposal, I had to go with them.

My family life was completely on hold, which made my wife, Kim, unhappy, since I was never home. We were actually deployed about three hundred days a year.

When I asked for leave to attend my sister's wedding, I was told that I couldn't go. I got the same answer when my second sister was married. I still regret missing their weddings.

I wasn't allowed to visit my uncles when they were dying. Nor was I given permission to attend their funerals.

During this time, I got a call from my parents, who were living in Westerly, Rhode Island. Because they knew I was very busy, they never asked me for anything. But this time my mom and dad said that my younger brother, Rick, was in real trouble and needed my help. He was drinking heavily and doing drugs; he had even attacked his wife and daughter with a Buck knife I'd given him for Christmas.

That night I sat down and wrote Rick an eleven-page letter. I spoke from my heart. I wrote:

Rick, you and I both were going down a road of trouble since we were kids. I diverted off—thanks to the Navy. But you've kept down the path, and now you're in all kinds of trouble. You're not working, you lost your family, you're having cocaine seizures, you're stealing cars. I know. You're going down a dead end road and you will end up dead or in prison. These are the only options for guys who lead the life you are living. You've got to stop. I love you. You're my only brother.

Please allow me to ask you just one favor. First, please stop drinking, drugs and partying for thirty days. Just stop. If you can't, let me send you to rehab and I'll pay. That's the only favor I'm going to ask you for the rest of my life.

I went to my assault team officer and asked him if I could go to Rhode Island for the weekend. I told him that my brother was in a lot of trouble and I needed to help him.

The officer said. "Sorry, Doc, but we can't afford for you to be away now."

I decided to go anyway. The only person I told was my swim partner, Clell.

I said, "Clell, if we get recalled, you know where I am."

"Okay."

"Maybe I'll lose my job, but it's my only brother and I have to do this."

The next day, I flew to Providence. My brother, Rick, picked me up on his Harley. He had long hair, a beard, and a black leather jacket— the same motorcycle-gang regalia I wore before I joined the Navy.

Rick had been a tough, well-built guy, but now he looked sickly and skinny. We rode directly to a biker bar. By the time we sat down, it was around eleven in the morning.

I turned to my brother and asked, "Rick, is this all you do, just hang out and party?"

He answered, "No, I stay here until nine or ten at night, then I go out partying."

"Did you come here to reprimand me?" he asked.

"No," I answered. "I came here at the risk of losing the best job I ever will have to hopefully save your life."

The two of us sat next to each other at the bar. To my right stood a gray-bearded biker with patches all over his leather vest.

He turned to me and said, "Your brother is a wild man. He comes in here every night and does eight balls [an eighth of an ounce of cocaine] with all the coke whores. They crawl all over him. He's crazy."

I said, "That's why I'm here."

The bartender set some beers in front of us.

I turned to my brother again and said, "Rick, I wrote you a long letter last night. It will be easier for me to give you the letter than for me to tell you all that it says."

I handed him the letter, and he started reading. I could tell he was moved. When he finished reading it, he folded up the letter and stuffed it in his pocket.

A minute or so later, the bartender came over and asked Rick if he wanted another drink.

Rick said, "No, I'm on the wagon."

That's all he said. He's been on the wagon ever since. Today, almost thirty years later, he's a successful businessman, with a wife and two wonderful children. And I'm so proud of him.

He still rides with motorcycle clubs and attends big bike rallies but is completely against drinking and doing drugs, and he has helped hundreds of people who are trying to end their addictions.

When I returned to the team the following Monday, the officer hadn't even noticed that I'd left. And I decided that if I wanted a life, I needed to train some of the other guys on the assault team to be medics.

So I started planning a mini goat lab and recruited four guys, one from each of the four boat crews, to attend.

Just before I started to train them, I received word that the new CO, Captain Murphy, wanted to see me. (Captain Thomas E. Murphy replaced Captain Gormly in early 1986.)

Captain Murphy said, "Sorry, Doc. But that goat lab you had planned—we're going to have to cancel it."

"Why, sir?"

"The team is under such close scrutiny, I don't need the press to find out that we're chopping up goats. I was shot in the leg in Vietnam. I didn't need somebody who chopped up goats to save me."

I said, "I understand, sir. But you can't cancel this."

The officer in charge of my team, who was sitting beside me, said, "Don, he's the CO. Let it go."

"I know, but this is important. We're going to have an accident one day, and we don't have enough medics in my team to cover everything we do."

Captain Murphy eventually got tired of hearing me talk and relented. He said, "Okay. Your medics can go to goat lab. But no one else."

My point was that we didn't have enough medics. In fact, we had only one, and that was me.

But I had received permission to conduct the goat lab. So I typed up forms for eight people, now two from each boat crew, and made them all "medics." I had no authority to do so, but I did it anyway.

Then I ran a week-long goat lab and taught the eight medics how to perform cricothyrotomies and cut-downs, how to insert chest tubes and make splints, and so on. All the ABCs of combat medicine. And I made all of them advanced trauma medical kits, which they wore.

Less than two months later, my boat crew was called to do a demonstration at Fort Bragg in North Carolina for a group of VIPs.

First, we rehearsed. Each four-man team flew in on separate Black Hawk helicopters. The helos flared and hovered about thirty feet over the tarmac as we fast-roped down, two men from each helo at a time, wearing gas masks, camo, and all our ███████.

Once we all got on the ground, we lined up and faced the reviewing stand, which was going to be packed with senators, congressmen, admirals, generals, and other VIPs. The rehearsal was rough, because one of our Black Hawks came in on a hard landing. Then a platoon of Rangers rappelled down from ropes after us, and a few of them broke ankles.

██

The Black Hawks approached the tarmac and flared. My partner and I fast-roped down, but when the second two started descending, one of them—a SEAL named Mark—got hung up. The strap from his M5 got stuck on something in the helo.

I shouted up at him from the tarmac, "Mark, come on down."

His weapon sling had dislocated his shoulder, and he was hanging from it and in a lot of pain.

He shouted back, "I hurt my shoulder."

I said, "I'll look at it when you get down here."

He cut the sling and came down, and our eight-man assault team ran up past the side of the reviewing stand. I saw that Mark's right shoulder was dipping way down, obviously dislocated.

As I was examining Mark, I saw the CH-53 carrying the Rangers approach. It hit its back rotor on the tarmac and bounced about seventy feet into the air. The rear ramp was open, and, as I watched, a soldier came out the back door just as the tail of the helicopter swung left. Then I saw a large pink burst, and the soldier flew through the air and landed in the dirt.

I was standing about a hundred meters away with my mask, body armor, and ▮ gear still on. I threw down my MP5 and ran as fast as I could to the downed man.

He was lying facedown in a pool of blood with his helmet still on. I turned him over and saw that his entire face and most of his head had been sliced off.

I took a deep breath.

Then I looked to my left and realized that there were six other bodies lying on the ground.

I hadn't even noticed that the helicopter had thrown those bodies out as well. People in the reviewing stand had ducked down and were screaming. They thought the helicopter was going to explode.

I had been so focused on the first soldier who had fallen out that I had experienced ocular exclusion (aka tunnel vision).

But as luck would have it, all eight guys that I had put through goat lab were there with their advanced emergency medical packs. They did what they had just been taught to do and went to work on the six soldiers who were torn up and had broken bones.

One guy was having trouble breathing, so I tried sweeping his mouth for broken teeth or bones. When I saw that the airway obstruction was down in his windpipe, I made a one-inch incision below the larynx and heard a loud whoosh as all the blocked air came out.

Then I inserted an airway tube that I had in my kit and started breathing into it. Mouth-to-cric.

After the medevac helicopters came to take the injured soldiers to the hospital, ██████████████████████████████████████ ██ ██ ██ ████████████████

So the VIPs returned to their seats and we continued on with the shooting and climbing demonstrations. We did double taps, but guys weren't hitting the targets as tightly as usual. I also noticed that people were looking at me funny.

Afterward, I went to the bathroom and saw that I had blood all around my teeth because of the mouth-to-cric breathing.

But the six soldiers survived, and Mark from our team was fine. Afterward, me and the eight guys I had put through goat lab received lifesaving medals.

* * *

Soon after the incident at Fort Bragg I was sent to Chile with two men from ▮▮▮ Chilean president General Pinochet, who had seized power in a bloody coup back in 1973, was growing increasingly unpopular. There was talk of another coup to depose General Pinochet, and three of us were tasked with surveying possible escape routes and finding safe houses, in case fighting broke out and the U.S. embassy and U.S. citizens had to be evacuated.

I flew to Panama wearing civilian clothes. With my longish hair and beard, I seemed to fit right in with the other people milling around the terminal in Panama City. But I couldn't find the two guys from ▮▮▮

So I called the command and was told to go to my hotel. Still no sign of the guys from ▮▮▮ There was a band playing downstairs, so I went down to check out the scene and drink a beer.

Then, because I was wide awake, I drove fifty miles across the isthmus to the enlisted club at Fort Amador and had a few drinks there.

I returned to my hotel room hours later. There were still no messages. So I went down to the bar, which was full of people drinking and dancing. I surveyed the crowd and saw two well-built guys standing against the wall, observing the area, their arms crossed in front of their chests. They wore big watches and were the only two in the bar who weren't participating in the fun.

I walked up to one of them and asked, "Are you Sergeant H.?"

He said, "Shh! Nobody's supposed to know we're here."

"Well, Sergeant, I traveled all over the country tonight and saw about a thousand people, and you guys definitely stand out."

On the flight down to Santiago, Chile, one of the ▮▮▮ guys talked about free-fall training. He explained how they practiced countless jumps in a wind tunnel. Then their riggers checked their chutes twice as they packed them. Finally, they did a jump, which was recorded on video and supervised by two instructors. Everything was by the book.

I told him about that tough old Vietnam-era SEAL who always had a can of Budweiser in his hand, how he'd asked us who hadn't jumped before and then had us all jumping the next day.

At ST-6, we thought more out of the box, which suited me just fine.

CHAPTER TEN

ST-6/Divorce

Blame it or praise it, there is no denying
the wild horse in us.

—*Virginia Woolf*

At ST-6, when we were recalled for training or for real-world ops, we had an hour to get ourselves assembled in the team room to receive the warning order. The warning order gave us basic information about the upcoming mission. It started with a brief, concise statement: This will be a jump op. Boat crew three will conduct a raid on this building, which is located at this position, at this time and date.

The warning order included the topography of the land we were going into, the enemy forces we'd be going up against, the location of the nearest friendly forces, and the location and number of civilians in the area of operation.

Once we started planning, the amount of detail and specificity depended on the amount of time available. In Grenada, the guys used street maps and tourist maps because they had had little time to plan.

Typically, we started our discussion with preliminaries—who is on the op, what are the jobs, what gear is required. Then we analyzed the specifics of the situation on the ground.

Part of the warning order was a general outline broken down into phases. Phase one might be how we would insert (boats or helicopters, and what types), followed by the infill, including primary and secondary insertion.

The general outline also included information about the recon team, where we would meet up with them, and what info they had provided so far.

Depending on the operation, the commanding officer, executive officer, operations officer, or assault team officer would then talk briefly about what was going to happen during each one of the phases. In most instances, he concentrated on the insertion, infiltration, and actions at the objective, which were usually the most critical components of an op.

The officer also provided specific information about what was required from each operator on the team.

The warning order covered all the basics. Following the warning order, after we had some time to sort out the gear for the op, a patrol leader's order (PLO) was prepared with the help of every member on the team.

All of the above topics covered in the warning order—infiltration, insertion, position, weapons, concealment, deception, ROE—were now broken down and discussed in detail.

Specific tactics were always determined by the team or element entering the engagement. Each assault team on ST-6 had a different standard operating procedure based on the skills and experience of its individual operators.

Once the entire team was present and we had a full muster, we'd synchronize all of our watches. Then the PLO was presented by various leaders of the team. They'd brief us on the weather forecast, moonrise, moonset, phase of the moon, sunrise, sunset, tides, currents, how deep the water was, natural boundaries, vegetation, landmarks, and so on.

The PLO provided specific detailed instructions to every assault team member on the op. Regardless of whether the mission required movement through jungle, desert, mountains, or urban areas, if the insertion or extraction was from sea, air, or land, it indicated all responsibilities and all fire positions—who covered right, who covered left, and who carried the grenades, Claymores, and any specific equipment.

In the case of a combat swimming op, we'd indentify who the swim buddies were going to be and review the hand and arm signals that would be used on the surface and underwater.

In certain missions we reviewed the procedures for body searches.

As in the ███████ op, the rules of engagement were discussed in detail. They're extremely important, because today's wars are fought with restrictions in terms of who operatives are allowed to fire at and under what circumstances, and there are rules for taking prisoners, seizing property, and interrogating enemy soldiers.

Most civilians probably aren't aware of the emphasis placed on ROEs and how they define and modify every U.S. military engagement.

We always designated a loss-of-communication plan too, and we answered the following questions: What signal will be used for withdrawal or extraction? Will we be using a 40 mm, a flare, IR chemical light, or an IR strobe? Would we come to report fifteen minutes past the hour, or every other hour?

All SEALs are experts at concealment and deception. And many of our ops included a deception plan. For example, we might blast off a lot of demo to make it sound like a hundred guys were storming a beach when in reality we were staging a night jump miles behind enemy lines.

We'd talk about how to get in, how to get out, and how to stay concealed, and remind one another of the importance of noise and light discipline. It's amazing how well sound travels at night, especially over water.

Usually we'd use only hand and arm signals and radio communications, when they worked. If we needed to communicate something between squads or boat crews, we'd talk in a whisper. SEALs are expert at sneaking in and out of an area completely undetected. We do it all the time.

All of us learned about forty-five hand and arm signals in BUD/S. There are signals meaning I see enemy personnel; I see a danger area; stop; listen; enemy hutch three hundred meters to my three o'clock; and many more. They're pretty basic, but in the pitch-darkness, they don't work. That's when we use a low whisper passed down the patrol formation.

In the PLO we'd discuss the challenge and reply we'd use to identify friendly forces. For instance, if you moved into a wood line and heard someone say, "Three," you'd answer, "Four." Because the code was seven.

We might simply use a red lens flashlight, but most often we used NVGs and IR, since we did practically everything in the dark.

SEALs are experts at inserting, causing all sorts of destruction, and then leaving the enemy to wonder, *What the hell happened?* It always sickens me when I'm in the field and see a bunch of MRE wrappers. It signals to the enemy that the U.S. military was here. Large, inexperienced units tend not to worry about leaving their trash behind for the enemy to find.

SEALs typically don't cook in the field, because we don't want to be detected by smell. That's why we don't use soap, shampoo, or cologne before going on an op.

We don't break branches, and we don't leave tracks. We also use the cover of darkness, when it's available.

We avoid crossing bridges and walking through open areas. Do our best to stay off roads or open trails. And we try to move so that we can't be tracked. No footprints. No turning over rocks. Move carefully through vegetation. No scrapes or broken branches.

Movement is always limited by weather and the type of terrain.

As for direction finding, our point man, rear security, and patrol leader generally use GPS, but the system fails on occasion due to equipment malfunction, cloud cover, or poor safelight reception. So, in spite of the technology at our fingertips, we still train and rely on good old-fashioned maps and compass techniques. We all know how to ascertain time and direction by looking at the sun, moon, or stars.

Our point man focuses on the sounds, or lack of sound, from native animals and birds. He knows that when birds fly off, it might mean movement nearby. He also listens for geese, dogs, or other animals that can give away position.

If we heard a dog barking or another animal making noise, we had to know what to do. Usually we either laid low in hopes it would move on or had specific plans and methods for taking out early-warning creatures.

Included in every PLO was a list of contingency plans—the what-if list. What if you're delayed on your insertion, someone is wounded, or a helo or insertion vehicle goes down?

What do we do if we're compromised? What happens if you run into an enemy patrol? What happens if you're separated from your squad or platoon? What do you do if you encounter extreme weather?

Every single operator has a primary and secondary duty. If the point man went down, rear security took his place. If the medic was incapacitated, someone was designated to take his place too.

We always had a loss-of-comms plan. What do we do if we can't establish comms with one another, or with HQ?

We had procedures for calling in air support and rendezvousing with another patrol, unit, vehicle, or vessel. These were also discussed in the PLO.

We'd talk about what to do if we encountered the enemy or surprised a local unit. And how to behave if we were captured.

██

██

A cover for action might be: I was walking down this street looking for this particular building.

A cover for status might be: I'm working as a counselor for the U.S. embassy. Since I was a medic, I always used to say I was helping out at a certain relief agency that was providing medical support to the locals. It worked like a charm.

██

██

You have to be able to live your cover. So you practice it and know it well.

Many SEALs have attended SERE School and are practiced in the techniques of survival, evasion, resistance, and escape. We know that if captured, we should try to escape as soon as possible. During SERE School, we're taught how to resist interrogation. That's one reason it's very difficult, if not impossible, to get any worthwhile info out of a SEAL.

Typically, the corpsman briefed the search-and-rescue plan and the location of the nearest medical facility. Then the commo guy would brief the comms portion of the PLO. The point man would discuss the primary and secondary insertion and extraction routes; the team tactician the specific actions at enemy contact. We all prepared and briefed our specific portion of the mission to our fellow team members and to HQ personnel attending the PLO.

Specific equipment and clothing was also briefed. Were we going to wear ▬ gear, desert camo, or flight suits?

Then we specified the first-line gear we'd be carrying at all times for the specific mission. First-line gear usually included a sidearm, a knife, and an escape-and-evasion (E & E) kit—compasses, flashlights, maps of the area, local currency, and medical gear.

Second-line gear was defined as the equipment we were going to need for our first twenty-four hours of survival—water, MREs, and extra ammo. It was carried on a harness, a vest, or a belt, depending on the op. Second-line gear had to be worn at all times except when sleeping in a tent, barracks, or hotel, in which case it was kept at the foot of the bed.

Today, in operations in the Middle East, SEALs keep their second-line gear on a belt or in a vest and don't leave the base or garrison without it.

Third-line gear incorporated the things needed for longer-time survival—we called them comfort items—and was usually carried in a backpack, a go-bag, or a bailout kit. It might include extra food and extra ammo, a weapon-cleaning kit, a large orange-colored air panel (to mark your location), a smoke grenade, Claymore mine, a larger medical kit than what you carried with your first-line gear, possibly a butane stove, and maybe a jungle hammock to keep you off the jungle floor.

If an operative was leaving the base or hotel in a car, third-line gear was usually kept in the backseat or stashed in the trunk.

First-, second-, and third-line gear were always prioritized according to the country we were going to and the mission. The gear could change during the mission based on the security level. All this was specified in the PLO. It was part of our planning.

Each SEAL also carried specialized equipment needed for his role in the platoon. So the commo guy carried the satellite phone and radio, and the medic was responsible for the more advanced emergency medical kit. I carried morphine and specialized medical equipment that enabled me to perform a cricothyrotomy, put in a chest tube, or do a cut-down if needed.

Crics, chest tubes, and cut-downs are essential parts of combat medicine. Crics are used to establish airflow when someone's airway is blocked or damaged; I'd simply slice the person's throat just below the Adam's apple and insert a plastic tube to reestablish breathing. Chest tubes are needed for penetrating wounds to the thorax. And cut-downs are required when you can't get an IV into someone who is wounded.

Once outfitted, the team assembled outside. Typically, every operator carried a blowout patch—a four-by-four-inch battle dressing used to control major bleeding—in his lower left cargo pocket. If that man was hit, everyone on the team knew to use his blowout patch.

Outside, we'd do a sound check, jumping around to make sure our gear didn't rattle or create any noise during movement. Often, we had PJs (Air Force Pararescue) or CCT (combat-control technicians) accompany us through training and on missions. Combat-control technicians were experts at establishing and maintaining communications.

Then we'd do a weapons check by firing off several rounds to verify that each weapon was in optimum working order.

Next, we'd stage a rehearsal. We were sometimes able to plan ahead and create a mock-up building, ███████████████████████████ If we didn't have time to mock up a building, we'd draw the floor plan on the cement.

We'd execute a walk-through first and review all the commands and procedures. When we worked with U.S. SWAT teams, we'd draw the room, house, or building plan in a parking lot, drive up to the structure, disembark from the vehicle, take cover, simulate the breach into the building, and rehearse actions on the objective.

Any information missing from the PLO was requested in an essential elements of information form (EEI) that was sent up the chain of command.

Sometimes the patrol leader would answer our questions. Other times the questions were handled by intel officers, the commanding officer, or even the task force commander.

The PLO was then briefed again by the senior officers—sometimes an admiral or a general. We'd do our final inspections, and the mission was launched.

Once the mission was over, the senior officer on the mission prepared a post-operations report.

The phases of a mission are:

- Pre-mission
- Insertion
- Infiltration
- Actions at the objective
- Exfiltration
- Post-mission

We went through many middle-of-the-night recalls, warning orders, and PLOs at ST-6 in the mid-1980s to the late 1990s, sometimes getting as far as loading up the aircraft, only to have the mission aborted at the last minute for reasons that were out of our control. A lot of my fellow operators at the team grew increasingly frustrated.

Some guys actually left for other teams in search of real-world action. We called it chasing the rainbow. ST-2 had the European the-ater, which was busy with counterterrorism. ST-4 was doing counter-narcotics work in Colombia and Central America.

Despite the lack of real-world missions at ST-6, we continued to train nonstop. Because I was the lead climber on ███████ I was given the opportunity to work with some of the world's top climbers, guys like Jay Smith and Charlie Fowler.

Jay and I, along with other climbers in ███████ were the first to ascend a new route at Devils Tower in Wyoming—the monolithic volcanic thrust of rock that rises 1,267 feet and was used as a location for Steven Spielberg's *Close Encounters of the Third Kind*.

Charlie Fowler and I completed a first-route climb together in Red Rock, Nevada. Days later, he did a climb with ███████ and fell to his death during a rappel.

Charlie had told me that if he ever died while climbing, it would happen during a rappel. He was one of the greatest climbers I've ever known.

Working with experts like Charlie and Jay, I became increasingly proficient. I climbed ships and oil rigs and scaled the faces of some of the tallest buildings in downtown Los Angeles at night.

During the late eighties, ST-6 did live-fire ops in U.S. cities all the time, which was pretty remarkable. We fired live rounds into targets in front of bullet traps in various buildings in heavily populated areas. If someone had happened to miss the target, the rounds could eas-ily have passed through a wall and into a home. But we were surgical shooters, and a miss usually constituted nothing more than a four-inch group at center mass.

During training ops, we took down buildings at night. One team fast-roped from helicopters on the roof while the ground assault team fought its way up from the ground floor. Once, we caused so much commotion that the *L.A. Times* actually wrote an article reporting that men from mysterious black helicopters were invading the city at night.

Another time, when we were training on an oil rig off the California coast, the helicopter we were in hit a crane on the rig as it started to ascend. With the rear rotor damaged, the helo fell forty feet off the rig, skimmed the ocean, and eventually made a hard landing on a public beach. Fortunately, we all got out safe. But the looks on the bathers' faces when they saw a dozen longhaired guys emerge from a downed helo, wearing flight suits and carrying weapons were priceless.

As we ran across the sand, one stunned woman asked, "Who are you guys, and what happened?"

I couldn't tell her that we were SEALs who had been assaulting an oil rig, so I said, "Our helicopter was hit by a seagull."

Next day, the headline in the *L.A. Times* read: "Black Op Helo Hit by Seagull Crash Lands on Beach."

The officers on the assault teams—████████████████—were in constant competition to see who could work their guys harder and make them more war ready. ████████████ were run by the officers. But at ████ where I served, the enlisted men were in charge.

Maybe that's why we had a reputation for being the rowdiest. We worked like beasts and partied hard.

Most of us, including myself, found it hard to shift down during the little time off we had with our wives and families. Instead of enjoying home life, I wanted to be in high gear, living for the moment, feeling that tomorrow could be my last day. I wasn't emotionally equipped to settle down with my wife, Kim, the sixty or so days a year I wasn't away from home.

My swim partner and I used to beat the hell out of each other, just for fun. When on the road or out in the field, every night we came back to our room (we were also roommates) and attacked each other like Inspector Clouseau and Cato from the Pink Panther movies.

Once our administrative senior chief joined us while we were messing around, and I put him in a headlock and stuck his head in the toilet. He reported me, but the charge was dismissed.

One night I was lying in bed with Kim in our house in Virginia Beach when, just after midnight, I heard someone jiggling the door-knob on our front door. I whispered, "Hey, Kim. I think someone's trying to break in."

I grabbed the loaded .45 I kept under my bed and crawled down the hallway. The front door was to my right. I crawled past the living room, went out the back door, slithered out, and ran around to the front. I was excited. My plan was to surprise the guy from behind and bang his head against the front porch while I held him at gunpoint.

But as I was coming around, a car took off from the front of my house and sped by at seventy miles an hour. It was going so fast, I couldn't read the license plate number. Disappointed, I returned to bed.

The next day I was back at work at ST-6 when my teammate Dave came up to me and said, "I hope I didn't bother you guys last night. I got so shit-faced that I went to your house instead of mine and was trying to get in the front door. My house key wasn't working."

I shook my head and said, "Dave, you're not going to believe what almost happened."

We dressed like civilians, and tried to look like civilians. But it didn't work all the time. Once, a group of us walked into a bar in Puerto Rico. I knew that we needed a cover, so I said, "Guys, let's say that we're in a band."

One of the guys on my boat crew said, "Yeah, we'll say we're called Head East and we just reunited."

We started talking to a group of girls, and before we knew it, someone on the stage announced that there was a band in the house called Head East. Our cover worked until one of the girls asked us to sing one of our songs.

Another time we were on a dive trip to Key West. We were thirty fit guys with long hair and beards sitting around a hotel pool and trying not to look like we were in the military. But the girls wouldn't come near us. They assumed we were gay.

Each of us was given a stipend for clothes. We were supposed to buy two suits and a couple of casual outfits. But some guys, including me, didn't know anything about buying or wearing fancy clothes.

One guy on the team, whom we called Dirty Dan (he truly earned his name), used to shop at the Salvation Army. He'd show up in used striped pants, a worn checkered jacket, a plaid shirt, and shoes that were a size too big for him. We thought it was a joke, but it wasn't.

Turned out he was spending all his extra stipend money on guns. Other guys blew their money on motorcycles or cars.

Guys had different ways of blowing off steam. I worked out and raced in world-class multisport endurance competitions. Others entered shooting competitions or sniper matches. Some raced motorcycles or cars. Many competed in hand-to-hand defense meets. Some of the guys on the team were incredible musicians. A precious few were family men.

Hazing was a popular activity, especially on birthdays and when guys were getting married. As the medic, I kept the medical records, so I knew the guys' birthdays and instigated most of the hazing.

If a guy was getting married, we'd shave off his pubic hair and eyebrows. On a teammate's birthday, we'd make him play a game called a shot or a shot.

We'd put paintball .38 rounds in the freezer, then lay out ten to twenty shots of tequila. We'd ask the guy which one he wanted, a shot or a shot.

If he chose the paintball shot, we'd fire it at his bare stomach, which stung bad and left a big red welt. Guys would alternate back and forth.

This went on for an hour until the guy was throwing up from all the tequila and his stomach was covered with welts.

Sometimes we'd wrap the birthday boy in duct tape and throw him in the ocean.

As my thirtieth birthday approached, I knew I was next, and I tried to come up with a plan to keep the thirty guys on my team off me. On the day itself we happened to be working in the kill house at the ████████████ Thirty of us had driven there, two men per car.

I remembered that when I was a prison guard one of the inmates had smeared feces all over himself and came out with his arms held wide. And all of us had backed off. Sounded like a plan.

So I stole all the car keys and locked them in one of the cars. I kept the keys to one car, but not mine. I figured that when they came for me and I ran, they would think I was planning to escape in my car. This way I would misdirect them. Besides, since I'd be covered with shit, I didn't want to get it all over the upholstery of my own rental car.

I said to one of my buddies, "Pass the word that no one's going to want to get near me. If they do, they'll regret it."

"What do you mean?"

"You'll see."

During break, the guys started to approach me. I was sitting on the ground in my flight suit, my plastic baggie filled with feces beside me. The plan was perfect, but the guys beat me to the punch.

Just as I was preparing to smear the shit all over my flight suit, one of the guys came up behind me and got me in a choke hold. I came to duct-taped to a medical backboard in the trunk of a car that was traveling down dirt roads at fifty miles an hour, the trunk's lid banging down on my stretcher. Just before they closed the trunk, the guys had stood over me pouring hot sauce down my nose and mouth. And that was just the beginning. They got me good.

Kim and I had been together since she was a teenager back in Rhode Island. She had driven with me to BUD/S and stayed with me through my three years in California, where we married in 1982. Now we were living in Virginia Beach in a house we'd bought.

She was a wonderful person and I loved her, but I didn't give her the time she deserved. She wanted a life together. Instead, I was an adrenaline junkie, addicted to the high energy and action of SEALs.

One night I returned at two in the morning from a dive trip to Puerto Rico and found no one home. So I knocked on the neighbor's door and asked if she knew where Kim was. She said no.

As I turned to go back home, I heard my neighbor talking on the phone. I heard her say, "Kim, you'd better think quick. Don's home."

About thirty minutes later, a car pulled up and Kim and this guy named Pat came into our house.

I watched them enter, thinking, *What do I do now? What do I do?*

I felt like I'd been kicked in the stomach, but I realized that it was my own damn fault. I'd been living for the moment. Having fun. Thinking of no one but myself. Sadly, we divorced. Kim later remarried and had two boys. I still wish her the best.

I tried to pick up the emotional pieces and move on. The first months were rough. Then, at the end of 1989, ST-6 sent me to language school in Monterey, California. My German teacher was a petite, blue-eyed beauty named Shannon Bailey.

We called her Frau Bailey. She referred to me as Herr Mann.

All of us were crazy about our sexy German teacher—especially me. The attraction was mutual. Even though Frau Bailey wasn't supposed to fraternize with students, the two of us started going for long rides together on my '85 Softail Harley. She introduced me to her beautiful three-year-old daughter, Chonie.

We dated and fell in love. But neither of us knew that the military action I had been craving would soon arrive.

CHAPTER ELEVEN

Panama

General Noriega's reckless threats and attacks upon
Americans in Panama created an imminent danger to
the 35,000 American citizens in Panama. As President,
I have no higher obligation than to safeguard the lives
of American citizens.

—*President George H. W. Bush announcing Operation*
Just Cause, December 20, 1989

Panama is a narrow neck of tropical land populated by 3.5 million
people and intersected by one of the most important strategic waterways in the world—the Panama Canal. Back in the late 1980s it was
run by a short, pugnacious military dictator named General Manuel
Noriega. Noriega had been the right-hand man of General Omar
Torrijos, who assumed power in a military coup in 1968 and insti-
tuted a number of progressive political, economic, and social reforms,
including initiating massive coverage of social security services and
expanding public education that transformed the country.

When General Torrijos died in a helicopter crash in 1981, General
Noriega seized control of the country and expanded the role of the
Panamanian Defense Forces (PDF) until they dominated Panamanian political life. Noriega, who had operated as a CIA asset, bought
the loyalty of PDF officers and their cronies with revenues from drug
smuggling and money laundering.

Under Noriega's rule, Panama became the major trans-shipment site for illegal drugs from South America bound for the United States. While elements in the PDF prospered, Noriega's regime grew increasingly repressive, and hundreds of political opponents of his regime were tortured and killed; hundreds more were forced into exile.

Political demonstrations against the regime were met with violence. A popular vocal critic named Hugo Spadafora was pulled off a bus by Noriega's men at the Costa Rican border. ███████

███

███████████████████████████████

███████████████████████████████

███

Several days later Spadafora's badly tortured, decapitated body was found wrapped in a U.S. Postal Service mailbag.

In 1987, alarmed by the growing criminality of the Noriega regime and angry about a PDF-directed attack on the U.S. embassy in Panama City, President Ronald Reagan froze U.S. military and economic assistance to Panama.

A year later, General Manuel Antonio Noriega was accused of drug trafficking, by federal juries in Tampa and Miami. In May of 1989, Noriega launched a new round of political repression after he was accused of trying to steal the recent national election. President George H. W. Bush protested loudly, demanding that Noriega end political repression and drug trafficking, and expressing concern about the secure functioning of the Panama Canal, which was vital to U.S. shipping and regional security.

Sometime in early 1989, the CIA, Naval Special Warfare, and other government and military units began to collect intel in Panama for a possible op to arrest Noriega and remove him from power.

I arrived there in November of 1989, shortly after a coup led by

Panama's Major Moises Giroldi had been violently crushed by Noriega's troops. The moment I landed, I felt the tension in the air. I had heard the stories about Noriega's out-of-control cocaine parties and about him throwing people out of planes.

I was stationed with a handful of other operators from ST-6 at Rodman Naval Station, which bordered the west side of the Panama Canal. We were there to assist Special Boat Unit 26 (SBU-26) with coastal and riverine operations. I also had orders to serve as SBU-26's training officer and to establish and run the Navy Special Warfare jungle training and the Central and South American MEDCAP program.

Rodman Naval Station was less than a mile away from the beautiful 5,425-foot cantilever Bridge of the Americas that spans the canal and links Central and South America.

On the night of December 16, 1989, I was driven in an armored vehicle to the airport to meet my girlfriend, Shannon, who was flying in to spend Christmas with me. Accompanying me was a young SEAL lieutenant also assigned to SBU-26, Adam Curtis, whose wife, Bonnie, was coming in on the same flight—a very rare occasion for any of us, especially in a hot zone.

The tension at the airport was palpable. You could see the anxiety about a possible U.S. military action in people's eyes.

After the plane carrying the women landed, Adam informed me that he was taking his wife out to dinner.

I said, "Be careful, it's getting bad out there. Shannon and I are going back to the base."

Adam Curtis and Bonnie dined at a local restaurant and were on the way back to his barracks when they were stopped at a PDF checkpoint. They were questioned and their car was searched.

Adam later stated, "While we were there, another group of Americans came to the roadblock, three Army guys and a Marine—all officers. They felt threatened, they gunned it through the roadblock, and five PDF soldiers turned and fired at the car. The officer in the back, an Army lieutenant named [Robert] Paz, was killed."

Adam Curtis and Bonnie were pulled out of their car and taken to a detention center, where they were interrogated and tortured. PDF goons hammered Adam's feet in one room while his wife was fondled and sexually harassed in another.

The next morning at muster, Adam wasn't there.

The captain turned to me and asked, "Where's Lieutenant Curtis?"

"I don't know," I answered. "Last time I saw him was last night at the airport."

According to various sources, President George H. W. Bush made the final decision to invade Panama after hearing about the murder of Lieutenant Robert Paz and the detention and torture of the Curtises.

By Sunday, December 20, assault units from Navy SEAL Teams Two, Four, and Six had infiltrated the country. At around midnight, Norman Carley, task unit commander for SEAL Team Two and former executive officer to ████████████ at ST-6, and four SEAL divers were aboard a CRRC in a stand of mangroves, waiting to attach a limpet mine to the *Presidente Porras* patrol boat.

"The commander of the whole operation, General [Carl] Steiner, thought that the operation had been compromised, and he moved up the time to execute the operation by a half hour," Carley recalled. "But the clocks and safety and arming devices on the explosives were already set."

As a firefight broke out nearby and grenades were falling in the water, SEAL diver Randy B. attached a limpet mine to the hull of the *Presidente Porras*. At 0100, a large blast shook the walls of buildings across Panama City. It was the first time SEALs successfully executed a limpet attack on an enemy ship of battle.

I was in base housing at Fort Amador, which was about four miles from Rodman, when Shannon and I heard an AC-130 gunship firing rounds at a target in Panama City. I telephoned work and they said, "Get in here immediately!"

I grabbed my gear and weapon and started running as fast as I could toward Rodman Naval Station. I was so excited!

A U.S. Army jeep speeding down the road saw me running and stopped. An MP asked at gunpoint, "Where the hell are you going?"

"My name is Chief Mann and I am on my way to Rodman. I need a ride."

They rushed me to Rodman. Minutes later I was on a river patrol boat with six guys from SBU-26. SBU-26 was commanded by a Navy lieutenant commander, Mike Fitzgerald, a tough Vietnam-era SEAL with more riverine experience than anybody else on the teams. The unit was made up of a headquarters element and ten patrol boat light detachments. Each detachment consisted of two boats with crews.

Our first frag order of the night was to confirm the reported sniper fire that was coming from the Bridge of the Americas.

We fired up the PRB (patrol river boat), basically a beefed-up Boston whaler armed with MK-19s and twin .50s, and approached the bridge. As soon as we emerged from the shadows, we started taking fire. The snipers had the advantage of concealment and elevation. With rounds ripping into the water around us, we trained our twin mounted .50-caliber machine guns on the snipers. They ducked behind some metal beams and fled.

At the same time a few miles away, SEALs from ST-4 were coming ashore in small inflatable boats near the Punta Paitilla airfield. Their mission was to seize the small civilian airfield and disable Noriega's Learjet so he couldn't escape. But the element of surprise had been eliminated because of the explosion on the *Presidente Porras*. Also, the runway was well lit by landing lights, and the AC-130 Spectre gunship that was assigned to provide air cover was unable to launch.

Those weren't the only problems the SEALs encountered. They had been told that the airstrip wasn't guarded. But the intel was wrong.

SEAL Dennis Hansen, a lieutenant at the time, was the platoon officer in charge. "As we advanced, I heard yelling," Hansen remembered. "The plan was to tell the Panamanian security guards to go away. This seemed to work well until we got to Noriega's plane hangar. There, a gunfight broke out after a brief exchange of words. The platoon adjacent to mine was directly in front of the hangar. They were to disable the plane. About half of the platoon was wounded. I sent my assistant officer in charge and his squad to support the platoon that was in contact. They took effective fire also, killing my AOIC and wounding a couple of other men."

Four SEALs died in the firefight: Lieutenant John Connors, my good friend; Chief Engineman Donald McFaul; Boatswain's Mate First Class Chris Tilghman; and Torpedoman's Mate Second Class Isaac Rodriguez III.

A very good buddy of mine, Carlos Moleda, was shot in the chest and leg. Another teammate, Mike P., thought Carlos was dead and used his body as a shield as he returned fire.

I was with Mike when he apologized. He said, "Sorry, Carlos, but I thought you were dead and I couldn't get low enough, and needed anything in front of me to block me from the incoming fire."

Fortunately, Carlos survived. Even though he never recovered use of his body from his sternum down, Carlos went on to compete in several Ironman and ultra-distance athletic events in his wheelchair, and he has won many!

Years later, while I was training with Carlos at Fort Story, Virginia, I saw him racing down a steep hill on his wheelchair bike at close to thirty miles an hour when his foot slipped off the footrest. I watched as his limp foot scraped down the road. When I ran over to Carlos to check on him, his foot was a bloody mess. He shrugged and said, "I guess that's going to take a while to heal." It took over a year.

Carlos is still competing in the world's most challenging events with the use of just his arms and shoulders.

Our next assignment was to capture Noriega's yacht, which was docked on the south side of the canal. The SBU-26 executive officer, Johnny Koenig, who could out-PT, outswim, and outrun most SEALs who were twenty years younger, received the order and wanted to accompany us.

The general in charge ordered him to stay.

Meanwhile, our patrol boat had almost finished backing away from the pier and was turning right. Johnny hung up the phone, ran down the pier, jumped in the water in full uniform, web gear, and weapon, and swam to the boat. Johnny wasn't going to let anybody tell him that he couldn't go into battle with his men.

The crew helped him board the vessel, and he went on the op.

Noriega's yacht was at least forty feet long with quarters for at least eight, ocean fishing rods and reels, and a wine cellar. We pulled up within fifty meters and observed the vessel with our .50-cals locked, loaded, and aimed at the craft. We had no idea how many people were aboard or if the yacht had been booby-trapped with explosives.

Our Spanish speaker got on the horn and announced that those onboard had thirty seconds to surrender before we blew their boat out of the water. About ten seconds later a hatch to the lower deck opened, and a guy stuck his arm out and waved a white T-shirt.

I was the first to board with my M16. Three other SBU-26 guys followed me. I saw a group of eight Panamanian SEALs hiding in the cabin and motioned for them to drop their weapons and come out.

Through our Spanish speaker, I ordered them to strip down. Since there were so many of them and the deck was small, I directed them to stack on top of one another, head to toe.

When one of the Panamanians refused, Johnny Koenig yelled to our Spanish speaker, "Tell him to strip down now, or we'll shoot him!" The Panamanian complied. We tie-tied them and hauled them back to Rodman, where we made a makeshift prisoner compound out of barbed wire. We'd cleared the yacht, and before the night was over we captured around two hundred PDF enemy soldiers.

At around midnight (eleven hours after the launch of the invasion) we approached within five hundred meters of another enemy vessel with our weapons ready. When we moved within two hundred meters, the interpreter yelled in Spanish, "Come out, or we're going to blow you out of the water!"

Everyone was off safety, fingers on triggers. The captain said, "Let's move a little closer." We pulled to within fifty meters, going bow to broadside. I was thinking, *This is insane! We're getting too close. A firefight between the two crews is going to be brutal.*

We were so close we could almost smell them. Suddenly a hand holding a little white handkerchief emerged from one of the cabin windows, and we gave a collective sigh of relief.

We captured another dozen armed PDF soldiers.

Little by little we gained control of the Panama Canal—blocking boats from entering, and stopping boats on the canal and searching for arms and enemy personnel. Meanwhile, U.S. Army and Marine battalions supported by airpower attacked the PDF's central headquarters (La Comandancia) in downtown Panama City and seized Fort Amador from the PDF in a nighttime air assault.

At some point during the night we exchanged fire with half a dozen PDF soldiers along the shore and tore them up pretty bad. We put the bodies in body bags, but when we returned to Rodman, nobody knew where to put them. So we decided to stash the bodies in the meat locker at the Rodman Enlisted Club with the steaks, hamburgers, fruits, and vegetables.

I found this somewhat disturbing because I ate lunch there almost every day.

When the U.S. military documentation people arrived a couple of days later, they asked me to open two of the body bags and turn the bodies over so they could photograph the faces. These particular bodies had been riddled with bullets. When I pulled one of them from the side to flip it over, the top half pulled away and separated from the bottom. It left me with a very unpleasant image that I'll never forget.

A couple of days after we invaded, we were ordered to report to the Caribbean side of the canal, where the U.S. Army had attacked a Panamanian fishing boat and killed everyone aboard.

We arrived at around noon of a steamy hot day about twenty-four hours after the engagement.

An explosive ordnance disposal team had already searched the fishing boat for explosives but hadn't removed the remains of the boat captain and six PDF soldiers, who were rotting in the sun. The smell, as you can imagine, was disgusting.

We had orders to clean up the sixty-foot vessel and tow it into harbor. The captain of the boat had been shot in the head with a large-caliber round. All that was left of his head was a small portion of his Afro. Maggots were in the process of eating away what was left of his brains. Behind him, against the cabin wall, was a large smear of blood.

I used this later when I trained guys in CQB. Since the captain had been standing next to a metal wall, it was easy to see that rounds had skipped off the flat surface and hit him. So stand away from hard surfaces during combat.

I said to the command master chief, the warrant officer, and the six SBU-26 guys who were with us, "Body remains, throw overboard. Marijuana, coke, or any drugs, just place it all in a pile. Anything that looks like it could be intel, put it over here."

We threw some loose marijuana in the water, and we watched the fish devour it.

While the SBU-26 guys were cleaning and disinfecting the boat, the CWO and the master chief were doing their engineering and mechanical work to ensure the vessel was fit to transport. It was my job to inspect the hull, shaft, and screw to see if the underside of the boat had sustained any damage during the attack.

Typically in the Navy, we dove with swim buddies. But I was the only one doing this inspection dive. So after I suited up and started to make my way down the ladder, I said to the master chief, "If you need me for anything, just bang three times on the deck and I'll surface."

The master chief picked up something that looked like a small pipe and banged it on the deck of the boat.

"How's this?" he asked.

"Great."

My dive took about forty minutes. There wasn't any obvious damage to the hull, shaft, or screw, and though I hadn't heard any banging, the master chief did tap a bit about the boat, taking soundings.

Soon after I surfaced, we attached the enemy craft to our patrol boat and towed it to Fort Amador. We arrived at about 1600, tied the Panamanian boat to the pier, and set up a large GPL (general-purpose large) tent about thirty meters from our boat. Opposite the tent, about fifty meters from the ship, was a big Dumpster. Behind us stood the fire department, which was adjacent to the Army's jungle survival school.

We heard sporadic shooting and rocket explosions in the distance.

Once we got the tent up, I said, "Guys, throw those old bloodied uniforms in the Dumpster, then take a break. You've been working hard."

A few minutes later, three Army guys walked over to our PB—Captain Mike O'Brien, a major, and a sergeant.

Captain O'Brien asked, "Do you mind if we take the stuff, the uniforms, you're throwing away? We're starting a war museum."

I said, "Sure. Help yourself."

Captain O'Brien and the sergeant jumped in the Dumpster and started handing stuff out to the major. Then the sergeant climbed out.

Sometime during the day, that piece of pipe that the master chief had banged on the deck of the boat and then used to take soundings throughout the vessel had gone in the Dumpster.

I was sitting in the tent at around 2145 hours when I heard a tremendous boom.

Captain Mike O'Brien had leaned over to pick up the pipe, which really was a live LAW rocket round, and it had exploded. (Typically you would never see a LAW rocket round outside of its tube.)

All of us in the tent grabbed our weapons. I ran outside in the dark and saw trash scattered everywhere.

The major and the sergeant were screaming, "*Help!* Get help!"

We all had our first-line gear and second-line gear next to our cots—which included weapons—and I had my Special Forces medical kit, which was part of my second-line gear. I did what combat medics are trained to do in medical emergencies first: establish that the scene is safe.

The major and sergeant were screaming but weren't hurt.

Captain O'Brien lay on the ground outside the Dumpster looking about as dead as a person could look. His left lower leg above the knee had been blown a hundred meters away. His right hand and most of the fingers on his left hand were gone. Both of his eyes were hanging out of the sockets by the optic nerves. And thousands of pieces of shrapnel had ripped into his face and body.

All of the combat medical training I'd received immediately kicked into place. I looked at his chest and listened and felt for any signs of breath from his mouth and nose. I saw that his chest was rising, which meant that he had an airway and was still breathing. His upper left arm had a major arterial wound that was pumping out fresh bright red blood. I covered it with my hand and then quickly applied a blowout patch.

His left femur was completely exposed. But with a traumatic amputation like that, the vessels constrict and seal up, so the bleeding was minimal.

The major knelt beside me. The sergeant, some Army Rangers, and all of the SBU guys eagerly offered to assist me.

I opened my SF medical bag—which was a little bigger than a one-day backpack—and started issuing instructions.

I said, "You. Take this Kerlix and wrap up that leg.

"You, wrap that arm."

All the time I was talking to the captain, saying, "Sir, we are going to take good care of you, you are in good hands, my buddy is going to place a bandage over your hand." And so on.

In a serious injury you need to calmly talk to the patient. Hearing is the last sense to go before death. Even when the patient doesn't respond, there's a chance that his hearing you might prevent him from going into a deeper stage of shock. In the unfortunate cases where the patient doesn't survive, at least the last thing he hears is a friendly soothing voice.

As in any trauma case, I constantly monitored the captain's AVPU scale—another great lesson from goat lab. AVPU (which stands for *alert, voice, pain, unresponsive*) is a tool for assessing level of consciousness. If the person is awake, opens his eyes spontaneously, and responds to questions, he's alert. In that case, I would make a mental note or ask someone to record *Alert 1545*.

The patient is one step lower on the scale if he doesn't move or open his eyes spontaneously but does respond to a voice; in other words, if the patient makes any sort of groan or movement when I ask, "Are you okay?"

Below that is pain—that is, responds to painful stimuli only. For example, the patient moans as you apply a splint or IV. I might also tweak the person's ear or rub the sternum with the knuckle of my middle finger to see if there's any response.

The worst case, other than death, is when the victim is unresponsive to both voice and pain.

Initially, Captain O'Brien was totally unresponsive. I tweaked his ear and did a sternum rub, but no response.

I monitored his airway constantly, because an airway can become obstructed at any time by bleeding, vomit, mucus, broken bones, teeth, or swelling. Just because the patient has an airway during your initial assessment doesn't mean that it won't close during your treatment.

Captain O'Brien had an airway, and we had stopped most of the bleeding. Now I needed to get fluids in as quickly as possible. Since he'd lost so much blood, he needed a blood-volume expander— Ringer's lactate. But I had a hard time finding a good vein because all of his limbs were injured. I finally managed to get two large-bore IVs in his good arm, then pumped in 4,000 ccs of Ringer's lactate.

Within twenty minutes, I'd gone through everything in my SF medical kit.

The captain's pulse was over 140 beats per minute. His heart was beating this fast because his brain was crying out for more oxygen.

If a patient's pulse was 110 and his breathing rate was twenty, and then I checked three minutes later and his pulse was 130 and his breathing was thirty, and then two minutes after that, it was up to 160 and forty, that meant something was seriously wrong; I'd need to correct it quickly or the patient would die.

What had been killing Captain O'Brien was all the leaks. Now that we had stopped them, his heart rate and breathing started to stabilize. Then he moaned and began moving around a little bit. He'd gone from being unresponsive to responding to pain. A step in the right direction. His pulse was getting stronger and his breathing was becoming deeper too.

Suddenly, he asked in a whisper, "Hey, what happened?"

I said, "Sir, what's your name?"

"Captain Mike O'Brien."

"Do you know what just happened?"

"No, but I went to pick up a flashlight."

That told me that he saw the live rocket round in the Dumpster and went to pick it up.

He asked, "How come I can't see?"

As a medic, I couldn't say, *Because your eyes are hanging down your face.*

It was my job to keep him as comfortable as I could.

I said, "You're going to be fine, sir."

He asked, "How come I can't feel my hand?"

I said, "We'll look at that. We just called medevac."

Half an hour had passed since the explosion. It seemed that medevac was taking forever.

Captain O'Brien asked, "How come I can't feel my leg?"

He got to the point where he was actually joking about his condition. He said, "At least if I still have my nuts, my wife will take me back."

The man's courage was amazing.

I'd moved to Captain O'Brien's side and left a guy I didn't know in charge of keeping the captain's head and neck immobile, something you always have to do in the case of a traumatic injury because of the possibility of damage to the patient's spinal cord.

When I saw him starting to move the captain's head, I said emphatically, "Don't move his head!"

"It's okay," the man responded. "I'm an Army doctor."

"Well, if you're a doctor, how come I'm doing all this?"

The Army doctor said, "His neck isn't broken. I can tell."

"You don't have x-ray fingers," I shot back. "So you can't tell. Hold his head still."

After forty-five minutes the medevac team arrived and flew Captain O'Brien away. He ended up being treated at the Army burn center in Texas.

Later he sent me a letter. He told me that he'd lost one eye but had partial vision in the other. He'd been fitted with a prosthetic leg. Surgeons removed a toe off his foot and attached it to his hand so he had opposing fingers on one hand, which meant he could grasp objects and lift them up.

The experience reinforced an important lesson: Don't lose your cool when you see someone who is grotesquely injured. Stay calm and proceed to treat him the way you've been trained.

Afterward the Army conducted an investigation. They found out that three LAW rockets had been fired at the boat, and the EOD guys had recovered only two.

So the story came together. And I'm very happy to report that Captain Mike O'Brien is doing well.

CHAPTER TWELVE

San Blas Island

War is hell, but that's not the half of it.
—*Tim O'Brien*

Within two days of the launching of Operation Just Cause on December 20, 1989, most PDF units loyal to General Manuel Noriega had either disintegrated or surrendered. Twenty-four U.S. troops had died during the takeover of the country—including four SEALs on the runway. More than 200 PDF soldiers had been killed, and another 1,905 captured. Unfortunately, the *New York Times* reported, between 202 and 220 Panamanian civilians had also perished.

Still, according to a CBS poll, 92 percent of all Panamanian adults supported the U.S. incursion. Seventy-six percent wished the U.S. had intervened earlier.

The fighting had pretty much ended, but Manuel Noriega was still at large.

Christmas Day 1989, he and four of his henchmen, including the former head of Panama's secret police, fled to the Apostolic Nuncio—the de facto embassy of the Vatican—and sought asylum.

American soldiers promptly set up a perimeter outside the building, while Secretary of State James Baker sent a strong message to the Vatican asking them not to grant the former despot diplomatic immunity.

When Vatican officials refused to turn Noriega over to the United States, the Army turned to psychological warfare (psy ops), surrounding the building with armored vehicles and blaring rock music over loudspeakers—including some of my favorites, the song "I Fought the Law" by the Clash and the album *Appetite for Destruction* by Guns N' Roses.

Ten days later, Noriega went outside for a walk around the Nuncio grounds and was grabbed near the gate by what he described as a "gigantic, enormous" American soldier. He was tackled, handcuffed, and whisked off to Howard Air Force Base in a waiting helicopter.

Two years later, on September 16, 1992, Noriega stood in a Miami courtroom listening to a federal judge sentence him to forty years in prison for drug trafficking, racketeering, and money laundering. He was later extradited to France, where he's still in prison.

While the Noriega drama played out in Panama City, we continued to patrol the canal and board suspicious vessels. We encountered hundreds of *cayucos,* which were homemade, cutout-type vessels sometimes powered by outboard engines. Usually they were manned by a husband and wife, and maybe a couple of young children.

Since the *cayucos* were too small to board, we'd stand on the deck of our PRB and shout instructions in Spanish that meant "Open that container."

Often we'd find small quantities of marijuana and cocaine onboard.

We also detained fishing boats with small four- to eight-man crews, as well as giant cargo ships. No matter the size of the ship, I'd board with three or four armed SEALs and/or SBU guys, look around, and review the bills of lading. Many times we were badly outnumbered. But we wanted everyone to know that we controlled the local rivers and the canal.

We conducted searches day and night, seven days a week, and seized huge amounts of cocaine that was being smuggled up through the canal from Colombia. Once, we had to wear plastic gloves as we were carrying off the shrink-wrapped packages because the cocaine was seeping through the plastic. We were getting wired and starting to grind our teeth.

Initially some of the SBU guys were intimidated to work around SEALs. After I'd been with them for about a month or so, I said to a group of them, "Whenever you guys are at a party or bar and the team guys [SEALs] are around, you SBU guys would all sit down, stop having fun, and get quiet. That's wrong. I mean, you guys kicked ass in Vietnam and now you're kicking ass down here and in South America. You're every bit as good at what you do as we are at what we do."

A couple of nights later, a pudgy little guy from SBU-26 went up to some SEALs in a bar and said, "Senior Chief Mann said that except for the trident, we're just as good as you."

The SEALs beat the hell out of him.

I told the SBU guy that he didn't get the right message. I wasn't telling him to mouth off. I wanted him and his teammates to hold their heads high and take pride in the fact that they were professional warriors.

My buddy Lieutenant Adam Curtis had returned to SBU-26 after he and his wife were released by the Panamanians. One day we were patrolling the canal together when we received a report about a boat that was attempting to smuggle one of Noriega's officers out of the country.

We pulled up to a forty-footer, sounded the siren, got on the bullhorn, and ordered the boat to stop. When it did, four of us boarded— me, Adam, and two others.

After we had searched the vessel and not found the Panamanian we were looking for, one of the crew members told us that the man had crawled under the deck and was hiding in a very tight bilge area at the bottom of the boat—a long tube-like container, about twenty- four inches in diameter and twenty feet long.

Lieutenant Curtis started to take off his gear so he could squeeze inside.

I said, "No, LT, you're not going down there."

He said, "I'll go."

I said, "No, you're an officer. I'll do it."

We both wanted to crawl in and catch the guy.

I squeezed through the tight opening, holding my .45 in front of me, and squirmed my way through. It was pitch-black and I couldn't use a flashlight because I'd give away my position.

I remember thinking, *If the guy is armed and he shoots, there's no way he will miss me.*

Turned out the Panamanian wasn't down there, but he was cap- tured later.

The following day, I was asked to go to Howard Air Force Base to assist a Special Forces Reserve unit that had been sent down for Operation Just Cause with orders to trek through the jungle of San Blas Island and capture one of Noriega's officers. This particular Panamanian general had a reputation for being a sadist, and he had recently decapitated one of his servants for serving bad wine.

The SF Reserve unit was composed of a warrant officer and twelve soldiers—all of whom had recently been recalled. They were poorly trained and in terrible physical condition. In fact, their medic was so fat that they didn't think he could make it over the difficult terrain. That's why I was asked to join them on the op.

I accepted the offer and took two Navy guys with me—a lieutenant and an E5 who were both preparing to go to BUD/S.

The San Blas Islands are actually an archipelago of 378 islands and cays—49 of which are inhabited—that string out along the Caribbean coast of Panama nearly all the way south to the Colombian border. They're home to the Kuna Indians, who worship the ancient god Erragon.

The islands are as close to a tropical paradise as you can get—powdery soft beaches, clear blue-green water, gently swaying palm trees, and tree-covered slopes and mountains.

We packed our rucks for what was supposed to be a weeklong trek through the jungle.

The SF warrant officer was a big man, weighing about two hundred fifty pounds and standing about six two. As three of us from SBU-26 and eleven SF Reserve guys listened to him give the patrol leader's order, I took notes. As the only SEAL on the op, I didn't want to be overbearing, but the PLO sounded incomplete.

At one point I said, "Warrant, I didn't hear the loss-of-comms plan."

The WO grinned and answered, "You guys in the Navy....We don't need any loss-of-comms plan, because our radios work."

That was a bullshit answer coming from an inexperienced operator. You always have a loss-of-comms plan. Comms fail often, and for a variety of reasons.

I said to the lieutenant and E5 I'd brought with me, "If the shit hits the fan, we will stick together."

We set out early the next morning into the jungle. It was extremely hot and humid. The terrain was steep. The SF guys were noisy and smoking nonstop. They had to take frequent breaks because they weren't used to carrying heavy gear.

A platoon is supposed to move quietly and use hand and arm sig-

Pre–SEAL deployment, Futenma
Marine Corps Air Station in
Okinawa, Japan, 1980

Pre–SEAL deployment,
U.S. Marine Corps
MASH tent in Pohang,
Korea, 1980

The SEAL Team One Foxtrot Platoon, 1983

Platoon training in the Chocolate Mountains of Niland, California, with SEAL Team One, 1983

In Korea with SEAL Team One, 1984. Frigid weather, in a whiteout. After the op, I had to be treated for frostbite.

Climbing caving ladder to helicopter, 1985

SEAL Team One
at Camp Kerry,
California, 1985

SEAL Team Six lead-climber
training in Yosemite National
Park, 1986 and 1987

SEAL Team Six jungle-warfare training in Puerto Rico, 1988

Weapons training, Niland, California, 1988

SEAL Team Six, 1987

Climbing an oil rig
in Grand Isle, near
New Orleans, 1989

SEAL Team Six, 1989

Shooting a
.50-caliber
machine gun,
1989

Navy Special Warfare jungle school in Panama, 1990

My CWO2 commissioning ceremony, 1993

Eric Olson pinning on my CWO3 insignia, 1996. Captain Olson was my commanding officer and is now the highest-ranking admiral in the SEAL Teams.

My retirement photo, from 1998. I was actually standing in a river in running shorts getting ready to go on a paddle when the photographer arrived.

Training wannabe SEALs at Naval Amphibious Base, Little Creek, Virginia, 2004 *(Will Ramos)*

nals. Every member is supposed to have assigned responsibilities—the point man, rear security, automatic weapons, and so on.

This platoon would patrol for twenty minutes, then the WO would call out, "Okay, guys, let's take a break."

When a platoon on patrol takes a break, it's supposed to establish 360-degree security weapons at the ready. But this WO would plop down on the log or a rock, take off his boots, rub his feet, then eat a sandwich.

He'd say in a booming voice, "These friggin' boots are killing my feet."

Meanwhile, all the SF guys would take out their cigarettes and light up.

The first day out, we were walking through the jungle when one of the SF soldiers ran up to the warrant and said: "Hey, sir, I left my AT-four against a tree the last time we took a break."

An AT-4 is a powerful antitank grenade and rocket launcher. Any twelve-year-old could have picked it up, snuck up behind our very noisy patrol, and blown us all away.

Instead of castigating the soldier, the WO shouted, "Break!"

Then he turned to the soldier and said, "We'll wait here while you go back and get it."

If a SEAL ever did that, he'd be relieved from SPEC WAR—but a SEAL would never do that! When the SF Reserve soldier returned, the WO simply said, "Good job. You found it."

After the mission, he probably put the guy in for a medal. It was pathetic.

We were about half a day out when a local Indian came down the jungle path on horseback. Through our interpreter, the WO asked, "If we pay you, can you get us some horses to carry our gear?"

He pulled out a big wad of money and said that he wanted to hire a dozen horses and twelve Indian guides.

The Indian guy said, "*Sí*, señor." And took off.

We waited in the same spot for hours before the Indian came back with the guides and horses. All the SF guys piled their gear on the horses.

I told our guys, "We'll carry our gear."

Now we moved in this long, noisy circus caravan with all the Indians and SF guys with all of their gear on horseback. The three of us Navy guys walked in the middle of the patrol.

The horses had an amazing ability to climb up the steep mountain trails. They were better at it than the SF guys, who had to stop all the time and were constantly complaining about the heat, humidity, insects, their sore feet, and their tired legs.

The WO had all of the comms loaded on one of the horses. As the horse was climbing a particularly rocky, narrow mountain trail, it lost its footing and fell hundreds of feet into a deep ravine. That was the end of all our communications equipment. We didn't even attempt to retrieve it.

At the end of the first day, instead of being stealthy and setting up camp with half of the guys sleeping while the other half kept watch, the WO had one of the Indian guys lead us to a Kuna village. It featured a group of huts that had sides made of reeds and roofs of thatched palm fronds.

As the older Indians lounged in hammocks, younger women wove *molas*—layered lengths of fabric intricately cut and sewn into various colors and designs. Their calves were wrapped in loops of beads, and they wore bright yellow and red blouses that highlighted their tanned skin. Large gold hoops adorned their ears and noses.

It was like a scene out of *National Geographic*. But we definitely didn't belong there.

The WO pulled out his wad of money and asked through the interpreter, "How much will it cost for us to stay here and have you cook us dinner tonight and breakfast tomorrow?"

He negotiated a price with the local chief and we stayed the night. While we were there, I'm sure one of the kids from the village ran ahead to warn the Panamanian general. The WO didn't seem to be the least bit concerned about that.

As a matter of fact, next morning after breakfast he asked the local chief, "Do you know where General X is?"

Talk about giving away our objective. By this time I'm sure the whole archipelago knew where we were going.

We lodged in local villages all of the three nights it took us to get in.

The farther we got, the slower we seemed to move. When we arrived at the general's mansion, on the fourth day, it looked like the set of a movie—a gaudy, modern villa smack in the middle of the jungle with stables, a beautiful modern kitchen, and fancy tile floors.

As the WO started to walk up the driveway, I stopped him and said, "Warrant, we need to do a recon of the area first. The general's probably gone anyway, but we should do surveillance for a while and watch what's going on before moving in."

The WO smirked at me and said, "You've seen too many movies. Don't worry about it."

It took all my restraint not to deck him right there.

He and a couple of his men starting walking up the long driveway, as obvious as sitting ducks. As they approached the gate, a young male servant came running out of the house.

The Spanish speaker in the group asked, "Where's the general?"

"Oh, he left two days ago."

Big surprise.

For the next twenty-four hours we searched the house, stables, and property for drugs and weapons, but we didn't find anything. The whole mission seemed like a big waste of time, resources, and energy.

My only consolation: I slept in the general's bed and took his shaving gear. It's very high quality and I still use it.

I want to point out that I've worked with many exceptional SF guys throughout my career, but those reservists were terrible. I could have taken a troop of kids and been more successful.

Five days later, me and the other two Navy guys were back at Rodman Naval Station on the other side of the isthmus. That afternoon Lieutenant Adam Curtis and I were lying on the pier when our captain, Mike F., walked over and said, "The secretary of defense wants to meet with you."

We stood up, buttoned our shirts, and straightened out the dirty, sweaty camo uniforms we'd been wearing for three days as two black cars pulled up and a group of Secret Service agents in dark suits emerged. Behind them walked Secretary of Defense Dick Cheney.

Seven of us stood at attention. The captain made the introductions.

When he got to Adam, who was standing to my right, Captain Fitzgerald said, "This is Lieutenant Curtis. He's the one who was kidnapped with his wife driving back from the airport."

Secretary Cheney nodded and said, "That was the straw that broke the camel's back. That's when we decided to invade."

As the new year, 1990, began, our pace at SBU-26 didn't slow down. In fact, many of my teammates from ST-6 requested orders to SBU-26 because they wanted a piece of the action. Chasing the rainbow.

Our patrols started to expand up and down the Pacific coast of Central and South America, and throughout the rivers and waterways from Panama all the way to Bolivia. We were now on the front lines of the war on drugs, which had been declared by President Richard Nixon in 1971 and grown in intensity during the presidencies of Ronald Reagan and George H. W. Bush.

The "war" was actually a campaign of foreign military aid and military intervention, with the assistance of participating countries, the goal of which was to reduce or eliminate the sale of illegal drugs.

Over the next two years, I worked with SBU-26 conducting hundreds of VBSSs (visit, board, search, and seizures) throughout Central and South America. We seized hundreds of tons of marijuana and cocaine. But our enthusiasm was quickly dimmed by the rampant local government corruption.

Whenever we entered a foreign country that was cooperating with us—Colombia, Venezuela, Honduras, and so on—we'd always meet first with local officials, and they'd brief us on where we could operate. Inevitably they directed us to little villages in the jungle. We'd raid family-run cocaine labs that had fifty-gallon drums and burn down some huts. Seize drugs and equipment.

But it didn't take long for us all to realize we were attacking the tip of the iceberg. The big drug dealers and labs were being protected by corrupt government officials and were, therefore, untouchable.

Another component of the war on drugs was something we called mobile training ███████████████████████████████

██

██

███████████████████████

Many of the guys we trained were conscripts with no gear, no training, and little funding. Also, they understood that they had to operate within the political restraints of their country and region. So they weren't allowed to fully execute their jobs.

Still, we taught them how to shoot, patrol, and establish comms.

One of the MTTs we conducted took place in Riberalta, a little town of about 78,000 on the edge of the Amazon basin in northern Bolivia. The town was primitive and filthy, like something out of the

Wild West, but with lots of mosquitoes, and everybody rode a motorcycle.

It wasn't unusual to see a family of four riding on a Suzuki 125—the wife on the back of the seat, one kid on the gas tank, and another one on the handlebars. Cars and trucks were luxuries that few of the locals could afford.

For some reason, the people who lived there dumped their sewage upstream, so the water we cooked and bathed with was badly polluted. Even though we were careful about what we ate or touched, all of us got sick.

One day we were in our room and the LT said, "Hey, Doc. There's some guy outside selling rolls."

All of us were hungry, so I went to check these rolls out. They were covered with seeds and in a plastic bag, and they looked clean. They tasted great.

We must have eaten a hundred of them over the next couple of days. One night we were chewing on the rolls when the LT stopped and closely inspected the seeds.

"These aren't seeds," he shouted. "They're moving!"

The seeds turned out to be tiny bugs. But they tasted better than anything else we ate during that deployment.

Before we departed Panama, the commanding officer called me and the LT into his office and said, "Guys, I want you to make sure that nobody gets in trouble. I'm sending you down with a couple of trucks, our best boats, and I want them back looking like they do now, no scratches, dents, or dings."

We were in Riberalta about a week more when one of the SBU-26 guys, a petty officer third class named Hutch, was driving one of the trucks down a dirt road to a four-way intersection when this eleven-year-old boy on a Honda 125 cut in front of him. Hutch slammed on the brakes but still hit the boy with the truck.

The boy flew off the bike, hit the road hard, and lay on the ground unconscious. Bolivian authorities arrested Hutch and threw him in a tiny, filthy, barbaric-looking jail cell.

The boy, meanwhile, was loaded into the back of a vehicle and dropped off at the so-called hospital.

I received a call over the PRC-77 radio to get to the hospital ASAP and was there in ten minutes. When I examined the unconscious eighty-pound, eleven-year-old boy, I saw that his pupils were unequal and not reactive to light—a sign of serious head trauma. Otherwise, he was breathing fine and didn't appear to have any other injuries.

The hospital looked like a dirty garage—so filthy and ill equipped that you wouldn't want to use it to work on your car. I introduced myself to the doctor on duty and told him that I was an American medic and was there to help the unconscious boy.

The doctor said, "Do not interfere. The boy will either live or die. Don't bother this process."

What?

"Doctor," I said. "I don't want to cause trouble here, but I insist that we take care of this boy immediately. Check his vital signs, do pupil checks, and order an MRI and a CAT scan as soon as possible."

He became very agitated, but I wouldn't take no for an answer.

It was obvious to me that we needed to get the boy to a real hospital. Brian L., also from ST-6 and executive officer at SBU-26, searched for a plane and pilot; he tracked down a confiscated drug plane and we used that to fly the boy to a real hospital in the city of Santa Cruz. (Note: Brian L. is now one of the highest-ranking admirals in SEAL teams.)

There I met a Bolivian doctor who had trained in the United States and had actually saved the life of a SEAL buddy of mine in Vietnam.

He assembled his OR team, which was made up of an anesthesiologist; an assistant, who wore flip-flops; and myself.

I asked him, "Where can I wash up?"

He said, "Don't worry about that."

None of the team scrubbed up or wore surgical masks or gloves.

The impact of the accident had caused the boy's brain to slam forward against the front of his skull, then push back again—coup-countercoup, it's called. His injury required brain surgery.

As the Bolivian doctor spoke to me in broken English, he took a scalpel, cut along the top portion of the boy's head, then peeled down his face, exposing his skull.

Then, as I held the boy's head, the doctor picked up an old hand drill that you wouldn't want in your toolbox and started to drill into the boy's skull.

As he was doing this, the doctor asked me, "So, how's the pussy in Panama?"

I said, "Fine, Doc. But don't you think we should pay attention to what you're doing?"

As he drilled, he used a piece of gauze to catch the tiny bone fragments that were falling free from the boy's skull.

The doctor drilled six holes in the boy's head. I initially thought he was just drilling the holes to relieve the pressure on the boy's brain. Instead, the doctor took a wire saw, put it in one hole, and started to saw through the bone. Then he did the same thing to the next hole. Once he'd finished with all six holes, he lifted off the top of the boy's skull and placed it on a table.

The boy's exposed brain was about the size of his fist and mostly gray.

While the Bolivian doctor continued to talk to me, he reached down and started to cut away pieces of the front of the boy's brain that had turned black.

He said, "Black brain, no good."

He was correct. The black parts of the brain were necrotic and would have caused infection and resulted in the boy's death.

When he was finished with the frontal lobe, the Bolivian doctor sliced off the black parts of the temporal lobe and the back of the brain.

I said, "Doc, you're cutting away so much of his brain. Is he ever going to be okay?"

"Oh, yes. He'll learn to work around it. He'll think differently. But he'll be okay."

As I watched, the doctor took a piece of IV tubing and cut some slits in it. Then he placed the tubing on the boy's brain and pushed it down, so that the blood drained away. He said, "Look, drainage tubing made in Bolivia," and he laughed.

Next, he picked up the skull section and put it back, saying, "Look, it's just like a bowling ball."

As I watched in a combination of wonder and horror, he mixed some liquid with the bone fragments and then used that as a superglue to hold the skull section in place.

He carefully peeled the face back up over the skull and lined up the nostrils and eye sockets.

"That's it!" he announced.

Miraculously, the boy recovered. Months later, he was back on his motorcycle riding around town.

While I was attending to the injured boy, the LT was trying to get Hutch out of jail.

During the three days it took him to negotiate Hutch's temporary release, Lieutenant Mike R.—who had a really sick sense of humor—continued to mess with him. He told Hutch, "I have bad news. The Bolivians won't let you out of here, and they're planning to give you the death penalty."

He also walked in one day and said, "Sorry, Hutch, but the boy died. You killed an eleven-year-old boy."

When Hutch started to scream, the LT said, "I'm only kidding."

Once the LT knew Hutch was being temporarily released, he called us together and said, "I want you guys to load the plane quickly. I'm going to pick up Hutch, then we're going to fly out of here illegally, as fast as we can."

I thought, *That's a pretty ballsy move.*

Later that night, as we were loading the C-130, the LT drove up in a taxi with Hutch. As soon as they boarded, he ordered the pilot to fire up the engines.

We were pulling the rest of our gear up the back ramp when two platoons of Bolivian soldiers arrived and surrounded the plane, their weapons drawn.

They yelled in Spanish, "If you try to leave, we'll shoot you."

The LT refused to back down. Instead, he said, "Okay, guys. Open the cruise boxes and break out your weapons."

It was going to be like the gunfight at the O.K. Corral.

We closed the ramp and taxied down the runway as all of us held our breath. Thankfully, the Bolivians (many of whom we had just trained) let us leave without firing a shot.

But when we returned to Panama, we caught hell. The commanding officer who had told us not to cause any trouble was pissed. And rightfully so.

CHAPTER THIRTEEN

El Salvador

What does not kill me, makes me
stronger.

—*Friedrich Nietzsche,*
Twilight of the Idols

My former German teacher Shannon and I were married in 1990, and she eventually moved to Panama with me. But even though we loved each other, our marriage got off to a somewhat rocky start.

When Iraqi troops invaded Kuwait in August of 1990, President George H. W. Bush launched Operation Desert Storm to thwart Iraqi aggression. In Panama, where I was still stationed, I heard over the radio that the U.N.-authorized coalition force of thirty-four nations led by the United States was in dire need of special operators who were also medics, and I wrote to the SEAL commodore in Coronado, California, requesting orders to be assigned to the invasion. When Shannon found out, she protested strongly.

With good reason. She was pregnant with our daughter, Dawnie, who was born on March 22, 1991—which was one of the happiest days of my life.

Months before Dawnie was born, I had been sent with a group

of ST-6 SEALs to help provide security to a regional drugs summit being held in the beautiful colonial city of Cartagena, Colombia. Tension was extremely high. Officials feared that Colombian drug barons would take revenge for the recent arrest of their friend and ally Manuel Noriega.

██ who, in the style of machismo, wore black armbands with DAS printed boldly on them and roared through the streets on trail bikes.

We were staying at the same local hotel as the presidents of Bolivia and Peru. As ST-6 SEALs, we tried to remain low-key, but the seriousness of the summit didn't stop the presidents and their friends from partying all night with loud music; people laughing, dancing, and screaming; and naked women being thrown in the hotel pool.

President George H. W. Bush was more discreet, arriving in the morning on Air Force One. After the Boeing 747 taxied to a stop near the terminal, the president emerged and waved from the top step of the stairway. At least, I thought it was the president. But when I looked closer, I saw that the man was not the president but an almost perfect double. When he wasn't shot at or attacked, the real president emerged from the plane and was whisked quickly to an armored limo.

Since BUD/S, the pace of my workouts hadn't let up. In addition to doing the required daily SEAL PT, I was on a thirty-year mission to work out every day. I hadn't missed a workout since February of 1978, and that included fifty-mile trail runs, two-hundred-mile bike rides, twenty-four-hour mountain-bike rides, and fifty-mile kayak paddles.

In the fall of '91, I was training with four guys from SBU-26 for the Run Across the Isthmus—a fifty-two-mile run across Panama, starting at the Atlantic coast and following jungle paths and railroad beds to the Pacific Ocean. The first man who won it, in 1940, was a future World War II hero named Fay Steele.

The guys at SBU-26 weren't as committed to training as I thought they could be. Having some idea of the toll that fifty-two miles through the heat and humidity was going to take, I invited them over to my place and warned them by saying, "This is going to be the most miserable day of your life."

As I was talking, I felt a series of sharp pains on the right side of my abdomen that caused me to double over.

One of the SBU-26 guys asked, "Don, are you all right?"

"Yeah," I answered. "I think I just have a slight case of food poisoning."

A few minutes later I started feeling nauseous, and I ran to the bathroom and threw up.

Shannon said, "Don, you better not do this stupid race. You're sick and need to see a doctor."

I said, "I'll be fine."

The guys I was planning on running with that night had never run an ultramarathon. So I explained to them the importance of hydration and electrolyte replacement, bringing extra shoes, and considering race tactics.

After they left my house, Shannon saw me lying on the sofa in pain, holding my side, and she said, "I can't believe you're doing this!"

Not about to let a little discomfort stop me, I answered, "I'm running the race."

She said, "If you do, I'm out of here." Then she picked up our baby daughter, took my stepdaughter, Chonie, by the hand, and left the house. (She was gone for two days.)

We were living in Navy housing at Fort Amador, which faced the canal, with SEAL neighbors on both sides.

Now I was alone, dry-heaving green bile, and feeling like someone had thrust a rusty sword in my side. The pain was so bad that when I tried calling the hospital, my eyes couldn't focus enough to read the numbers.

When I stumbled out of the house, a neighbor's wife saw me and screamed, "Don, what's the matter with you? Oh my God!"

I asked weakly, "Can you take me to the hospital?"

She and her husband helped me into the backseat of their Volkswagen Bug and sped to the nearest hospital. I was in so much pain that I fell to the floor of the car and curled up in the fetal position.

The moment the emergency room orderly opened the door, I hurled all over his shoes. Turned out that I was in the process of passing kidney stones and had to spend the night. Regretfully, I never got to run the race.

During my three years in Panama, I had a full plate of responsibilities. When I wasn't on missions, I directed the three-week Naval Special Warfare jungle-survival course in Panama, which was held in jungles filled with crocodiles and poisonous snakes. We taught members of the Naval Special Warfare community advanced-weapons tactics; small-unit-patrol techniques; how to plan and conduct small-unit missions; how to recon an area; how to tactically cross rivers; how to make improvised tools, set traps, and fish; food and water procurement and preparation; and jungle navigation.

The course culminated in a four-day SERE exercise designed to test each student's ability to survive alone or in small groups while in hostile territory.

The crocodiles and snakes weren't a joke. After I left, an Army soldier who was attending the course disappeared. It's presumed that he was eaten alive by a crocodile.

Once, when I was leading a group of trainees on a run down a jungle road, I looked back to see how they were doing and saw a strange, whirling haze. While trying to figure out what it was, I was surrounded by a swarm of killer bees that started stinging me without mercy.

Soon all of us were jumping and screaming, looking like we were doing some kind of crazed Pygmy dance. The only way we could get away from the bees was to run a quarter of a mile and jump in the ocean. By that time, we were all covered with welts.

Another time, when I was driving down that same road, I saw an Army platoon sitting in a group. Two soldiers were huffing and puffing, and the face of one had turned white.

I stopped the jeep I was driving and asked, "Are you guys okay?"

"Yeah, we're fine."

I pointed to the one guy who looked liked he was having a particularly hard time and said, "He doesn't look okay to me."

One of the soldiers said, "He was stung by some killer bees and is allergic to bees."

"Well, you are not fine. Where's your medic?" I asked.

"He's lost."

"Then where's your sergeant?"

"He's with the medic."

In the few minutes we were talking, the soldier lost consciousness. So I loaded him in my jeep, took him to a tent we had set up along a river, and administered Benadryl, epinephrine, and oxygen.

He woke up, looked at me, and asked, "Who are you?"

I didn't tell him how lucky he was to still be alive.

In addition to directing the jungle survival course, I ran the Medical Civic Action Program (MEDCAP) throughout Central and South America. This was an extension of the same program that had been used in Vietnam in which free medical care was administered to poor peasants and intel was gathered that could be of value in planning future operations.

I ran similar events in Honduras, Bolivia, Colombia, El Salvador, Peru, and Nicaragua. First, I'd get a grant of seventy thousand dollars from an organization that managed Central and South American military aid, and I'd use it to buy medical, dental, and veterinary supplies. Then I'd recruit volunteer doctors, nurses, and medics from the different military hospitals and clinics in the United States and Panama. I'd look for dentists, OB-GYNs, and veterinarians too.

We'd strategically select a remote area filled with poor people in need of medical attention and set up field tents. We'd have a dental tent, an OB-GYN tent, an admin/registration tent, and a general sick-call tent where everyone came in to be checked.

Once we put out the word that we were going to be there, hundreds of men, women, and children streamed in, often accompanied by their farm animals. Some would walk for two or three days, then stop and bathe in a nearby river. They were proud people who wanted to look their best.

The native women were remarkable. They'd arrive dressed in their finest clothing. Some had never seen a dentist in their lives.

The people sat on the wooden dental chair, and the dentist would pull their bad teeth without using Novocain. The men and boys would cry. But the women never complained. We pulled bad teeth, rotten teeth, and teeth that looked like they might go bad. We used a fifty-gallon barrel to hold all the bad teeth. By the end of the week, it would be a quarter filled.

Meanwhile, the veterinarians and some of the medics would go into the fields and inoculate the cows, goats, and sheep.

Some of the people who attended were suffering from serious injuries that hadn't ever been treated. I remember one girl limped in with a club foot. We managed to get her a flight to an Army hospital in Texas for treatment.

Another father and son carried in the almost lifeless body of a teenage girl. She weighed about seventy pounds and was running a 106-degree temperature; her unconscious body was hot to the touch. Upon examining her, we found that she'd had a spontaneous abortion and part of the fetus was still stuck inside her. It was infected and she had become septic. She'd probably had no more than an hour left to live when her father put her in my arms.

We worked on the girl for hours, and she survived.

I staged a number of MEDCAP programs in El Salvador. Since 1980, a civil war had been raging there between the military-led government, which was supported by the United States, and leftist rebels of the Farabundo Marti National Liberation Front (FMLN).

The MEDCAPs we held there turned out to be great sources of intelligence. We'd set them up in the foothills of the Sierra Madre, near FMLN strongholds. Grateful patients would tell us where the rebel camps were located and what routes they used to smuggle in weapons.

I was wearing many hats in Panama—running missions and serving as director of the jungle survival course, director of MEDCAP, and liaison to SEALs who were deployed to Panama.

I also supported many of the military operations in El Salvador. The first SEAL funeral I attended was for Lieutenant Commander Albert Schaufelberger, who had been the security chief to the American military advisers stationed in El Salvador. Schaufelberger had been waiting to pick up his friend outside Central American University when he was approached by an FMLN gunman, who shot him three times in the head. In accordance with Schaufelberger's sealed instructions, his ashes were scattered in the Pacific from a SEAL patrol boat.

I arrived in El Salvador toward the end of the conflict. By the time the government and the FMLN rebels signed the Chapultepec Peace Accords, in January of 1992, approximately seventy-five thousand Salvadorans had died.

From my point of view, the Salvadoran conflict was unique. For one thing, the Red Cross seemed to be openly supporting the rebels. Whenever we saw a Red Cross ambulance, we knew the rebels were nearby. In the evenings, armed fighters from both sides of the conflict would frequent the same restaurants and bars. We knew who they were, and they knew us.

One night I was on a joint SEAL–Special Forces op with an experienced SF operator named Chito. The two of us were lying in long grass dressed in Salvadoran garb—Levi's, jungle-camo tops, and ball caps. We had a wheelbarrow filled with automatic weapons and ammo that we were supposed to push for about twelve kilometers, to a rendezvous point.

While we were lying in the grass in enemy-controlled territory waiting to launch the op, Chito couldn't keep his mouth shut. Maybe he was nervous. Maybe he had a lot on his mind.

For whatever reason, it was the beginning of a strange night.

He started to tell me that before joining the Army he'd been the lead singer in a punk rock band called Luke, Puke, and the Vomits. No kidding.

And he told me about some songs he wrote dealing with the many intense things that had happened in his life. Like the time the remains of his best friend were returned from Vietnam. Or when his girlfriend was badly injured in a motorcycle accident.

He explained the elaborate stage act he'd worked out. Before his band performed, Chito would buy sheep intestines from a butcher shop and hide them in a plastic bag that he taped under his shirt. At the end of a particularly dramatic song, he'd take out a knife and slash the bag so that it looked like he was cutting his stomach and his guts were spilling out.

I liked Chito, but he was wound tight. The more he spoke, the more agitated he got. He'd been in El Salvador for years and was frustrated. He said, "We keep pushing human rights on the Salvadoran army troops, but every morning they find the headless body of another of their fellow soldiers in the river."

As he started to tell me about visiting his girlfriend in the hospital after her motorcycle accident, I heard something moving toward us in the pitch-black night.

"Chito, be quiet!"

We slithered through the chest-high grass and hid behind a large tree. I was on the right; he was on the left. The sound was moving closer and growing louder. We had our fingers on the triggers, safeties off. I could feel Chito about to explode.

He said, "On three, we'll rush them!"

"No, Chito," I said. "Let them come to us. We have cover. We're undetected."

He said, "No, let's go get them."

"No. Listen to me, Chito."

The noise grew louder, and the object crept closer. Our hearts were pounding. Our weapons were pointed at the noise. We were ready to fire when a big black bull emerged from the grass and stared at us.

We laughed our asses off.

A few minutes later we started moving through the high grass toward the Pacific coast again, Chito pushing the wheelbarrow.

We stopped after a bit because Chito was out of breath. I felt something at my foot and scratched it. Then I said, "Chito, let me push the wheelbarrow."

Now I was pushing the weapons-and-ammo-loaded wheelbarrow. Even though it was past midnight, the air was hot and sticky. Both of us were sweating.

I felt something on my leg under the faded old Levi's I was wearing.

Chito was talking, telling me about how he loved this one girl even though she had been with a lot of men. He said when he last saw her in the hospital her jaw was all wired up and she'd said, "Chito, I can't suck your dick, but you can rub it on my lips if you'd like."

Then I felt something near my knee and stopped to scratch it. A few minutes later, whatever it was moved to my groin.

I stopped and said, "Chito, shine the flashlight on the front of my pants."

"Why?"

"Just do it, okay?"

I opened my pants and saw a small black snake. I stared at it; it looked back at me. Then I grabbed the damn thing and flung it as far away as I could.

Chito loved that.

An hour later, we arrived at the coast, where we met another SEAL, named Johnny. We were supposed to rendezvous with an SF medic also, but he hadn't arrived.

So the three of us—me, Chito, and Johnny—sat on a bluff overlooking the shore waiting for the asset we were scheduled to meet. Suddenly, round things started rolling down on us from the land above. We couldn't tell what they were or where exactly they were coming from.

Johnny and I climbed up the bluff to look.

He whispered, "Come here! Come here!" And pointed to a camouflaged hatch door in the ground.

We both drew our weapons as Johnny lifted it up.

Hiding in the little hole in the ground was the SF medic, surrounded by coconuts.

Johnny asked, "What the hell are you doing down there?"

"I thought you guys were the enemy," he answered. "I was trying to scare you off."

We once again laughed our asses off. It was that kind of night.

We finally met our asset and delivered the wheelbarrow filled with weapons and ammo. Later, we set our demo at a choke point in the river and waited for the rebel boat to arrive. It was a twenty-foot wooden boat with a small cabin.

We waited as the boat puttered down river. Then we saw a huge flash, followed a split second later by the sound of a big explosion.

Mission success!

When I returned to Panama, I learned that I'd been selected for promotion to chief warrant officer (CWO)—an officer grade above senior enlisted rank but below the grade of commissioned officer. If I'd chosen to stay enlisted, I could have gone directly back to ST-6 after my tour in Panama was complete.

But since I'd decided to go the warrant route, I had to serve with another team as a freshman warrant before I could return to ST-6. I accepted the position as the SEAL Team Two training officer at Little Creek, Virginia.

My wife, Shannon, however, wasn't ready to go. She loved living in Panama and wanted to complete the language course she was teaching. So she, Chonie, and Dawnie stayed in Panama for another ten months. I checked into ST-2 and missed them a lot.

Because of the experience I gained in the Central and South American waterways, I taught VBSS to all the platoons. I was also the director of weapons training, winter-warfare training, the MOUT (military operations in urban terrain) course, and ST-2's PT program.

ST-2 was known for having the toughest PT of all the teams, partially because of the difficult winter-warfare training they'd been through and the counterterrorism ops they ran in Europe.

But when I saw what they were actually doing—some flutter kicks, push-ups, and sit-ups on the grinder, then one run through the obstacle course, a two-mile ocean swim in good weather, and a six-mile run once a week—I was disappointed and made it my mission to step up the PT.

Instead of their running the obstacle course once, I bumped it up to three times, followed by a three-mile run. And after that, I made them complete the cycle twice more, for a total of nine times through the obstacle course and three three-mile runs.

One morning, the CO, Captain Joe Kernan (who is now an admiral), asked to join us. We were doing lunges across a football field when he said, "Doc, this is pretty hard. I guess you've been picking up the PT pace."

I said, "Yes, sir, and I'm going to pick it up even more."

I didn't know it at the time, but the older guys on the team were starting to complain about the PTs becoming too difficult. The young guys, meanwhile, were eating them up.

After the lunges, each guy lifted a buddy on his back and sprinted across the field, then did more lunges. I worked the team up to nine times through the obstacle course, twelve-mile runs, and two-mile swims, even in frigid cold and pouring rain.

My XO called me in his office one morning and said, "Look, I can't move my arms." I thought he was joking at first, but he wasn't.

All the department heads were complaining that their men were exhausted from the PTs and were falling asleep during the day. But I didn't let up. I considered my tough PTs a badge of honor. Like they had taught us in BUD/S, "The more sweat and tears you put into training, the less blood you shed in war."

One time one of the SEALs' elbows, wrists, and shoulders locked up on him during PT. He was cramping so bad it looked liked he was experiencing rigor mortis.

The CO heard about it and said to me, "Doc, that was a rough PT."

Then the master chief said, "Doc, I keep hearing these PTs are too tough. Everyone is so tired they can't do their work. You've got to ease up."

The SEALs on ST-2 started calling me Warrant Officer Manslaughter. Even all these years later, people are still talking about the brutal PTs I ran at ST-2.

I always pushed myself just as hard as I pushed the people I trained. Probably harder. Years before this, when I was at ST-1, I came very close to dying from overtraining. In addition to all the work required of a SEAL and the PT I was doing with the team—which included two hours of PT each morning—I'd ride my bike to the Coronado pool every day before work and swim two to four miles with the masters swim team. During lunch I'd run 13.1 miles (in under ninety minutes), and after work I'd ride forty to sixty miles or go to Nautilus.

Weekends there were even more grueling. Saturdays, I'd swim 4 miles and bike 156 miles. Sundays, I'd bike 120 miles and run 20 miles. I was working out a minimum of sixty hours a week.

With all the training I was doing, I barely had time to replace all the calories I was burning. I was so lean that when I took a breath, you could see all the veins in my chest and abs. My commanding officer looked at me one day and asked, "Doc, where is the other half of your body?"

One day when I walked up to the pool, my coach noticed that my skin had turned a greenish hue and that my ankles were badly swollen and had red spots all over them, as though I'd been bitten by some kind of insect.

He told me I needed to take a break. But I couldn't—I was training for the longest triathlon in the world: 3.1-mile swim, 156-mile bike ride, and a 32-mile run. I felt I could win it.

After the four-mile swim workout, the coach and I went for a twenty-mile run at a sub-seven-minute pace. He said, "You're sweating, and you never sweat. You'd better take a break."

When I got home, my wife at the time, Kim, was alarmed by my appearance. I looked in the mirror and saw that my skin had turned green.

I asked Kim to run me a hot bath. After that, I figured, I'd rest.

But I was in so much pain that I couldn't walk from the bedroom to the bathroom. So I crawled on my hands and knees and passed out in the hallway.

I woke up in the Balboa hospital in San Diego. The doctors informed me that I had a torn rotator cuff, a compressed spine, plantar fasciitis in both feet, and a torn quadriceps muscle in my left leg. My skin had turned green because my liver and kidneys were shutting down. And my weight, which was normally around 185, had dipped below 140.

The doctors called it the worst case of overtraining that they'd ever seen.

I had to stop doing PT, forgo the ultra-distance triathlon, and spend time in the hospital. I hated backing down. And it wasn't the only time injury forced me to do so.

During a sniper-training mission with ST-2 at Fort Pickett, Virginia, I went out to check the hides the snipers were constructing. Sometimes the snipers' hides were so good, I'd walk to within three feet of them and still not see them.

So instead of walking through the woods like I usually did, I decided to ride my new Trek Y22 mountain bike, figuring that afterward I'd pedal through the nearby hills and forest, despite not having a helmet.

After checking the hides, I went for a ride and crossed a long wooden bridge. The roadway was made of long six-inch-wide planks of wood that had inch-and-a-half gaps between them. When I saw the gaps, I braked to slow down, but then I immediately started scolding myself, saying, *What kind of pussy am I? I've ridden and raced all kinds of bicycles and motorcycles and I'm worried that I can't keep the wheel of my bike on a six-inch-wide board?*

I swore to myself I wouldn't slow down when I crossed it on the way back. An hour or so later, I looked at the bridge and hit it at about twenty-five miles an hour without even thinking of braking.

Lights out!

I woke up on the side of the bridge feeling sunshine on my face and wondering why I was sleeping outside. Then I noticed a sharp pain in my right leg. Stuck in it was a ten-inch-long splinter, and another six-inch splinter was sticking in my forearm.

All the water had trickled out of my water bottle, and I'd suffered a head injury and been unconscious for some time.

I pushed myself hard and often paid the price.

In fact, I can't count how many times I've pushed myself to unconsciousness. We have a saying in the teams that I never liked: Too much can-do can do you in.

I like to think that the only thing that should ever be done in moderation is moderation itself.

In Fort Pickett, as I mentioned, I ran the military operations in urban terrain course. We had a setup that looked just like a village, with cars we could set on fire and all kinds of buildings. I often worked with a British SAS (Special Air Service) soldier who had conducted numerous ops in Northern Ireland.

One afternoon, we took a break so the guys from ST-2 could do their helo-rappel requalifications. The SAS sergeant and I sat on the ground watching them rappel about seventy feet from a helicopter and onto the ground behind a building. A big 230-pound SEAL named Steve was the one first out. He went to brake by putting his hand behind his back, and his Ka-Bar knife came out of its scabbard enough to cut the rope, causing him to fall fifty feet.

The ground shook when he hit it.

Steve broke both his hands, both ankles, his back in two places, and had an open femur fracture in his leg.

I treated Steve with the help of a SEAL corpsman. Although Steve was in tremendous pain, he never lost consciousness. After he was splinted and bandaged, Steve was medevaced out by the same helo he'd fallen from.

Meanwhile, Mike, whom I'd worked with in Panama and who was the LT in the platoon, happened to be videotaping the whole thing. The Navy later used the tape to show new corpsmen how to treat traumatic injuries.

Shannon, Chonie, and our baby daughter, Dawnie, finally arrived in Virginia Beach from Panama. I found a home that Shannon liked, and I thought it was a perfect place to raise a family. But work required me to spend a lot of time away.

Sometime in 1994 I returned to Virginia Beach after a month in Fort Bragg, North Carolina, where I was running a weapons and CQB course, to find the grass on the lawn high, the light bulbs and toilet paper gone, and our house completely empty. Shannon had packed up and moved across country. She hadn't even left a letter.

Even though I had sensed that the breakup was coming, I was devastated. Physical pain I could take, but emotional distress was harder to handle.

CHAPTER FOURTEEN

Back to ST-6

Goldfinger could not have known that
high tension was Bond's natural way of
life and that pressure and danger relaxed
him.

—*Ian Fleming*, Goldfinger

My second wife had left me and taken everything, including my
nine-year-old stepdaughter and our four-year-old daughter, leaving
me down in the dumps and living alone in our empty house in Virginia Beach. No furniture. No TV. Not even a toaster. I bought a
cheap futon and slept on that.

Weekdays I spent training the guys at ST-2. Weekends, even
though I stayed busy running, cycling, paddling, and lifting, were
tough.

One Saturday afternoon, a SEAL buddy of mine named Bruce
called me and invited me to a barbecue. I didn't feel like going out, so
I said, "Thanks, Bruce. But I think I'll stay home."

When he mentioned food and beverages, my ear perked up.

Bruce said, "Come on, Don. It's a great sunny day; ride your bike
over. I'll meet you halfway."

I got on my Harley and rode from my home in Virginia Beach

about five miles to the local 7-Eleven, where Bruce was waiting on his chopper. His Harley was more radical than mine, with ape hangers and very loud upswept fishtails.

I eased off the throttle and heard the loud *bup-bup-bup* of my motor—a sound that some people find annoying but that always fills me with excitement and expectation.

"Follow me," Bruce said with a wild smirk on his face.

What's going on? I wondered.

He led the way to a nice neighborhood just two miles outside of the SEAL Team Six compound. One of our SEAL buddies opened the wooden gates when he heard us approaching. Wafting through the air was the welcome smell of barbecue.

I saw about a dozen guys I knew from the teams, all of them holding beers and grinning like cats that had just eaten canaries. Beyond them were six young women lying on lounge chairs, either topless or entirely naked.

Immediately, I was like, *Wow! This is cool.*

One of the girls said, "We were just playing a joke. Bruce told us you needed some cheering up."

"Thanks. Hey, before you get dressed, would you mind posing with the bikes?"

I borrowed Bruce's wife's camera and figured, Why waste a great opportunity?

They complied. It was my introduction to a group that we called Frogs on Hogs—which now includes over two hundred SEALs who own Harleys and who often get together to ride on weekends and to hang out.

Even though I was still feeling down because of my second failed marriage, riding with the guys helped me clear my head. On Memorial Day weekend 1994 we rode to the Rolling Thunder motorcycle rally in Washington, DC, to raise awareness of the plight of prisoners of war and soldiers missing in action. Something like fifty thousand bikers from all over the country assembled in the Pentagon's north parking lot then rode together up and over the Memorial Bridge, past the Capitol, and then down Constitution Avenue to the Vietnam veterans memorial wall, near the Lincoln Memorial's reflecting pool.

As waves of bikes carrying Vietnam vets and their supporters rumbled past the rear of the White House, we passed a relatively small group of gay marchers on their way to Capitol Hill. Talk about a contrast in lifestyles.

President Bill Clinton, who had recently been sworn into office, was scheduled to speak to the bikers. When he took the stage, over half of the people in attendance turned their backs on the commander in chief who had dodged the draft instead of fighting for his country in Vietnam.

Frogs on Hogs continued. Though the group was made up exclusively of men, we did decide to admit one woman, named Debbie, a former Navy LT who had recently retired.

She was full of life and rode a Sportster that her dad had willed to her. Debbie had been dating an ST-6 guy named Tom, and they got engaged. One rainy Saturday afternoon, Deb called Tom and asked him to meet her at Harpoon Larry's bar on the beach.

Tom said no but told her to come home afterward and he'd make her dinner.

But as soon as he hung up the phone, he changed his mind about the bar. So while Deb was on her way, Tom got on his bike and rode past my house to meet her at Harpoon Larry's.

Deb's bike hit a slick patch on the wet road and flew over the sidewalk and up four steps that led to a hotel lobby. The front wheel of the bike climbed up the wall, then the bike flipped over and landed on top of Debbie.

As Tommy rode past the hotel, he saw an overturned bike with a rider trapped underneath. He ran up to help the biker and, seeing that it was his fiancée, fell to pieces. Tommy called me immediately. I was there in a flash.

But there was nothing I could do to help Debbie.

The accident had ruptured her aorta, and she quickly bled out. I watched as she took her last breath.

Thrills and danger ride together. That's the way it works.

While I was still the training officer at ST-2, I accompanied a Delta platoon to winter-warfare training in Alaska. The forty-five-day course started with the basics of survival in a frigid landscape around the Buskin River—we set up snow caves and slept in them, worked with avalanche beacons, did cross-country and downhill skiing, pulled sleds, made fires, fished, procured food and water, and conducted small-boat drills in Seward Bay, which, because it's salt water, doesn't freeze in the winter.

The last forty-eight hours of the course was a tough final training exercise (FTX), which included a two-thousand-meter cold-water ocean swim, a river crossing via high line, and long-range navigation through the mountain wilderness to infiltrate and establish covert surveillance of a target site. We had to accomplish all this while carrying seventy-five to ninety pounds of operational gear each, including weapons and ammo.

Accompanying the platoon during the winter training were two SEAL LT reservists. As we made igloos and snow caves, skied, and trekked through the mountains, they kept asking me about my background as a multisport athlete.

One day, the two of them pulled me aside and told me about something called the Raid Gauloises. They said that it was the world's premier long-distance multisport endurance race and that it had been created in 1989 by a man named Gerald Fusil. The five-hundred-mile race included mountain biking, kayaking, white-water rafting, running, rock climbing, and swimming, and it required each competitor to be part of a five-person coed team. It was named after its original sponsor, which in an ironic twist was the Gauloises cigarette company.

The Navy reservists asked if I would be interested in coaching, training, and leading a team.

I said, "I don't know if I'll be able to, since I have a lot of responsibilities as the training officer at ST-Two."

"We already checked with your commanding officer, Joe Kernan, and your executive officer," the LT reservist responded, "and they said that as long as Don can still do his job, it's his call."

"In that case, absolutely!"

They explained that they wanted to build a team around two men, Mike Sawyer and Mark Davis, who had already raised a lot of money from an organization in Chicago that included NBA superstar Michael Jordan and heavyweight boxing champ Mike Tyson.

Mike Sawyer (who was a world-class sprinter) and Mark Davis (a weight lifter and former WNBA coach) planned to be the first African Americans to compete in the Raid Gauloises, which was known as the world's most difficult endurance competition.

The first thing I had to do was select two more athletes to complete the team, which was named Team Odyssey. At least one of them had to be a woman, so I chose one of the toughest people I've ever trained with, Juli Lynch—an exceptional athlete, a world-class ultra-distance marathoner and cross-country skier. She stands five feet tall, weighs about a hundred and five pounds, and is tough as nails.

Rounding out the team was another SEAL, Erik Liebermann, who was not only one of the best athletes in the teams but also an exceptional navigator.

The next Raid Gauloises would be held in the Patagonia region of Argentina in late 1995. Which meant that we had a little more than a year to prepare.

Mike and Mark were cousins and incredible athletes, but neither of them was really a trained outdoorsman. In fact, they both hated the water and didn't like being out in the woods at night.

So a large part of the fifty thousand dollars that they raised from various sponsors was spent on sending them to climbing, kayaking, and mountaineering courses. The five of us also met once a month for three-day nonstop workout sessions, usually in the White Mountains.

We assembled in southern Argentina in late November of 1995. The area we would be racing through, Patagonia, was a million square miles featuring a harsh combination of ice, snow, glaciers, mountains, heat, and relentless Antarctic winds.

Race officials informed us that we would be required to ride horses using wooden saddles, like the native gauchos; don snowshoes and crampons; and risk altitude sickness and avalanches—all the time carrying all of our food and gear. They estimated it would take the fifty-five-person teams seven to ten days to complete the five-hundred-mile course. Most teams would average fewer than two hours of sleep per night.

The reward? Forty thousand dollars to the winning team, which would barely cover the fifteen-thousand-dollar entrance fee and the additional money we had already spent on travel, equipment, and training.

We weren't in it for the money.

Despite all the time they'd spent on training, Mike and Mark began lagging behind from the start of the race. Erik and Juli were always way ahead of them. And I was running back and forth trying to keep the team together so we wouldn't be penalized for being dispersed.

Mike and Mark were made up of fast-twitch muscles, which are better suited for sprinting and lifting than for long treks. Like Erik and Juli, I was born with mostly slow-twitch muscles.

Fast-twitch muscles contract and expand quickly, but get tired fast. Slow-twitch muscles are more efficient at using oxygen to generate fuel, and can fire for a long time before they fatigue.

Mike and Mark were great guys but constantly complaining. The white-water sections scared them. When we got to the smoother sections of the river, we had to pull their kayaks. They weren't very good at the climbing or biking sections either.

Day three we'd climbed to about twelve thousand feet when a bad storm started blowing in. We now had to cross a rocky peak that was covered with snow and ice.

Juli and Erik went up the side of the cliff without a problem.

I noticed some loose rock and warned the two cousins that they shouldn't climb one behind the other; the person ahead might dislodge a rock that would tumble down onto the guy below.

I ascended and waited with Juli and Erik. The three of us were sitting on the side of the mountain taking in the incredible scenery around us and wondering when the next storm was going to hit when we heard some rocks come loose, then the sound of rocks falling, and then a bloodcurdling scream.

Mark and Mike hadn't wanted to be separated. So Mark had ascended the cliff with Mike right below him, just like I had warned them not to do. Mark had knocked a rock loose; that had caused a rock avalanche, and...*bam!*

I climbed down to them and found Mike holding his right hand, which had been smashed by a boulder. He was in shock as he looked down at the bloody stump of flesh—all that I could see was a little piece of the palm.

I quickly wrapped his hand with the military OD green triangular bandage that I was wearing as a headband and yelled to Erik, "Set up a tent. Tell Juli to activate the emergency personal-locator beacon!"

Juli activated the beacon, and the race organizers in Argentina dispatched a medevac helicopter, which arrived forty minutes later. In the meantime, I bandaged and splinted Mike's hand and stopped the bleeding.

We found a small ledge on the side of the mountain for the helo to land, and when it did we carried Mike aboard. Fortunately, the helicopter took off minutes before the storm hit, otherwise Mike would have had to wait until it blew over.

His cousin Mark was an emotional wreck, so I said to him, "Mark, you might as well leave the race. Take care of your cousin."

But Mark was determined to finish.

Next, we had to descend twenty-five hundred feet down the side of a snowy mountain and climb over another range. The ride was a blast. You basically sat on your backpack, used your ice pick to steer, and glissaded all the way down.

Juli went first, then Erik.

Before I left, I asked Mark, "Are you sure you're going to be okay?"

He answered, "I'll be fine; I just need a minute. You go ahead."

I went down like a shot.

At the bottom Erik and Juli asked me, "How do you think he's going to do?"

As we watched, Mark stumbled, fell, and tumbled all the way down the mountain. Before he even reached the bottom, we started to set up the tent and radio for medevac. He was badly broken up.

After Mark was medevaced, all that remained of Team Odyssey was me, Erik, and Juli. We flew through the rest of the course, passing twenty-seven teams in the next two days. Late in the race, I sank into a patch of quicksand.

Also, during two days of continuous paddling, I saw a beautiful Chinese girl in a traditional costume emerge from the water just in front of my canoe, and I stopped paddling. Erik, who was sitting behind me, asked, "What's the matter, Don? Are you okay?"

"I don't want to hit the girl." Of course, there was no girl.

The three of us made it to the finish along with about half of the teams that had entered, but our finish was unofficial because we didn't have a full team.

That was my first adventure race and I loved it. I was getting tired of the triathlons, with just the three sports. Adventure racing was much more exciting. By this time I had competed in over a thousand endurance competitions and I was looking for something more—and I had found it. So I immediately started planning and training for the next Raid, which was going to take place in South Africa in 1996.

That summer I was training with a group of athletes who were interested in participating too. Five of us paddled for twelve hours, then drove to the mountains in western Virginia and ran with packs and boots for fifty miles. Following that we mountain biked for another fifty miles with backpacks.

After we returned to Virginia Beach, we rode our bicycles another sixty miles at high speed (about twenty-three miles an hour, average).

As soon as the bike ride was over, I flew to Atlanta with a group of ST-6 operators to provide liaison and security to the Atlanta Summer Olympics, where 10,320 athletes from 197 countries were going to compete in 271 events. We landed, were briefed about the area we would be operating in and the mission, and were told we had ten hours before we had to report to FBI headquarters.

We were staying in a military barracks near a small park outside of Atlanta, which we were told was a known site of drug deals and homosexual hookups. Beyond the park stood several wooded mountains. Even though I was exhausted, I did a twelve-mile mountain-trail run.

On the way to the barracks, I stopped at the base gym to finish my three-day nonstop workout. I crushed myself on the leg-extension machine. Usually I could lift 340 pounds, but this time I could only lift around 30—I was beat!

Wanting to push myself until I didn't have anything at all left, I started to run back to the barracks, passing through the park that we had been told to avoid. When I stopped behind a tree to urinate, I pissed pure blood.

I'd done this other times during ultra-distance runs and wasn't particularly concerned. But now I felt light-headed and collapsed to the ground.

I woke up minutes later by the tree, with my shorts down, wondering where the heck I was. I couldn't even remember the name of the city, or the state.

I pulled up my shorts and started to walk. And as I did, my head started to clear.

Later, when I explained to the guys on the ST-6 security detail what had happened to me, they joked to the FBI guys that I'd been assaulted in the park.

On the night of July 27, 1996, thousands of spectators gathered in the town square area of Centennial Olympic Park for a late-night concert by Jack Mack and the Heart Attack, whose big hit was "Cardiac Party." Sometime around midnight, someone planted a green U.S. military field pack containing three pipe bombs surrounded by nails underneath a bench near the base of a concert sound tower. The bombs weighed more than forty pounds and used a steel plate as a directional device.

Security guard Richard Jewell discovered the suspicious field pack and alerted Georgia Federal Bureau of Investigation officers. Nine minutes later, the bomber called 911 and alerted authorities.

I was on duty at the operations center with an FBI agent when we got the call. It went something like "My brother-in-law is a nut. He told us that he built a pipe bomb and that he would be famous at these Olympics."

We'd received dozens of similar calls.

But we decided to take this call seriously and alert authorities, who started to clear concertgoers from the park. At 1:20 a.m., while Richard Jewell and other security officials were in the process of ushering people out, the bomb exploded, killing one woman and injuring over a hundred others. Another man, a Turkish photographer, died from a heart attack while running away from the blast.

President Bill Clinton condemned the bombing as "an evil act of terror" and vowed, "We will spare no effort to find out who was responsible for this murderous act. We will track them down. We will bring them to justice."

Thirty-four-year-old Richard Jewell was initially lauded as a hero. But three days it came out in the news that the FBI was treating him as a suspect. They conducted several searches of the house where he lived with his mother. Several months later, the investigating U.S. attorney cleared Jewell of all charges.

The investigation stalled until early 1997, when the Atlanta bombing was linked to two other bombings in the Atlanta area. After a massive manhunt, fugitive Eric Robert Rudolph was arrested in Murphy, North Carolina, and sentenced to life in prison.

As the advanced-training officer at ST-6, I organized and conducted elaborate training exercises—capability exercises (CAPEX), we called them. Sometimes we'd rent commercial cruise liners for a week at a cost in excess of a million dollars and practice taking them down.

Often we deployed all three SEAL assault teams, along with the snipers, breachers, and coxswains, and worked with helicopters and ships. We would spend an entire week climbing up the sides of the ship from the cigarette boats, rappelling down from the helos, taking down the ship's ballroom, disabling the engines, and defusing elaborate IEDs. It was an exercise in coordination with the air assets, boat assets, assault teams, and ship crews.

We also practiced jumping from passenger jets. We'd be sitting in a Boeing 727 with the passengers in the front of the plane and our parachutes stashed in the luggage compartment. Once we got close to our target, we'd move to the back of the aircraft, which would be partitioned off by a curtain.

We'd open the door to the luggage compartment and retrieve our parachutes, then crank open the back door of the jet. The first four guys would position themselves on the stairs. When the green light went on, they jumped. Then the rest of the team would run down the steps and jump. We needed to exit quickly so that the separation between all the jumpers in the air wasn't too great. We usually achieved a tight stack and flew, bumping canopies.

We even had passenger jets specially designed so the seats would turn around to make room for us to don our chutes. We practiced this often.

In addition to being the ST-6 advanced-training officer, I served as the weapons of mass destruction (WMD) officer, which became the most important program that ST-6 was involved with at the time. We went from a counterterrorism team to a counter-WMD team. Part of my responsibility was to help track and recover approximately two hundred nuclear weapons that had gone missing when the Soviet Union disintegrated in 1990.

A large number of these had vanished from Soviet stockpiles in the Ukraine, Belarus, and Kazakhstan, which had been part of the

Soviet Union. Pyotr Simonenko, head of the Ukrainian Communist Party, admitted to reporters, "Out of 2,400 nuclear warheads which were on Ukrainian territory, only 2,200 can be accounted for. Nobody," he said, "has any idea where the other 200 deadly warheads have gone."

Maybe he didn't, but we did. Most of them were recovered. But a number of former Soviet nukes found their way to North Korea, where they were being hidden in large underground tunnels.

███

███

███████████████████████████████ door was not a problem. But breaching tunnels fortified with layers of concrete and steel was a completely different challenge.

Upon learning that there were tunnels of similar size and reinforcement throughout Europe, we coordinated training with some of our NATO counterparts. We surveyed their tunnels to test their vulnerability to an attack. This was very valuable information to the host nation and also taught us a great deal about what it would take.

Many of the tunnels had been built during World War II to serve as bomb shelters. In Norway, there was one twenty-six miles long that served as a hydroelectric plant. Another tunnel had been converted into a huge underground ice-skating rink.

I can't say much more about the WMD program except that it was a success. The team I worked with also helped locate and recover a number of former Soviet nuclear scientists who were selling their bomb-making expertise to other countries.

But not everything at ST-6 was so life and death—or limited to official business. Once I was traveling with a new ST-6 corpsman named Reed to do some Pararescue training with the PJs in Albuquerque, New Mexico.

As we checked into the hotel, I noticed some pamphlets on the front desk advertising local activities. One devoted to a balloon festival caught my attention.

I turned to Reed and said, "Hey, Reed, why don't we go jump out of a balloon this weekend?"

He looked at me like I was crazy and answered, "I don't know, Don. We don't even have parachutes."

"We'll have to find some."

First, I had to see if I could find a balloonist who would let us jump from his hot-air balloon. Everybody I contacted said no.

Eventually I located this old hippie with a gray beard and long hair. He said, "Sure, dude. But last time I let a jumper out, I smashed into the mountains and ripped off my kneecap."

He explained that when someone jumps out of the basket, the balloon loses so much weight that it goes spastic.

But he was a cool guy and willing to try again. He told us that he'd be going aloft early the next morning when the air was thick, which enabled the balloons to get off the ground. We agreed to meet at 0300.

Now Reed and I had to find chutes. At the time all of us at ST-6 were jumping with MT1X parachutes, which were also used by the Air Force. So we went over to the air loft at the USAF base and found the chief rigger. Reed and I were these longhaired guys who didn't look like normal military. And we didn't have our jump logs with us, because we hadn't planned on jumping during the trip.

I went up to the chief rigger and said, "I'm Chief Mann and this is my teammate Reed. We are both SEAL medics going through the PJ course. And we'd like to ask you if we could borrow a couple of MT1X chutes for a balloon jump tomorrow."

The rigger looked at me like I was crazy and said, "Sorry, Chief, but no way."

Another rigger who was packing reserve chutes on the other side of the room called us over after the chief rigger left.

He said, "Guys, I'll be on duty tonight, and see that table over there? The door will probably be unlocked, and there will be two MT1X parachutes lying on that table. If they happen to be gone when I come back, I'll need them back by tomorrow night."

We went out and bought him a case of beer, then returned later and took the parachutes off the table.

Reed and I didn't have jump boots, suits, helmets, or altimeters. Nor did we have time to repack the chutes.

We found our way to the large, open desert field where the Albuquerque balloon festival was taking place. Some balloons were already going up, and others were filling with heated air.

The basket could only accommodate two people at a time, so I climbed in first with the old hippie. He turned a valve, releasing propane from the tank, which caused the flame under the balloon to grow larger and fill the balloon with hot (lighter) air. The balloon started to rise gently from the ground.

Looking out from the basket, I was treated to an amazing sight— hundreds of different-colored balloons decorated the sky that changed hue by the second as the sun crept over the horizon.

I was taking it all in when the old hippie said, "Okay, dude. You can jump anytime."

I had made more than five hundred jumps, and every time I'd jumped, I'd had a jumpmaster with me who gave me a pre-jump inspection and spotted the jump.

This time I was on my own. I had no idea how high we were and how much time I had before I could deploy my chute.

I stood on the edge of the basket and watched different balloons sail by. When I saw a clear space around and under us, I pushed off.

It felt like a base jump, which meant that I was falling right away. When you jump from a plane that's moving at 120 knots, you're initially moving at 120 knots too.

But this was more like a bungee jump. I felt an initial rush, waited for the air that I was pushing through to get louder, then pulled. The chute opened, and I had only a few seconds of floating under the canopy before I landed.

Now it was Reed's turn. The balloonist landed and Reed went up and jumped.

After that it was propane and champagne, which is the motto of ballooners.

Teams and shit. What a thrill!

CHAPTER FIFTEEN

Retirement from ST-6

Whatever you do, you must pay the price.
—*Angelika Castaneda,*
world-class triathlete

One of the toughest people I've met in my life wasn't a SEAL; she was an Austrian named Angelika Castaneda. She and her identical twin sister, Barbara Warren (who died in 2008 after a bicycle crash in a triathlon), were world-class adventure racers, triathletes, and ultra-distance runners. Both were tall, blond, and beautiful, and had previously been high-fashion models. Angelika used to work as Farrah Fawcett's stunt double.

I recruited her to be part of my five-person team for the 1997 Raid Gauloises in Lesotho, South Africa. Even though I was still the advanced-training officer and WMD officer for ST-6, I had a ravenous appetite for new challenges and excitement.

In addition to Angelika, I recruited my buddy Lieutenant John Kainer, who had been stationed with me in Panama and was a member of SEAL Teams Two and Six. In late '96, the two of us traveled to the Gauley River near Summersville, West Virginia, to test the two remaining candidates for Team Odyssey—Special Forces Major Alan Holmes, an accomplished triathlete, and Nick Spaeder, a great athlete and platoon chief at ST-2.

In three days, the four of us paddled seventy-five miles and ran ninety miles with backpacks and boots.

We flew to Johannesburg in January, and I remember sitting with Angelika and a reporter at a restaurant a few days before the start of the Raid. I'd watched Angelika bonk badly during another competition—crawling on her hands and knees, defecating, and passing out—and I wanted to make sure that she ate enough before the race.

When I expressed my concern, she answered in her charming Austrian accent, "Don, I will not die on you. I might feel like I'm going to die, but I will not die. My body will eat from itself."

She was hard core.

We always used superglue to repair cuts, bruises, and blisters. It sealed the skin and helped prevent infection. But toenails were always a problem in long races. Sometimes they'd turn brown and black, and you had to peel them off. Other times, they'd fall off altogether.

As I was pulling out my seventh toenail of the race, Angelika reprimanded me. "Don," she said, "if you're serious about these races, you'll have your toenails removed before the race. Have them pulled out and have them sew the skin together so they don't grow back."

Of course, she'd already had hers removed.

We started the Raid in South Africa at the foothills of the magnificent Champagne Castle Peak, and then we trekked, rappelled, paddled, biked, and portaged our boats more than five hundred miles over some of the most unforgiving terrain on earth.

Unlike marathons and triathlons, adventure racing isn't about athletic performance alone. You have to plot and navigate the entire course, deal with team dynamics—which include the pain and emotional lows and highs—sickness, bonking, anger, sleep deprivation, and hallucinations. In addition, you face the challenges of Mother Nature—fog, rain, snow, lightning, strong winds, and brutally high heat and freezing temperatures.

The sport tests you in every way possible. I'm proud to say that Team Odyssey finished in the top ten out of the seventy top adventure teams in the world that year.

The next year, in October of 1998, Team Odyssey competed in the Raid Gauloises in Ecuador. Among the physical challenges we faced this time was scaling a 19,600-foot live volcano named El Cotopaxi (Neck of the Moon). I suffered altitude sickness on the climb but recovered to complete the event.

When I wasn't competing with Team Odyssey, I raced in ultra-distance marathons and bike races. And I was conducting SEAL training events for civilians. One of these events took place in Utah, right down the road from the home of NBA superstar Karl Malone. After the event, he invited our five-man SEAL training cadre to meet his wife and children.

I ran to his home from our hotel (twelve or so miles), which he got a huge kick out of. Towering over me, he asked, "In the SEALs, do they ever drop you in the middle of nowhere and you have to find your way back?"

I laughed and said, "Yeah. And sometimes you have to shoot your way out."

"Do they make you swim a lot?"

"Yes," I answered. "They do."

He had his two pretty little girls with him. At one point, he turned to them and said, "Tell this man, what does Daddy do besides play basketball?"

Without missing a beat, they answered, "All Daddy ever does is watch SEAL movies."

One of those movies was, unfortunately, *Navy SEALs*, a film starring Charlie Sheen. I say *unfortunately* because I was part of a group of SEALs who had been asked to serve as consultants on the movie. Chuck Pfarrer, who had been a SEAL at ST-6, based the script on real events. But, in typical Hollywood style, his original script was rewritten many times until it bore little resemblance to reality.

Over the course of the production, most of the SEALs who had been hired as consultants quit. Charlie Sheen constantly worried about getting hurt. He'd stop filming in the midst of an action scene to make sure the cameras picked up the pretty side of his face. He wouldn't have lasted a week in BUD/S.

In between training, racing, and working at SEAL Team Six, I was trying to sort out my personal life. One of the girls I dated was a beautiful Australian athlete and diver named Paula.

Once when we were diving together in the Caribbean, we snuck into a shark feeding, where three guys with bang sticks and a bucket of fish were feeding the sharks.

I said to Paula, "Let's swim down near the wall, so that nothing can get behind us."

The wall was about three feet above our heads. We saw big fish starting to surround the guys who were doing the feeding. Then, before we knew it, the water around us was filled with hundreds of fish, including seven or eight very scary-looking eight-foot sharks—bull sharks, reef sharks, lemon sharks, sharp-nosed sharks, and hammerheads. As Paula and I watched helplessly, one of them approached, jaws wide open, and at the last moment swam over our heads. I've never felt so completely out of control.

Though Paula and I shared many interests, we didn't have enough in common to forge a deeper relationship. For one thing, she didn't believe in God, while I do. Things that upset me, like people not respecting their country and burning the flag, she thought were no big deal.

One of the best divers, shooters, and jumpers, and also a plank owner ████████████████████████████ at ST-6 was a guy named Ray—he was a good friend and fellow corpsman. For a while, I dated his sister, Janna, and was very friendly with his whole family, including his wife and the mother of their two sons, Dawn.

One day while we were working together at ST-6, Ray told me that he and Dawn were getting divorced. I was sad to hear that because they were both terrific people and Christian and Dylan were great kids.

A couple of months later, Ray approached me again and said, "Don, I've found someone else and I'm moving on. But Dawn is lonely. Why don't you take her out?"

"Me? Take out your ex-wife? I can't do that."

He said, "No, really, take her to a movie or something. Call her up."

I'd always admired Dawn and found her very attractive but had never thought of her in a romantic way, and I didn't want to insert myself in the middle of a difficult situation.

But Ray kept urging me to call her, so I did, and one night we ran into each other at a local Virginia Beach hangout called Phil's Grill, where we talked and drank a couple of beers.

Then Ray called me and invited me to come over to his house for Christmas dinner. Dawn picked me up, Ray cooked dinner, and we all sat together at the same table—Ray, his new girlfriend, me, Dawn, and Christian and Dylan.

It was an unusual first date. But it soon became apparent to both of us that we were meant for each other. We shared the same values, liked many of the same things, and, more important, fell deeply in love. Dawn told me that ten years ago, back when she first met me, she would have wanted nothing to do with me because I was too wild. Now I was more mature and a bit more settled down.

Dawn moved into my empty bachelor's pad in Virginia Beach and turned it into a beautiful home. Christian, her older son, lived with us, while Dylan stayed with his dad. While Dawn and I were happy, it soon became apparent that twenty-year-old Christian was having a hard time.

From the outside, Christian had everything going for him. He was strong, good-looking, athletic, had graduated from high school with honors, and was great with kids. He went to church regularly and worked out.

But while he was attending college at Old Dominion University in Norfolk, Virginia, he started drifting and hanging out with people who were dealing drugs.

He'd come home late at night with his pants hanging down below his underwear, a hat worn sideways, and a glazed look in his eyes. He was a smart young man, but somewhat naïve about the world. I tried many times to warn him about the drug scene he was starting to enter.

I said, "Christian, you might not know it, but you've got everything in the world going for you right now. You've got a beautiful girlfriend, you're doing well in college, you're young and athletic. Don't screw it up. If you're having problems or are confused about something, let us know."

He maintained that he was fine. But soon we started seeing less and less of him. He'd sleep until noon, go to school, hang out with his friends, and come home sometime in the early morning.

Both Dawn and I were concerned about him, but we didn't know what to do. And Christian wasn't sharing anything.

One night after he and his girlfriend came back from a trip to Florida, the four of us were sitting around the dining room table eating dinner. Both Dawn and I were curious about the purpose of the trip.

So I said, "Hey, Christian, how was your trip to Florida?"

"Fine. I went there to chill for a few days."

"That's funny," I said. "Because you know my friend John, the FBI agent who lives down the street? He said something about your cell phone and having your cell phone number. Is there any reason he'd be following your cell phone?"

Upon hearing this, Christian's girlfriend dropped her fork and said, "Oh God. I'm feeling sick."

This confirmed our suspicion that Christian had gone to Florida to sell or transport drugs.

I called my brother, Rick, who was involved with AA and NA, and explained what Christian was going through. And I spoke to friends who worked in law enforcement and drug rehabilitation. They all said the same thing: You can't help someone with a drug or alcohol problem unless he wants help.

Both Dawn and I tried talking to him. Some nights I'd be up in his room until five in the morning trying to get through to him. But nothing we said seemed to work.

One night Dawn went up to his room and found sixteen thousand dollars in cash. She came down the stairs holding it in her hands and said, "Look, Don. Whatever Christian's doing, he appears to be good at it."

She said it in a sarcastic way. Both of us were very alarmed.

I said, "Hide it. It's dirty money. We're going to find something positive to do with it. But in the meantime, put it away."

A couple days later, Christian confronted her and said, "Mom, I need that money."

"Why?" she asked.

"I want to buy a Lexus."

"No, you don't," I said.

"I need a good car to drive back and forth to school."

"A Lexus? Come on, Christian," I shot back. "A Lexus would only advertise that you are in the drug culture."

He found the cash Dawn had hidden and added it to other money he had to buy the Lexus. I told him that he couldn't park it in the driveway. I was pissed.

He parked it on the curb in front of our house, and was coming home later at night and more infrequently.

One night, as Christian was driving back from a Snoop Dog concert, he was stopped by the police. They searched his car and found a couple of ounces of marijuana in the backseat. Christian was arrested, and the Lexus was confiscated.

Two uniformed policemen showed up at our front door to explain what had happened.

I said to the two young officers, "I don't blame you for arresting our son. If I saw someone driving a new Lexus away from a Snoop Dog concert, I'd follow them too."

One of the police officers said, "No, Mr. Mann. He was going eighty miles an hour through a red light and was sloped so far down in the front seat we couldn't even see his head."

Christian's father, Ray, took out a second mortgage on his house to raise the bail money to get Christian out of jail.

When Christian returned home, I sat him down and said, "Christian, now you've got a big strike against you. Your life is going to be a lot harder. I know. I've been there. I know the excitement, the adrenaline rush you get from the outlaw lifestyle, but you've got to stop. You can turn your life around. Look at me. I turned my life around and managed to change, and you can do the same."

A couple of months later, Christian was arrested again for possession of marijuana.

Now, for the first time, Christian seemed concerned. When I

spoke to him after his second arrest, I felt like he was hearing what I said.

"Christian, now you're really in trouble. I know that I've been saying this for a long time. But now you have no options. Turn in the names of the drug punks you're hanging out with. In order to save yourself, you've got to turn them in. You've got no other choice. They're not your friends, and they don't deserve to live in our society."

He did. Christian went to the police and gave them the names of a couple of the big drug dealers he was working for, including a thug called Marc. Christian also stopped dressing like a gangbanger and got a good job working at a hotel.

Marc and another drug dealer were arrested; they posted bond and were released within a week.

That weekend, Dawn and I were in Kentucky staging a five-day adventure race we had organized, the Beast of the East, when we got a call from Christian's girlfriend.

She asked, "Has Dylan called you yet?" Dylan was Christian's fifteen-year-old brother.

She sounded upset.

"Where are you calling from?" I asked.

"I just want to know if Dylan has told you anything yet about Christian?"

"What happened to Christian?" I asked, fearing the worst.

She said, "You'd better call the hospital right away!"

Oh God...I didn't want Dawn to know. I snuck off to a quiet room and telephoned the hospital.

The doctor attending to Christian told me, "Sir, you'd better get here quickly. Your son is very, very ill. He's got a head injury."

"What kind of head injury? What happened?"

"He was shot in the head."

I was the director of the race, and Dawn was running operations and handling all the staff and logistics. Luckily, we had an incredible staff who were able to take over.

Dawn and I got in our truck and I drove ten hours at a hundred miles an hour, stopping only for coffee and gas. During the trip, Dawn was on the cell phone with Ray, who was sitting with Christian in the hospital.

He said, "Get here quick. He's on a respirator and they want to take him off. His body's ballooning up."

Dawn said to him, "Put the phone up to Christian's ear."

She spoke in a voice full of love and emotion. "Christian, I love you. Don't try to hang on if you don't want to. Just let go."

It broke my heart to hear a mother say that to her son.

We drove directly to the hospital in Norfolk, arriving at sunrise, and ran up to his room. We had to push by a nurse, who actually said, "Would you people hurry up? We've got to get that boy out of there and clean up his room." It took all I had not to smack her across the face.

Ray stood in the room with Dylan, who was having a hard time looking at his brother lying there unconscious and breathing through tubes.

While Dawn held Christian, we all said a prayer for him. With tears in our eyes we walked out together. Minutes later Christian was taken off the respirator and died.

We found out later from his girlfriend that she and Christian had been sitting at home watching TV when he got a call from a girl who said she was interested in buying his car. We didn't know this, but apparently he'd decided to sell it and had placed an ad in the newspaper.

The girl wanted to see the car immediately. Christian told her that he was taking his girlfriend out and could not show it that night but could at another time.

But she insisted, and Christian relented, driving directly to the address she gave him in Norfolk. Two young guys walked out of the building and said that they wanted to test the car.

Christian, even though he had been working with drug dealers, wasn't street-smart at all.

He sat in the backseat and let the two guys sit up front. They drove to an intersection, stopped the car, and pulled Christian out. According to witnesses, this took place at around four forty in the afternoon.

The driver pulled out a revolver and shot at Christian six times. One bullet tore into his elbow, another ripped into his abdomen.

Christian lay on the ground screaming, "I've been shot! I've been shot!"

A small bespectacled man in his fifties named Bill heard Christian yelling and ran out of his house. He saw the shooter reloading his revolver, ran up to him, and tried to push the pistol out of his hand.

Bill's actions were heroic, but the shooter was stronger. He shoved Bill aside and raised the pistol.

As Bill yelled, "Don't! Don't do it!" the gunman shot Christian in the head.

Later, Marc was overheard bragging in a bar that he had executed the hit for two hundred dollars.

Reports of Christian's death were all over the evening news, along with footage of his blood on the street. Dawn watched, and then turned to me and said, "Don, I want to go there."

I said, "No, sweetheart. You don't want to go there now."

But she was determined to go. So I drove her to Norfolk and found the intersection. We saw the bloodstains, the bullet holes in the road, and the chalk marks the police had drawn. Dawn even got down on her knees and touched the dried blood. Then she said, "I want to ask the neighbors if any of them saw this."

We found seven eyewitnesses. One of them told us, "Stuff like this happens around here all the time. It used to be a nice neighborhood, but the gangs have moved in." When we met Bill, the man who tried to save Christian's life, Dawn hugged him and told him he was an angel.

A week or so later, we attended what would have been Christian's graduation ceremony from Old Dominion University. Governor Mark Warner of Virginia called out Christian's name, walked over to where we were sitting, and handed Dawn her son's diploma. Christian had graduated with honors.

All of us who had known and loved him were devastated.

As Dawn was going through Christian's things, she found his diary. In it he described in detail how he was trying to turn his life around. He wrote about his discussions with the police and about the drug dealers he'd turned in. One of them was named Marc. In the last entry, Christian wrote, *Marc is going to have me killed.*

He knew.

Tremendous anger mixed with guilt burned inside me. I kept thinking to myself that I was the one who had convinced Christian to talk to the police and turn in the drug dealers.

I felt that I had to track Marc down and kill him. It didn't take me long to locate his address in Virginia Beach, where he was living with his two young daughters.

I didn't want to harm his girls but I had no problem ending the life of the scumbag drug-dealing murderer who'd killed Dawn's son. After watching Marc's house and tracking his movements, I came up with three options for taking him out:

1. I'd knock on the door, ID him, and shoot him with my .45—twice in the chest, once in the head, the Mozambique drill.

2. I'd take him out from across the street with a long shot from my M4.

3. When I was sure that his daughters weren't home, I'd blow up his house with explosives.

I settled on the first option and had an alibi all worked out. But Dawn knew me well enough to intuit what I was about to do and asked me not to. She said, "I don't want his daughters to grow up as orphans."

She'd been following Marc's case in court. Once, when she was at the courthouse, she'd passed Marc on her way up the stairs. He turned and looked at her with a smirk, as if to say, *Yeah, I had your son killed, and no one's gonna touch me.*

I asked her to stop going. Marc was eventually arrested and served a jail term for another crime.

But the incident left terrible emotional scars on all of us.

A couple months later, Dawn and I traveled to Hawaii. While we were there we met an actor from *Baywatch* who told us that a huge storm was blowing into the northern shore, and it was attracting surfers from all over the world. He explained that it was a weather phenomenon that happened every six or seven years and suggested that we go surfing with him.

I said, "Thanks, but I'm not a surfer."

He said, "That's okay, dude. I've got this big board with me. And since you're an athlete, you'll be fine."

Dawn didn't want me to go, but I couldn't back down from a challenge. As soon as I got in the water, I started to realize that I'd made a mistake. The waves were immense, and the undertow was powerful.

Wearing a leash that connected my foot to the board, I paddled half an hour until I was almost half a mile out, past the surf zone where most of the waves were breaking.

I was so far out, I couldn't see Dawn, who was nervously pacing the beach, hoping I didn't hurt myself badly.

Exhausted by the long paddle against the current, I lay on the long board and watched the expert surfers—many of whom were Hawaiian—surf the pipeline the half mile into shore.

As I was lying there on my board, one of the Hawaiians gave me the thumb-and-pinkie Hawaiian wave and pointed to the wall of water behind me. "Hey, dude. This one is going to get you."

I looked behind me and saw this enormous wall of water collapsing. It hit me like a freight train, causing my board to shoot up and pull me with it into the air. Then I slammed down into the water. I felt like I was stuck in a huge washing machine, going up and down and spinning. All I could do was pray that the board didn't smash me in the head.

It reminded me of running out of air under the ship. I couldn't wait to surface and breathe, and I tried to remain calm.

When I started getting close to shore, I got my feet under me, grabbed my leash, and pulled it. At the end of it was a two-foot piece of surfboard. That's all that was left.

Dawn, who had seen pieces of my surfboard wash up on the beach, looked very relieved when she saw me emerge from the water in one piece.

She said, "Don't you ever, ever do that again!"

"Don't worry. I won't."

We were married that weekend.

In August of 1998, I reached my twenty-first year in the Navy. Twenty years served was the minimum requirement for retirement. Since there wasn't a lot going on in the teams, I decided to retire and dedicate myself to adventure sports, racing, and climbing.

It was a difficult decision, which meant letting go of the only job I had ever wanted—being a Navy SEAL. It also required my turning in my weapons, dive and jump gear, and beeper.

I could have stayed for another nine years and probably retired as a CWO5 instead of a CWO3.

But I figured that I was still young and fit enough to complete many of the great adventures I'd been dreaming of doing—including climbing the seven summits, starting with Mount Everest. I'd also have more time to spend with my family.

I didn't know how I'd make money, but I would work that out later.

Usually when guys retire from ST-6, it's a big deal with a formal ceremony. But I knew my parents couldn't make the trip, because my mom was ill with emphysema. So instead, I wrote a letter to all the guys at the command. I talked about how much I respected them and had enjoyed working with them at ST-6. I explained why I didn't want a big ceremony and ended by saying, *This is my good-bye.*

I was only forty years old and in excellent physical condition. I thought I'd be spending the next decade or two of my life training, racing, and climbing all over the world.

CHAPTER SIXTEEN

The Dirt Circuit

We rejoice in our suffering because we
know that suffering produces perseverance, perseverance produces character,
character produces hope. And hope does
not disappoint us.

—*Romans 5:3–5*

I put the same energy and commitment I had for SEALs into extreme ultra-distance endurance sports. Since I'd paddled, run, and biked the mountainous terrain of Virginia and West Virginia many times, I knew it was the perfect setting for a long-distance adventure race. It wouldn't be as dramatic as an event staged in a foreign country, but I figured by holding it in Virginia, I could keep the cost and entry fees low. Instead of having athletes pay twenty thousand or more each and race five hundred miles in ten days overseas, why not produce an event that was just as challenging, three hundred and fifty miles in five days here in the United States?

Together with Joy Marr, one of the first female river guides in the United States and an incredible athlete and event organizer, and Mike Nolan, another exceptional athlete, we founded a company called Odyssey Adventure Racing (OAR) and staged our first event—

the grueling Beast of the East. Soon, Dawn joined our team and managed all of the race operations.

I had to sell my beloved Harley-Davidson and mortgage my house to help finance it, but the Beast of the East was a great success. Soon after, my phone started ringing off the hook. Athletes loved the concept of my low-cost, grassroots adventure race and wanted to know if we could organize a shorter race that could be completed over a weekend.

So OAR produced a two-day race, the Endorphin Fix, which became known as the world's toughest two-day adventure race. Before we knew it, Odyssey Adventure Racing was producing up to twenty-one extreme sporting events a year—including Mega Dose, Odyssey One-Day Adventure Race, Jeep Kentucky Adventure Race, Jeep Kentucky Sprint Race, Expedition British Virgin Islands, Odyssey Triple Iron (7.2-mile swim, 336-mile bike ride, 78.6-mile run), Odyssey Double Iron, Odyssey Half Iron, Odyssey Off-Road (Xterra Qualifier), Odyssey Off-Road Iron (the world's most difficult triathlon), and the Odyssey Off-Road Half Iron.

The company motto was Your Pain Is Our Pleasure, and I meant this literally.

At OAR, we trained thousands of athletes and helped grow the sport of extreme ultra-distance racing. By the year 2000 OAR had become a burgeoning business, and adventure racing was starting to gain mainstream appeal in the United States.

But we had a competitor in Hollywood producer Mark Burnett (who went on to fame and riches with the TV show *Survivor* and many others). Mark saw money to be made in the burgeoning sport of adventure racing and organized a televised race called the Eco-Challenge. But many of the serious competitors considered the Eco-Challenge to be a camping trip compared to the Beast of the East.

Mark started calling me all the time. He said, "Don, you're the hamburger stand down the street that everybody likes going to, but let's face it, I'm the McDonald's. Let's join forces. If anybody wants to do an Eco-Challenge they'll have to qualify by doing the Beast first."

The idea appealed to me, but there were two problems. One, I was in it for the love of the sport, and he was in it to make money. And two, he wanted a big cut in my sponsorship money and race fees, which meant that I would lose control of my own events.

Meanwhile, Odyssey Adventure Racing was planning the first world championship, Beast Alaska. Soon, I started getting phone calls from some of the world's greatest adventure racers. It turned out that Mark had contacted many of the athletes who had registered for the Beast Alaska and were listed on OAR's Web site and offered them free airfare and sponsorship if they did the Eco-Challenge instead.

One of the most accomplished women in the sport, Jane Hall, called me from New Zealand in tears. She said, "Don, I'm so sorry, but I'm just a poor athlete and had to accept Mark's offer."

My next call was from world-champion adventure racer Ian Adamson. He also told me he had received a call from Mark and was dropping out of the Beast Alaska to race in the Eco-Challenge.

Over the next couple of weeks, we lost many of our competitors and a potential broadcast deal with the USA Network. They signed with Mark Burnett instead.

In 1998, I received a call from the U.S. Navy Recruiting Command. They said, "Hey, Don, the Marines have the Marine Corps Marathon. The Army has the Army Ten-Miler. Do you have any ideas for the Navy? We need a way to recruit SEALs."

I said, "I train guys who want to become SEALs all the time. I put them through two-day-hell weekend training. "

A few weeks later, I sat down with the people from NRC, a group of lawyers, and some Hollywood producers and presented my plans for a televised forty-eight-hour event called the SEAL Adventure Challenge that would include running through mud and sand, PT drills, diving, and shooting.

They loved it.

I said, "Whatever you do, be careful. Because if Mark Burnett hears about this idea, he'll steal it."

Months later, Mark Burnett announced that he was developing a new TV show called *Combat Missions*, which was very similar to SEAL Adventure Challenge. *Combat Missions* ran for one season and disappeared.

Despite the challenges I faced in the business end of the sport, my love for extreme-distance adventure sports only grew stronger. It helped that I was training and competing with the world's most elite adventure athletes.

In April of 2000, I competed with Team Odyssey in the tenth Raid Gauloises, in the Himalayas. Rounding out the team this time were the Crane brothers—Adrian and Dick—Terri Schneider, and Andrew Matulionis. Back in '83 Dick and Adrian had trekked the length of the Himalayas (3,500 kilometers) in 101 days, carrying only ten pounds of gear, including a camera, one water container, and a pair of socks and one outfit each.

The rivalry between the brothers, who are also best friends, was intense. In 1985 Dick rode a bicycle up Mount Kilimanjaro (19,500 feet), thereby setting the world record for the highest altitude cycled. Adrian broke that record two years later when he bicycled up Chimborazo in Ecuador, approximately 20,500 feet.

Both Terri and Andrew were elite adventure racers. Terri was an Ironman champion, while Andrew was the Iditasport one-hundred-mile champion.

Sixty-nine teams took part in the tenth Raid Gauloises. After two days of acclimatizing to the high altitude of the Tibetan Plateau (average elevation: 14,800 feet), we started on foot with Mount Everest at our side, then completed 800 kilometers of horseback riding, mountain biking, and more trekking. By this point all of us in Team Odyssey were suffering from altitude sickness.

We'd also been warned before the race about possibly running into Maoist rebels who were fighting to overthrow the government of Nepal. During a fifty-mile trek/run section of the course that ended at the Nepalese border, I had to take a bathroom break and told my teammates to continue without me. So I set down my Kelty pack and trekking poles and ducked behind a tree.

But when I returned, I encountered two very unfriendly-looking fellows armed with machetes standing over my pack. When I moved to pick it up, they blocked my way. I started to back off, then quickly lurched forward and grabbed my trekking poles. Now I had something in my hands to defend myself with.

They tried to stare me down, but I wasn't going to back away. Nor was I going to let them walk off with my pack. I mean, I had a race to finish!

After a few seconds, they turned away and disappeared down the trail.

I caught up with my teammates, and after reaching the Nepal border near Kodari, we continued, canoeing, white-water rafting, and kayaking down the turbulent Sunkosi River. This section concluded with three kilometers of canyoneering, where at one point we had to rappel down a six-hundred-foot waterfall.

Our next challenge was a twenty-three-kilometer section of white-water swimming, where we used fins to help us negotiate the rapids and avoid large boulders. It was like riding a very cold, wet roller coaster.

The race ended in Janakpur, Nepal, after 827 kilometers. Team Nokia from Finland won with a time of six days, twenty-two hours. Despite our best efforts, we finished more than two days later.

* * *

In late 2000, Dawn and I went to Hawaii to conduct a team-building event for Seagate Technology, the world's largest manufacturer of hard drives. CEO Bill Watkins had hired me to spend a week training two hundred of his employees in hiking, kayaking, mountain biking, and rappelling, in preparation for the corporate Seagate adventure race. He saw the race as a way to instill a greater sense of teamwork and accountability throughout his company.

After the race, Bill approached me with an offer. He said that he was willing to invest a million dollars of his own money if I would help create the world's greatest adventure race—which would be named Primal Quest.

Together with my wife, Dawn, our incredible race staff, and over two hundred volunteers, we planned, conducted, and directed Primal Quest Utah (2006), Primal Quest Montana (2008), and Primal Quest Badlands South Dakota (2009).

Primal Quest Utah turned out to be particularly intense, because competitors faced a course of approximately 420 miles and temperatures exceeding 110 degrees Fahrenheit. The four-member coed teams weren't allowed to bring support crews, so they had to carry more gear and all of their food.

Race disciplines included mountain biking, trekking, horseback riding, technical rope skills, mountaineering, kayaking, and whitewater swimming. The event was broadcast internationally as four one-hour episodes on ESPN2, with a one-hour recap and finale on ABC Sports.

The extreme temperatures had a tendency to produce hallucinations. At the end of one seventy-mile paddle section, a participant thanked me for carving the faces of his family members in stone cliffs along the river.

Also, someone captured videotape footage of a snake crawling onto the hot sand and burning to death. Fortunately our competitors fared better, though we did experience one close call when a male racer suffered heatstroke and fell off his bike as he rode into the town of Moab.

He quickly slipped into a coma and was immediately flown to the regional hospital, where they intubated him and attached him to a respirator. Days later, the athlete started to mumble. Someone handed him a pad and a pencil. He wrote that he wanted food.

Shortly after I retired from the Navy, a retired SEAL buddy called me and asked if I would be interested in serving as a weapons and tactics instructor. I didn't want to be tied down to a full-time position, but accepted his offer. Soon I was working as an independent contractor teaching weapons and tactics all over the world, including in Serbia, Ethiopia, Romania, Jordan, Iraq, Afghanistan, Yemen, and other countries.

Part of our mission was to train the security details assigned to guard friendly heads of state. The United States had a vested interest in keeping certain world leaders, prime ministers, and presidents alive. So we would train the protective details of many Middle East heads of state. This could be a challenge because compared to U.S. security, most of the Middle East protective details were very poorly trained, ineffective, and even dangerous. We also trained our allied military troops in marksmanship, CQB, small-unit tactics, defensive driving, and protective operations.

In Serbia I worked closely with an Army captain whose eyes would fill with tears when he talked about the atrocities he and his men had committed during the ethnic cleansing that had taken place there.

I completed one training assignment with ████████████ ██████████ operator and hero of *Black Hawk Down*. One night, while Paul and I were teaching low-light and no-light shooting to some Middle Eastern soldiers, I said to the translator, "Tell the men to be careful that their light doesn't go on accidentally. Because if the enemy sees it, they will shoot at the light."

Paul said, "That's exactly what happened to me in Mogadishu."

"What do you mean?"

"My light accidentally went on and I was shot at. But the skinnies missed, and then I put them all down."

I was in Israel when Prime Minister Yitzhak Rabin was assassinated by a right-wing Israeli radical who opposed Rabin's signing the Oslo Peace Accords. I watched as hundreds of thousands of Israelis took to the streets to light memorial candles and sing peace songs while angry mourners rioted.

A few years later, I was training a group of Palestinians in protective operations. One night after work I went out to dinner with a group of Palestinian officers, who started to open up after a couple of drinks.

One of them turned to me and said, "All we want to do is to be able to pray. Has anyone ever told you that you can't worship in your church?"

"No."

"Has anyone ever told you that you can't go home for three or four days?"

Another one of the officers said, "All we want is the land that used to be ours, and to be able to drive to church, drive home, and drive to work."

I was interested in hearing their perspective. Of course, they didn't mention the fact that Palestinians were hitting Israel with bombs and rockets all the time.

██

██

███████████████████████████

***

When my mother became ill, I stopped deploying as often. Memorial Day weekend 2001 I spent visiting her and my father in Myrtle Beach, South Carolina, where they had retired to a nice home near a golf course. My poor mom was suffering from emphysema and lung cancer and had to breathe through a respirator.

As I kissed her good-bye to return to Virginia Beach to pick up my daughter, my mom whispered, "Don, don't leave."

I said, "Don't worry, Mom. The nurse is here to take care of you. And I'll be back."

Again, she said, "Don't go." I saw fear in her eyes.

While my dad was down the road at the VFW, where he served as state commander, a thunderstorm moved into the area, and my parents' house was struck by lightning. The window between the porch and the bedroom exploded, and the porch caught fire.

As my mother lay in bed too weak to move or call for help, flames from the porch started to spread down the hallway. A neighbor saw the flames and ran into the house to try to rescue her.

The nurse who was with her disconnected my mother's frail eighty-five-pound body from the respirator and was running out of the room with my mother in her arms when the flames reached the oxygen tanks and the house exploded. The nurse survived, but my mother and the Good Samaritan neighbor died in the fire.

My father called me in tears with the awful news. I got into my car and drove as fast as I could back to my parents' home. All that remained was charred wood and ashes.

The first thing I did was visit the neighbor's wife to express my thanks and condolences.

She said, "I always knew that my husband was going to die helping someone. I'm just sorry he couldn't do more."

I couldn't believe the depths of her compassion and kindness. Her husband had died eight hours earlier trying to save my mother, and she was apologizing to me!

I drove to the morgue to view my mother's body. Her face was charred black. Even with all my combat medical experience and training, I couldn't take it. I broke down and ran into the woods in tears.

My mother had been afraid of fire her whole life. She'd always been so good to me, and she had asked me not to leave her.

I felt as if I'd let her down one last time.

I had to keep busy, and by the summer of 2001, I was spending about half my time doing weapons and tactics training and the other half training, racing, climbing, and producing extreme sporting events.

That changed when al-Qaeda terrorists attacked the World Trade Center and the Pentagon on September 11, 2001. My focus immediately switched to the war on global terrorism. Sports took a backseat.

On the day of the attack, I was at a U.S. base overseas training a group of Egyptian commandos in M4 marksmanship and weapons drills. Right after we heard the news, the chief of the base directed us to disarm the Egyptians, stay armed ourselves, and not allow the Egyptians to leave their barracks.

The air was suddenly thick with distrust. I understood that the world had changed immediately and that the United States would be engaged in a war against Islamic terrorists that would last for decades.

Since 9/11, I've been working to help defend our country in a number of different capacities—training people for BUD/S and teaching military, special-police units, and government agencies how to do VBSS; CQB; fast-roping; diving; shooting; urban, jungle, desert, and arctic warfare; and more.

I've deployed to the Middle East many times. In fact, I traveled to Afghanistan soon after the fall of the Taliban in late 2001 to train the security detail of President Hamid Karzai. I was with him in February of 2002 when he teared up after learning that one of his ministers had been assassinated.

When one of the Americans on my team in Afghanistan got sick late one Christmas night, I drove to a clinic to get some medicine for him. On my way I was stopped at an intersection that was blocked by a large tractor-trailer.

A British MP came up to my window and said, "Yo, mate, you might want to go the other way. This truck is filled with explosives and could blow up half the city."

The day after the incident with the tractor-trailer, I learned that one of our vehicles had gotten stuck in a mud-filled ditch just outside the city. I threw some chains in the back of my armored vehicle and drove to the site as fast as I could.

When you're trapped like that in a hostile environment, you have two choices: call for help and sit in your vehicle until help arrives, or have someone hold security while someone else tries to get the vehicle out of the ditch.

You try not to escalate the situation. Which means that you don't point your weapon at a crowd, instigating trouble. Instead, you constantly scan the area using all of your senses, looking in people's eyes and at their hands.

Hands hold things that can kill you. If you see someone raise a weapon, you have no choice but to eliminate the threat.

As I drove up to the scene, I saw about twenty Afghan men, women, and children closing in around the vehicle. Some of the men were armed. Practically everyone in Afghanistan seems to own an AK-47. They cost about fourteen dollars on the street, less than a pair of Nike sneakers.

I made my way through the crowd and saw that the American holding security was standing with his M4 pointed toward the ground and his mouth frozen open with fear. His partner, meanwhile, was trying to hook a line to the back of their stuck vehicle, without security.

Stepping into the middle of the circle, I motioned to the Afghans who had gathered to back away. I spoke in a firm voice because I didn't want to make them angry. They started to retreat, which gave us room to hook a cable to the vehicle, and we towed it out of there without incident.

Another time, a successful Afghan construction contractor I was working with was kidnapped and held for ransom. One night he'd entered his driveway, and a black SUV had pulled in right behind him; four armed men wearing balaclavas and CT gear got out. They hog-tied the contractor and drove him through several Afghan military checkpoints without being stopped, which is usually unheard-of.

He was taken to a house and up flights of stairs, where the kidnappers instructed him to call his family on his cell phone. They were demanding three hundred thousand dollars. His family managed to raise two hundred thousand dollars in a week. The kidnappers accepted the lesser amount and released him. I treated his injuries, which included a dislocated shoulder and some minor lacerations.

After the contractor was released, he told me that he was sure that officials from the Karzai government and local banks had been part of the kidnapping ring. It explained, he said, why his kidnappers were able to pass through government roadblocks without a problem and how they knew that he had a lot of money in the bank.

Things weren't any less complicated in Iraq, where I've also spent a good deal ████████████████████████████████

ST-6

Unlike many of the Afghans and Iraqis I've encountered, the Kurds, who occupy northern Iraq and make up about 17 percent of Iraq's total population, seem to appreciate Americans and what our country is trying to achieve.

The first time I arrived in Iraqi Kurdistan, my interpreter explained the absence of trees. "Saddam had them all burned down so that when he attacked, people couldn't hide behind them."

When I pointed out that there seemed to be many more women on the streets than men, he said, "That's because Saddam had the men killed."

Then when I noticed a large number of little boys and girls with cysts on their necks and faces, he said, "That's because the gas that Saddam used against us gets into the DNA and is passed from one generation to the other."

The terrain wasn't as brutal as the dictator had been, but it was pretty demanding. I was teaching a weapons and small-unit tactics course in the snow-and-ice-covered mountains not far from the Iranian border with a former ████ man and another security contractor. There was a two-thousand-meter mountain I wanted to climb, so I asked my colleagues if they wanted to do it with me.

The ████ guy said, "The mountain road is too dangerous. We might run across an IED."

"We can avoid the road and run up the side of the mountain and post-hole through the snow," I replied. "No one's going to place an IED on the side of the mountain where there's not even a trail."

We started out together, but I arrived at the top first. At the summit stood a little wooden hut.

After my two buddies arrived, I looked over a snowbank through the door opening and saw somebody's hand on an AK-47. Seconds later, four soldiers emerged and they held us at gunpoint.

With my hands held over my head, I tried to explain why we were there. Unarmed and wearing cold-weather workout gear, we hardly looked threatening. Nor did the Iraqi soldiers, who seemed to be in their late forties and fifties.

The one soldier who understood a little English translated for the others. They lowered their rifles and invited us into their little shack.

As we sat on a rug, they shared tea and bread with us and explained that they were on guard against foreign fighters sneaking across the border from Iran.

Sometime in 2005, I traveled two hundred fifty miles northwest of Baghdad to Mosul, Iraq, with three other Americans ██████████ ██████████ At the time, the ancient city of two million was the scene of constant and severe violence as its diverse ethnic, religious, and political groups vied for supremacy.

On December 21, 2004, fourteen U.S. soldiers, four American employees of Halliburton, and four Iraqi soldiers had been killed by a suicide bomber who entered a dining hall at Forward Operating Base Marez near the main U.S. military airfield at Mosul wearing an explosive vest under an Iraqi security service uniform. Another seventy-two Americans were injured.

After arriving and completing our mission, the four of us stopped at a safe house where American soldiers were defusing a rocket that had been placed near the front door. The chief who ran the building said, "You guys came at the right time. We need more shooters. We're being attacked all the time."

The four of us were armed and ready. But nothing much happened during the daylight hours other than our hearing rocket attacks and small-arms fire off in the distance. At night, as we prepared to leave, the chief said, "Great. Now that you guys are leaving, we will be attacked again."

The four of us climbed into an armored vehicle with our gear and weapons and headed to a deserted field on the outskirts of the city where we were scheduled to meet our aircraft.

As we drove, we heard the chief shouting over the radio, asking for the QRF (quick reaction force) to respond: "We're being attacked!"

We couldn't turn around. Instead, we waited in a darkened field for

INSIDE SEAL TEAM SIX

about forty-five minutes until a blackened six-seat prop plane landed. As we scurried aboard, the pilot shouted, "Hurry up! Hurry up!"

Recognizing his voice, I said, "Al?"

"Don?"

He turned out to be a pilot and a good buddy from ST-6 who is still flying high-risk missions all over the Middle East.

As I sat with him in the cockpit, he said, "When I first starting flying here, soon after the war started, I noticed all these little lights coming at me, like fireworks, and quickly realized that they were tracers and I was being shot at from the ground. But I love it! I love the action!"

Al approached the Baghdad airport, then started to corkscrew in so suddenly that I felt like my stomach was coming out of my throat.

As Al did this, he gave me a little smirk. It was the same little smirk he'd given me years earlier when the two of us were testing an

██████████████████████████

Al and I were going to jump out on an experimental tandem rig. It was actually two jumps combined into one, because soon after Al deployed his main chute, I had to release four points of contact with him before I could free-fall away from Al and pull my chute. Before I jumped, I said, "Al, I want to be released at eight thousand feet so I have plenty of time to do a cutaway." And knowing Al the way I did, I added, "I'm serious, don't mess around up there."

Al had a reputation of being one of those sky gods at ST-6, a man who would jump on the back of a new jumper as he was falling at 120 miles an hour to scare him shitless. Or he'd grab the jumper's feet and spin him in circles.

Al and I exited the bird at twelve thousand, five hundred feet, the two of us secured, my back to his front.

When we got to eight thousand feet, I yelled, "Okay, Al, I'm going to cut away now."

He said, "Wait, let's go over there."

He steered in an easterly direction for about a thousand meters as we fell to seven thousand feet.

I shouted, "Okay, Al, now!"

He said, "No, you were right. Let's go back over to where we were before."

Now we were less than six thousand feet and I was getting worried because I still had four release points to pull—two at my chest, two at my hips—before I could free-fall away from him and pull my chute.

"Al, now!"

We were down to five thousand feet and falling. Had it not been an experimental chute, I wouldn't have been so anxious.

"Al! Damn it!"

He smirked, then gave me the signal to release. I cut away from Al and had a good opening and a safe landing.

As I continue to work the dirt circuit—which is what we former operators call the Middle East—I keep running into retired SEALs like Al. Guys I've known for thirty years now. It's always great to see them. We've all turned gray and look a little weary but are still riding the operational train.

CHAPTER SEVENTEEN

ST-6 Today

Although I sacrificed personal freedom and many other things, I got just as much as I gave.... For all the times I was wet, cold, tired, sore, scared, hungry, and angry, I had a blast.

—*ST-6 Petty Officer First Class Neil Roberts in his "open in the event of my death" letter to his wife*

Today's ST-6 operators are very intelligent and have more combat experience than any unit in the history of the United States. They score far higher than average on standard military intelligence tests and are usually college graduates. Some even hold advanced degrees. In this era of unconventional warfare, they're called upon not only to possess battlefield skills but also to think on their feet, overcome fear, operate sophisticated high-tech equipment, and plan for every possible contingency.

Like one team member told me, "Given the pace of operations and all the things we're asked to deal with, mental toughness is more important than ever."

Today's SEAL training focuses on ways to rewrite primal and remembered fear. Researchers have discovered that once an animal learns to be afraid of something, that memory never vanishes from the amygdala, a part of the brain. But according to Dr. Gregory Quirk of the University of Puerto Rico's school of medicine, a person can supersede those bad memories stored in the amygdala by forming new ones in the brain's prefrontal cortex.

How? By repeating an action, any action, over and over, with the understanding that you are rewriting the bad memory.

Lieutenant Commander Eric Potterat, a Naval Special Warfare psychologist, compares the process to the making of world-class athletes. "Physically, there's very little difference between athletes who win Olympic gold and the rest of the field. It's like the SEAL candidates we see here. Terrific hardware. Sit-ups, push-ups, running, swimming, off the charts, superhuman. But over at the Olympic center, sports psychologists found that the difference between a medal and no medal is determined by an athlete's mental ability."

The elite athletes—the Wayne Gretzkys, the Laird Hamiltons, the Michael Jordans—know how to use the information they learn about how their body responds during a contest or a race. According to Lieutenant Commander Potterat, this is what separates them from the competition.

Just like some SEAL snipers I know, who, before lining up their targets, steady their hands by taking four very deep breaths to oxygenate their bodies as much as possible.

Of course, nothing prepares a warrior better than combat. And today's ST-6 operators are conducting live-fire missions all the time.

Most of the recent ops that they've been engaged in are rarely talked about and don't reach the press. But the pace is incredible, and the missions are highly dangerous.

Some of my ST-6 buddies played an important role in Operation Anaconda in Afghanistan during the U.S.-led coalition effort to rid that country of al-Qaeda terrorists ██████████████████

████████████████████████████████████
████████████████████████████████████
████████████████████████████████████
███

████████████████████████████████████
████████████████████████████████████
████████████████████████████████████
████████████████████████████████████
████████████████████████████████████
███████████████████

The first helo landed on a high slope near the east peak of Takur Ghar at 0245 hours on March 4 and was immediately struck by machine gun fire that ripped into the fuselage and cut the hydraulic line. With the severed line spraying hydraulic fluid everywhere and the chopper jerking this way and that, my friend Petty Officer First Class

████████████████████████████████████
████████████████████████████████████
████████████████████████████████████
████████████████████████████████████
████
████████████████████████████████████

In a letter Roberts left for his wife to be opened in the event of his death, he wrote, "If I died doing something for the Teams, then I died doing what made me happy. Very few people have the luxury of that."

His was the saddest SEAL funeral I've ever attended. As I looked around me, I was struck by how many of the current ST-6 members in attendance were badly scarred and missing limbs.

Since Neil's death, ST-6 operators have staged literally thousands of raids throughout the Middle East—taking out high-value targets, killing Islamic terrorists, rescuing hostages, and collecting intel.

██
██
██
██
██
██
██
██
██████████████████████
██
██
████████████████████████████████████

Since December of 2001, when the al-Qaeda leader was almost killed by U.S. bombs in the mountains of Tora Bora, Afghanistan, bin Laden had disappeared from sight. By 2011, many Americans believed that he was either dead or so deeply hidden that he would never be found.

But after years of painstaking detective work carried out by the NSA, the CIA, and U.S. military intelligence, the United States eventually pinpointed the location of bin Laden's longtime trusted courier Abu Ahmed al-Kuwaiti. CIA agents and satellite surveillance cameras tracked al-Kuwaiti's white SUV to a large concrete compound in the mountain resort of Abbottabad, which is an hour's drive north from the capital city of Islamabad. ████████████████
██
██

████████ named the Pacer, who was living in the compound surrounded by wives and children, was Osama bin Laden.

██

███

███

███

██████████████

███

███

███

███

███

███

███

███

███

██

███████████████████████████████████████

███

███

████████████████████████████ On March 29, President Obama met with his national security advisers in the White House Situation Room to review a plan to attack the compound with helicopter-borne commandos. Some military advisers favored destroying the compound with smart bombs. But President Obama vetoed that option because of the extensive collateral damage a bombing raid would likely inflict on the surrounding area.

████████████████████████████████ ST-6 ███████████

███

███

███

██████████████████████████████████

███

[REDACTED]

Four days later al-Qaeda released a statement confirming their leader's death and vowing revenge.

When President Obama arrived at Fort Campbell, Kentucky, on May 5 to congratulate the team and present them with a Presidential Unit Citation, he said, "I had fifty-fifty confidence that Bin Laden was there, but I had one hundred percent confidence in you guys. You are literally the finest small-unit fighting force that has ever existed in the world."

I know about a dozen members of the UBL assault team, and I'm enormously proud of them. Though I understand the public's curiosity, I see no good reason to reveal their identities, which is why I won't say more here.

The important thing is, SEAL Team Six had extinguished our country's number one enemy [REDACTED]

* * *

Soon after the bin Laden hit, the SEALs who went to Abbottabad were back on the job, launching new missions against terrorist threats.

The dangers the brave operators of ST-6 face routinely was tragically and dramatically underscored four months later on August 6, 2011, when seventeen SEALs (all but two were members of ST-6, but none of them had been on the mission to Abbottabad) were among thirty U.S. servicemen killed when the Chinook helicopter they were riding in was shot down during a nighttime mission in the Tangi valley along the Afghan-Pakistani border. From what I know about them, they were amazing men—in other words, typical SEALs.

One of the SEALs who died in the crash had lost part of his left arm and suffered a collapsed lung in Iraq but felt compelled to rejoin his unit.

Another one of the downed SEALs, Jonas Keisall, had told his mother, "If I die on a mission, I'll die happy because I'm doing something for my country."

It was a devastating blow to ST-6, and the biggest one-day combat loss to U.S. troops in Afghanistan. But the promise of ST-6 lives on. Right after the accident, the remaining brave operators at Six did what they always do. They picked up their weapons and went right back into combat, fighting the only way they knew how—fiercely, skillfully, and with courage.

Epilogue

Mother, tell your children not to do what
I have done.
—*unknown author, "The House of the*
Rising Sun"

Recently, I took my wife, Dawn, to visit my hometown of Methuen, Massachusetts, for the first time. My old buddies greeted us by blasting "Born to Be Wild" from the jukebox as we entered the Plantation, a bar only a quarter mile from my childhood home and the place where my dad and his friends had gone for years to meet up, watch football, and unwind after work.

Now it was a biker hangout with SUPPORT YOUR LOCAL HELLS ANGELS stickers everywhere, and Angels proudly displaying their colors on their leather vests and jackets.

The leather on the stools was worn and cracked, and the floor was dirtier than I remembered. And the locals who now frequented the bar had a tough, far-away look in their eyes that said: *If you look at me the wrong way, I'll kill you.*

I was thrilled to see many of my old buddies. A lot of them still had long hair and beards. Some were wearing the same black motorcycle jackets we'd worn thirty years earlier.

As we exchanged hugs and sat down to beers, I started to experience a strange sense of déjà vu. Or rather, a sense of what could have been.

My old childhood buddies began regaling Dawn and me with stories of their recent adventures. Even though the storyteller shifted from one old friend to another, the themes and narratives remained the same. Many stories went something like this: A group of us got really wasted, committed some sort of stupid crime, were caught, and ended up spending time in jail.

Some of my buddies—now in their late forties and fifties—were back living with their parents. And some of them had long police records, were in poor health, had no steady employment, and were addicted to drugs or alcohol.

As I looked into their faces, I thought: *This could have been me. This is the life I was headed for.*

Thank God for the SEAL teams!

I mean, I love my old buddies, but it was sad to see how so many of them had ended up.

The truth is: I found a way out and they didn't. If I hadn't made that trip to the Navy recruiter, I could have been sitting with them on one of those bar stools—if I were even still alive. But somehow I'd managed to channel the same wild energy all of us shared into something positive and useful. I'd become a Navy SEAL and a corpsman. I proudly served my country and had the opportunity to save lives.

I'm not saying I didn't make mistakes. My rough beginnings, my two failed marriages, my shortcomings as a father, my failure to achieve more as a SEAL and more as an athlete: those are just the tip of the iceberg.

But that day at the Plantation, at the same time as I was happy to see the people I'd been close to so long ago, I realized just how fortunate I'd been. First and foremost, I had had two wonderful parents who loved me and stood by me through thick and thin. And even though I was a rebellious kid, many of my parents' values did rub off on me.

I learned love of country from my dad. He'd been in the Navy, as had my uncles and my aunt. All of them had served proudly and with distinction during World War II. So even though I didn't realize it as a teenager, I was following a path that they had blazed for me.

My mom and sisters had taught me to be compassionate and always try to help those in need, which somehow translated into my desire to become a corpsman.

Both of my parents taught me to have faith in God and set goals for myself.

Goals have always been some of the sturdiest foundations in my life. Micro-goals, like winning a local triathlon or bike race; and macro-goals, like making it through BUD/S, becoming a Navy SEAL, getting selected to SEAL Team Six, and competing in the world's most difficult endurance events—setting my sights lets me have something to work toward and, in some of the hardest times, to have something to live for.

SEALs taught me the need to work as a team, to trust and support your teammates, and that a group of individuals working together toward a common purpose is much more powerful than the aggregate of their individual skills.

All the SEALs I've known—whether they were athletes, bikers, cowboys, muscle heads, or college students—have had one thing in common: their willingness to push themselves far beyond what they thought were their limits.

I was never the fastest, strongest, or smartest. So I've always felt that if I wanted to not just get there but get there up in front of the pack, I had to push myself harder than others.

I've been tremendously fortunate in other ways too. In fact, when I think of the number of times I narrowly escaped death, I almost can't believe it. Besides the ever-present chance during ops, there was the free-fall accident in Arizona, the time I ran out of oxygen diving in Key West, the training accident in the desert of California in the ambulance, and the live-rocket round in Panama.

Another time was when I was with ST-1 in Korea: Our entire platoon was getting ready to board a helicopter when a Marine came up to us and said, "We have a Marine with us with frostbite and hypothermia. Do you mind if we have this helicopter and you guys wait for the next one?"

We said, "Go ahead."

Twenty Marines boarded the helicopter and took off. We learned an hour or so later that it flew into a storm and hit a mountainside. Everyone onboard was killed.

Sometimes luck finds you when no element of training or experience can help you come out on top. Just recently while I was riding my Indian Chief—like the one my dad used to own—on a country road near my house, I came roaring around a curve and was hit in the face by a large vulture.

I was almost knocked off my bike and initially thought I broke my neck. The worst that came of it in the end was that I tasted wet vulture feathers in my mouth for months afterward.

I'm fifty-three years old and still competing at a fairly high level against twenty- and thirty-year-olds. I have nerve damage in my face and head from shrapnel that ricocheted off a piece of steel; hearing loss from explosions, helicopters, and weapons; skin cancer; two fractures in my back; a compressed spine; rib fragments in my liver; an enlarged heart; two torn rotator cuffs; patellofemoral pain syndrome in both knees; and chronic plantar fascia nerve damage and frostbite in both feet.

I also have the well of energy I had as a youngster still burning inside me, urging me to accomplish more and set new goals for myself. There are so many exciting things I still want to accomplish in this life while I still have time.

A big deal for me is to climb five more of the seven summits!

I attempted to summit Mount Baker in Washington State a couple of years ago as a tune-up for my Denali climb; I went with an SF guy, an adventure racer, and a mountain guide. We ran into a terrible storm with high, frigid winds. The SF guy lost his footing, fell backward, and tumbled a hundred meters over his large backpack and the sled he was pulling and suffered a head injury.

When I ran over to where he was lying in the snow, he told me that he had to get up and patrol the barracks. He thought he was back in the Army as an E-1.

After my wife and I climbed Mount Kilimanjaro, in 2008, we went on safari. One morning she thought she heard a lion outside our tent. But when she told the guard, he said, "No, those lions are far away, but because of the way the sound travels, they sound like they're close."

The next night she woke me up and pointed to the little tarp outside our tent where we washed up. A large lion was out there drinking our water and urinating, three feet away, with nothing between us except a thin piece of canvas. That day I had bought a spear from the Masai warriors, and I had it next to my bed. Dawn said, "Get your spear." I replied, "It would be like a toothpick in that seven-hundred-pound beast—let's just stay very quiet." It was another one of those helpless moments.

I'm proud that I still do the work I love—training people who deploy overseas in the global war against terrorism and men who want to become SEALs. But most important, I've been married for ten years to a wonderful woman, whom I love deeply. Between us we have three talented, smart children—Dawnie, Chonie, and Dylan—who fill me with joy and pride.

There's a reunion that Dawn and I look forward to every summer—the three-day gathering of SEALs that's held in Little Creek, Virginia. Thousands of current and former SEALs show up with their families—everyone from Vietnam-era SEALs like Medal of Honor recipient Bob Kerrey to current members of ST-6.

The whole history of SEAL teams is represented. Crusty ████ ████████ can be seen holding court with a beer in his hand, signing autographs and telling stories. At recent reunions, I've run into distinguished SEALs like Jesse Ventura (the former pro wrestler and governor of Minnesota), ████████████████████████████ ██████ and Medal of Honor recipients Thomas Norris and Michael Thornton have appeared.

I take special pleasure in seeing some of the officers I served under who have now become admirals. Guys like Joe Kiernan, Eric Olson, Ray Smith, Bob Harwood, and Brian Losey, who was with me in Riberalta, Bolivia, when the boy was hit by a motorcycle.

It's a tight-knit community of men, women, and families.

I'm always struck by how many former SEALs like me are still engaged in some sort of military activity. And I'm pleased by the number of guys who talk proudly about their sons who are going through BUD/S or serving on one of the teams.

Dawn's ex-husband, Ray, who is one of only three SEALs to have spent his entire career at ST-6, usually attends. At one recent reunion, Dawn and I were standing next to Ray and his new wife when a former teammate of ours walked up, looked at the two of us with our arms around our wives, and said, "You see the funniest things at these reunions."

Last time that guy had seen the three of us, Ray and Dawn were married to each other, and I was single.

Even though we gather to see one another and celebrate, the reality of war is always present. As the years pass, it pains me to notice an increasing number of current SEALs with prosthetic legs or glass eyes or otherwise scarred with battle wounds.

At the last reunion, I ran into Admiral Bob Harwood, who was the officer in charge of ██████████ when I was there. Bob turned to the guys he was talking to and said, "This is Don Mann. He's the toughest guy I've ever known in Special Operations."

Even if he said it to be nice, it was good to hear.

It also reminded me that any individual accomplishment I might have achieved over the years doesn't match the pride I feel in being part of one of the most exclusive and distinguished communities on earth—U.S. Navy SEALs.

The bond between teammates is as strong and unconditional as the promise all SEAL operators make to defend our country:

I will never quit. I persevere and thrive on adversity. My Nation expects me to be physically harder and mentally stronger than my enemies. If knocked down, I will get back up, every time. I will draw on every remaining ounce of strength to protect my teammates and to accomplish our mission. I am never out of the fight.

Glossary

AOIC Assistant officer in charge

ARS Alcohol rehab service

AVPU Alert, voice, pain, unresponsive

BMC Boatswain's mate chief

BUD/S Basic Underwater Demolition/SEAL

CAPEX Capability exercise

CCT Combat-control technicians

CO Commanding officer

COC Code of conduct

CONUS Contiguous United States

CQB Close-quarters battle

CRRC Combat rubber raiding craft

CT Counterterrorism

CWO Chief warrant officer

DEVGRU United States Naval Special Warfare Development Group

DT Defensive tactics

DZ Drop zone

E & E Escape and evasion

EEI Essential elements of information

EOD Explosives ordnance disposal

FMLN Farabundo Marti National Liberation Front

FN Fireman

FTX Final training exercise

GPL General purpose, large

HAHO High-altitude, high-opening

HALO High-altitude, low-opening

HQ Headquarters

HRV Heart-rate variability

HUMINT Human intelligence

IBS Inflatable boat, small

IED Improvised explosive device

279

IR Infrared

ISI Pakistan's Inter-Services Intelligence

JSOC Joint Special Operations Command

KIA Killed in action

LAW Light armor weapon

LPO Leading petty officer

LT Lieutenant

MEDCAP Medical Civic Action Program

MM Machinist's mate

MOUT Military operations in urban terrain

MREs Meals ready to eat

MTT Mobile training team

MWR Miniaturize, weatherize, ruggedize (Admiral Olson called it "moral welfare and recreation")

NPY Neuropeptide Y

NRC Navy Recruiting Command

NSWDG United States Naval Special Warfare Development Group

NSWG1 Navy Special Warfare Group One

NSWG2 Navy Special Warfare Group Two

NVGs Night-vision goggles

O-2 Navy lieutenant (junior grade)

O-3 Navy lieutenant

O-4 Navy lieutenant commander

O-5 Navy commander

OAR Odyssey Adventure Racing

OCONUS Outside the contiguous United States

OIC Officer in charge

OODA Observation, orientation, decision, action

Op Operation

OP-06D Naval Security Coordination team

OTB Over the beach

PDF Panamanian Defense Forces

PJs Air Force Pararescue

PLO Patrol leader's order

PRB Patrol river boat

PRODEV Professional development

PRT Physical readiness test

PT Physical training

QM Quartermaster

QRF Quick reaction force

ROE Rules of engagement

RPG Rocket-propelled grenade

SAS Special Air Service

SBU-26 Special Boat Unit 26

SDV Swimmer-delivery vehicle

SERE Survival, evasion, resistance, and escape

SF Special Forces

SIT Squadron integration training

SN Seaman

SOP Standard operating procedure

SOTIC Special Operations Target Interdiction Course

SPECTRA Specialized training

SPEC WAR Naval special warfare

ST-1 SEAL Team One

ST-2 SEAL Team Two

ST-6 SEAL Team Six

██████████████████

UBL Osama bin Laden

UDTs Underwater demolition teams

VBSS Visit, board, search, and seizure

VFW Veterans of Foreign Wars

WFO Wide fucking open

WMD Weapons of mass destruction

WO Warrant officer

XO Executive officer

Acknowledgments

Don Mann:

I owe an immense amount of gratitude to the men in the SEAL teams who I was lucky enough to serve with. They taught me some of life's most valuable lessons. Since BUD/S all the way through retirement and beyond, I have been honored to serve with every one of them.

This book would never have been possible if it were not for my coauthor, the very talented award-winning author, playwright, and screenwriter Ralph Pezzullo.

I am deeply grateful for all of the assistance I received from our editor, John Parsley, who took a very personal interest in this project, and his incredible team at Little, Brown.

I want to thank Heather Mitchell, our literary agent, and her very professional staff at Gelfman Schneider Literary Agents for all that they did to ensure this book project would become a reality.

And finally I want to thank my very understanding wife for putting up with me over the last ten years and for supporting me with this project that means so very much to me.

Ralph Pezzullo:

First, I want to express my appreciation to the amazing Don Mann. He not only gave me the opportunity to help tell his incredible story but also became my friend, for which I'm extremely grateful. And I want to thank the man who introduced us, fellow author and friend Tom Sawyer.

Thanks to the wise advice and effort of our agent Heather Mitchell of Gelfman Schneider, this book found the perfect home with Little, Brown and Company, our extremely talented and thoughtful editor John Parsley, and its superlative staff, including Nicole Dewey and William Boggess.

Finally, I want to thank my wife, Jessica, and my children, John, Michael, Francesca, and Alessandra, for supporting me with their love and understanding and putting up with my long absences during the summer—all for a very worthy project.

Index

INDEX

Mann, Dawnie (daughter), 195, 197, 205, 210, 275
Mann, Dawn (wife), 3, 231–40, 243, 247, 270–71, 274–76
Mann, Don. *See also* adventure sports; training; *and specific missions and SEAL Teams*
  childhood and youth, 26–38
  college experiences, 50–52
  fight with drug dealer, 43–48
  goals of, 272, 274
  high school experiences, 39–50
  luck and, 38, 140, 272–73
  mother's death, 250–51
  mottos of, 26, 243
  nicknames of, 25, 90, 97
  parents and, 26–27, 35–38, 49–50, 52, 59, 61, 71, 89, 141, 241, 250–51, 271–72
  retirement of, 240–41
  stepsons and, 231, 232–39, 275
Mann, Kim (wife), 37–38, 63, 71, 75, 114–15, 141, 159–60, 163, 208
Mann, Rick (brother), 49, 141–43, 233
Mann, Shannon Bailey (wife), 163–64, 167–68, 197, 205, 210, 211
Mann, Wendy (sister), 63
marathons, 52, 60, 66, 207–8, 229, 244

marijuana, 41, 174, 181, 189, 234
Marine Corps Marathon, 66, 244

Marr, Joy, 242
Matulionis, Andrew, 245
McCullen, Dave, 40
McFaul, Donald, 170

Medal of Honor, 275
Medical Civic Action Program (MEDCAP), 199–201

Mega Dose adventure race, 243
Methuen, Massachusetts, 27–28, 30–31, 270
metronomic heartbeat, 72–73
MH-47 Chinook helicopters, ███ ███ 269
MH-60 Black Hawk helicopters, 6, 144–45███
Middle East, 155, 248–49, 252, 257–58 | ███. *See also specific countries*
Milford, Connecticut, 49 50
military operations in urban terrain (MOUT), ███ 205, 209–10
military intelligence tests, 259–60
MK 15 underwater breathing apparatus, 85
MK-19 machine guns, 169
MK23 Mod 0 .45-caliber handguns, 86
MK43 machine guns, 86
mobile training teams (MTT), 189–94
Moleda, Carlos, 170–71
Morgan, Charles, 72–73
Morrel, Al, 124–26
motorcycles
  early experiences with, 28–39
  Frogs on Hogs, 212–14
  gangs and, 29–30, 37–38, 39, 49–50, 270
  Evel Knievel and, 28–29
  motocross racing, 35–37, 40, 51–52
  as transportation, 190, 211–12, 273
Mount Baker, 274
Mount Everest, 241, 246
Mount Kilimanjaro, 245, 274
Mozambique drill, ███ 110, 238
MP5-N submachine guns, 5, 110, ███ 132, 145

MT1X parachutes, 224–25
Murphy, Thomas E., 143–44
muscles, fast/slow–twitch, 217

National Security Agency (NSA), 263
Naval Amphibious Base, Little Creek, Virginia, 3, 102, 205, 275

INDEX

INDEX

U.S. Navy Underwater Demolition Teams
(UDTs), 57, 88–89, 102

████████████████████

USS Grayback, 106, 108–9

████████████████████

USS Nimitz, 103
USS Stethem, 118

████████████████████

Venezuela, 189, 200
Ventura, Jesse, 275
vertical de-rigs, 127, 139
Vietnam War, 39, 57, 90, 96, 97, 101, 104,
127
Virginia Beach, Virginia, 3, 88–89, 210,
211–12, 219, 232, 238, 250
visit, board, search, and seizures (VBSS),
189, 205, 252
visualization, 69, 129

warning orders, 149–50, 157
war on drugs, 188–89
Warren, Barbara, 227

████████████████████

Watkins, Bill, 247
weapons of mass destruction (WMD),
222–23, 227 ██
weapons training, 86, 109–10, 127–28,
131–32, 205, 210, 248–49, 251,
255–56
Western Pacific marathon, 66
Willis, Claude, Jr., 104
winter-warfare training, 113–14, 131, 205,
214
Womack Army Medical Center, Fort
Bragg, 134
Woolf, Virginia, 149

Yemen, ██ 248
Yosemite, 134

████████████████████

Zodiac CRRC (combat rubber raiding
craft), 12, 16, 18–20, 57, 84, 114, 168

About the Authors

DON MANN (CWO3, USN) has for the last thirty years been associated with the Navy SEALs as a platoon member, assault team member, boat-crew leader, and advanced-training officer, and, more recently, as program director preparing civilians to go to BUD/S (SEAL training). Up until 1998 he was on active duty with SEAL Team Six. Since then, he has deployed to the Middle East on numerous occasions in support of the war against terrorism.

RALPH PEZZULLO is a *New York Times* bestselling author and award-winning playwright and screenwriter. His books include *Jawbreaker* (with CIA operative Gary Berntsen), *At the Fall of Somoza, Plunging into Haiti* (winner of the Douglas Dillon Award for American Diplomacy), *The Walk-In, Most Evil* (with Steve Hodel), *Eve Missing,* and *Blood of My Blood.* His film adaptation of *Recoil* by Jim Thompson, directed by James Foley, is scheduled to reach theaters next year.